SUBLIME SUMMITS AND VANISHING WORLDS

Uschba, from above Latal

Also by Beatrice Teissier and published by Signal Books

Into the Kazakh Steppe: John Castle's Mission to Khan Abulkhayir

Russian Frontiers: Eighteenth-Century British Travellers in the Caspian, Caucasus and Central Asia

Beirut: Scarred City: Walks through Beauty and Brutalism

SUBLIME SUMMITS AND VANISHING WORLDS

*British Travellers, Adventurers and Agents
in the Nineteenth-Century Caucasus*

Beatrice Teissier

Signal Books
Oxford

First published in 2024 by
Signal Books Limited
36 Minster Road
Oxford OX4 1LY
www.signalbooks.co.uk

© Beatrice Teissier, 2024

The right of Beatrice Teissier to be identified as the author of this work has been asserted by her in accordance with the Copyright, Design and Patents Act, 1988.

All rights reserved. The whole of this work, including all text and illustrations, is protected by copyright. No parts of this work may be loaded, stored, manipulated, reproduced or transmitted in any form or by any means, electronic or mechanical, including photocopying and recording, or by any information, storage and retrieval system without prior written permission from the publisher, on behalf of the copyright owner.

A catalogue record for this book is available from the British Library

ISBN 978-1-909930-88-9 Paper

Cover Design: Tora Kelly
Typesetting: Tora Kelly
Front Cover: National Library of Scotland, Bell Vol.1, NLS Special Collections LS k. 160.b
Back Cover: Grove 1875
Frontispiece: NLS SC K 130.f
Printed in the UK by 4edge Ltd

Contents

Introduction 1
Acknowledgements 8

Part 1
War and Diplomacy 9
Circassia (1820s-1853) 9
The British: Black Sea Fever 14
Dagestan and Chechnya 27
The Crimean War (1853-56): Circassia and Dagestan 32
The British: *A Superior Man* and Others 33
Shamil and the Naib 37
Consuls 48
Expulsion 56
Looking to the Future 63
Travellers' Voices (1865-77) 65
The Russo-Ottoman War (1877-78) 69
New Consuls (1876-88) 74
The End of the War and its Aftermath 80

Part 2
Tiflis 99
The Caucasus Museum 109
Society and Dissent 115

Part 3
Ethnography 123
The Museum and the *'Civilizing Mission'* 125
Circassia and the West 131
The North 136
Chechnya: a scholar's journey 146
Svaneti 148
Dagestan 164
The Caspian 172

Part 4
Antiquarianism: 'A Wonderful Harvest' 186
Civilized and Primitive 187
Islam and Dagestan 194

Part 5
The Great Outdoors 207
'Stupendous Peaks': Mountaineering 207
Hunting: *'A Very Lively Time'* 220

Part 6
Images 233
The Alpine Club and Photography 242
Reflections 248
Conclusion 253

Appendix 261

Short Biographical Notes 275

Bibliography 278

List of Illustrations 288

Index 289

Introduction

Russia's 2008 attacks on Georgia and military interference in South Ossetia and Abkhazia on behalf of separatists, its grabbing of Crimea in 2014, and the invasion of Ukraine in 2022 have served as a reminder that geo-politics never sleeps in areas under Russia's former control or influence. Nor do local separatist movements. The Caucasus lives this history, past and present.

Gripped in a diagonal between two seas (the Black Sea and the Caspian), between the great land masses of Turkey to the west, Russia to the north and Iran to the south, and truncated down the middle by two mountain ranges, the Caucasus' history is one of territory claimed, lost and reclaimed. Its mountains, multiple valleys, impenetrable forests and rivers have long acted as barriers to be defended or to be overcome, while the steppe lands to the north have invited invasion and the coastal regions colonization. Perhaps

'Dykhtau and Koshtantau from the Salynan Ridge'

best known for its mountains, the land is not defined by them alone: it has multiple micro- and macroclimates, ranging from the sub-tropicality of the western coastline, the dense temperate forests along the line of mountains, the alpine highlands of Dagestan to the sub-tropical plains of Azerbaijan. The Caucasus has thus formed a coveted crossroads with access to the sea and desirable natural resources. It has never been able to escape its fatal geography.

Long before Russia, which became the dominant player in this area, chipping away at Caucasian Persian and Ottoman provinces during the eighteenth and nineteenth centuries, various empires - Roman, Achaemenid, Safavid, Ottoman - have fought over the region, while parts of it also suffered devastation by Mongols, Seljuks and Persians. Historically independent kingdoms such as the Armenian Arsacids and Bagratids, the Georgians under King David and Queen Tamara and various statelets in Dagestan were eventually doomed by invasion, co-option and infighting.

The Caucasus has always been highly complex: known from classical sources to be a melting pot of languages (some Indo-European, some unique to the region and some unintelligible to each other) and ethnic groups. Invaders added new populations to the mix of various native populations, particularly in frontier areas, while mountain regions remained fiercely independent. Groups were further divided by religious affiliations or influences irrespective of language: thus Christianity became the official religion of Armenia and Georgia from the fourth century, Islam was enforced from the mid-seventh century in Dagestan, and Russian Orthodoxy was partially imposed during the late eighteenth and nineteenth centuries over conquered areas. There were also indigenous traditions not belonging to any state religion. As the Russian conquest of the Caucasian Persian and Ottoman provinces progressed during those two centuries, Islamic 'holy wars' led by powerful imams (Mansur and Shamil) defined this conflict in Dagestan.

Today the Caucasus is still divided into zones of influence: Russia in the north and Dagestan, Georgia fighting for true sovereignty, Azerbaijan independent, Armenia increasingly isolated. In the wider world the Caucasus is mostly known from news

Introduction

flashes about Russian interference and aggression in Georgia, the war between Armenia and Azerbaijan over Nagorno-Karabakh, local demonstrations over Georgia's membership of the European Union, and as a semi-exotic tourist destination for the culturally curious. But it still seems distant.

What is it that made British travellers adventure there in the western and northern parts of the Caucasus during the nineteenth century while other individuals resided or travelled there as consuls or agents? There had been no tradition of British interest in the region itself and the impetus at first seems to have come with the opening up of the area by Russia, a vested interest in Black Sea trade, and anxiety over Russia's claims on the eastern (Circassian) Ottoman coastline and in the south-east Caucasus as it might affect Britain's relations with Persia. Then came a more focused commercial interest in the Black Sea, reactions to Russia's escalating designs on Ottoman territory and the future of the Ottoman Empire, and weighing up the potential geopolitical significance of parts of the Caucasus for Britain.

The representative sample of men and one woman (Robert Lyall 1825, Edmund Spencer 1837-39, James Bell and John Longworth 1840, George Poulett Cameron 1845, John Ussher 1865, Douglas Freshfield 1869 and 1896, Annie Jane Harvey 1871, Arthur Cunynghame 1872, John Buchan Telfer 1876, Florence Craufurd Grove 1875, James Bryce 1877, Clive Phillipps-Wolley 1881 and 1883, Oliver Wardrop 1888, John Abercromby 1889) and consuls whose work is discussed below is extremely varied both in terms of profession (merchants, scientists, military men, scholars, diplomats, writers, agents and sensation seekers) and age. This book, aimed at the general reader, explores the nature of the travellers' observations regarding the Caucasus and Britain's relations with Russia in light of the latter's *modus operandi*, their arguments (if any) and their contribution to knowledge of the Caucasus.

Some travellers had clear aims, such as political observation or sport, others were more focused on history or antiquarianism and language studies, but most would echo the words of professional travel writer Edmund Spencer from one of his prefaces, that his

Sublime Summits

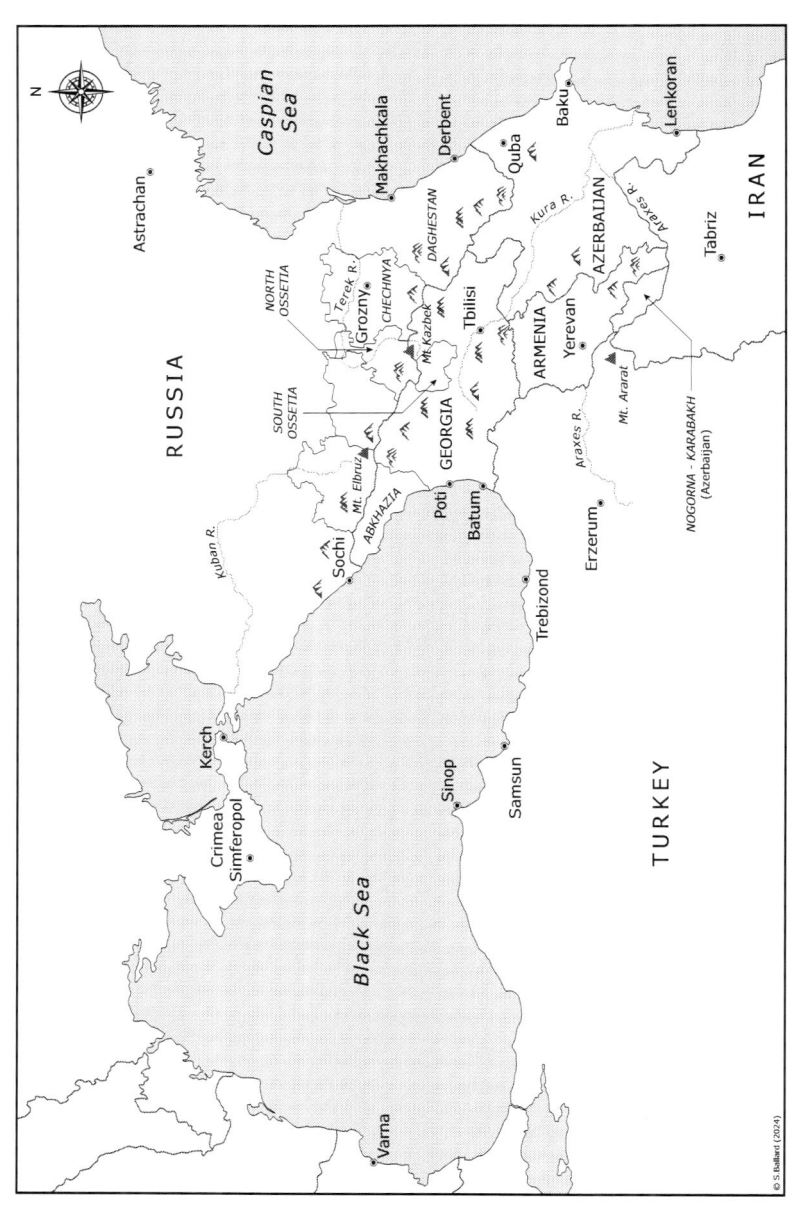

INTRODUCTION

books were 'something more than a narrative of Travel, as they contain a variety of notes and observations, on the social, moral and political condition of the countries through which I travelled.' Politics were also being played out. A number of travellers, whether on official business or not, reported to the Foreign Office. The consuls were there on official business and their despatches give month by month details of eventful and uneventful developments.

Travel at the time was also fuelled by the popularity of the travel writing genre and the competition for exotic locations driven by publishers like John Murray and Henry Colburn. The Caucasus was little known by the British, even those who were familiar with Russia and had toured Crimea. They did not really know what to expect on the ground, particularly in the first half of the nineteenth century when the region was still at war. Some who were versed in the classics were aware of the myths and legends associated with the Caucasus and had read previous travellers' reports, such as Pallas, de Montperreux and Klaproth, but it was still mostly *terra incognita*. They would also have been alerted to press reports on Russia's war in the Caucasus. Yet the majority do not seem to have read or been motivated by the romanticism of the Caucasus as demonstrated in Russian works such as Pushkin's *The Captain's Daughter* (first translated by G.C. Hebbe, 1853).[1] As the century progressed, they read each other's books, and extracts were published and reviewed in the press, fuelling competition.

Those in the diplomatic service, meanwhile, would have been made aware of political developments through consular offices or 'residents' and other contacts in Moscow, Constantinople, Trebizond, Baghdad, Basra or Tehran.

The historical context of the times was dramatic for such observers in the Caucasus. They witnessed the consequences of Russia's wars with Persia and the Ottomans, its gradual and brutal colonization and destruction of different parts of the Caucasus, the Crimean War and Russia's conquest of Central Asia on the sidelines. They saw the Circassian and the beginnings of the Armenian genocides, the forced transfer of populations and new settlers. They experienced the rule of very different tsars (Nicholas

I, Alexander II, Alexander III), Russia's administrative, economic and infrastructural development as it controlled more of the area, and Britain's changing and ambivalent relations with Russia. They engaged with various Caucasian chiefs and tribal peoples and saw parts of the area few had seen before.

The travellers followed different routes into the Caucasus: some from Crimea and the Circassian (later Russian) coastline, others from Russia and the north Caucasus. Travel would have been impossible without assistance from the Russian administration. Thus, all passed through Tbilisi (then Tiflis) in Georgia, Russia's main administrative centre, whether to obtain papers, pay their respects to officials, buy provisions, or find local guides and recuperate. Assistance or goodwill from local peoples, particularly in remote areas, was not always a given, but there was hardly ever a real threat. Consuls, located on the east coast of the Black Sea and Tiflis, whether short- or long-term, tended to stay put in their posts with short trips into the interior or to Tiflis.

This book discusses in six Parts topics most addressed in the material: War and Diplomacy; the city of Tiflis; Ethnography; Antiquarianism; Sport; and Illustration, arranged chronologically and by the four regions which brought the travellers and others to the region: Circassia and the west, Georgia (Tiflis), the northern Caucasus range and Dagestan with forays into Armenia and the Caspian. Georgia was not the focus of the travellers' interests, except for Wardrop's *The Kingdom of Georgia* (1888), and this is dealt with in Part Two. The Parts are subdivided into sections mixing historical context, the authors' paraphrased voices and commentary.

A note on place and tribal names

The sources use a range of different spellings for place names, some of which cannot be identified. The places that can be identified have been left in their original form in the text followed by the modern name in parentheses. Where tribal names are interchanged with area names and vice-versa this is made clear in the text.

The illustrations

All images and captions in this book, except for most of the 'calling cards' reproduced in the Appendix, are taken from the publications of the travellers and writers discussed (see Part 6).

1 Respectively www.peterharrington.co.uk (bookseller) and feb-ru/feb/pushkin/bilio/pie/pie/-od-.htm (Slavonic section of New York Library)

Acknowledgements

I am most grateful to the Nizami Ganjavi Centre for supporting this project. Special thanks go to the scholars who have helped with references and identifications (Warwick Ball, Irina Demetradze-Renz, Professor Edmund Herzig, Caspar Meyer, Ketevan Ramishvili, Vanessa Winchester), to Alexander Morrison for his critical reading of Part I of the book, and to my editor James Ferguson.

Warm thanks to the many people who have otherwise helped with advice, comments and hospitality: Timothy Blauvelt, the Demetradze-Renz family, Tamara Grdzelidze, Beka Kobakhidze, Lika Mamatsashvili, the ladies at the Georgi Leonidze State Museum of Georgian Literature (Tbilisi); Ramaz Obaladze (Kutaisi), Gillian Evison, Simon and Dillian Freeman, Vanessa and Peter Winchester (Oxford). The friendly technical help of the staff at the National Archives, Kew, the National Library of Scotland and Special Collections of the National Library of Scotland, the Edinburgh University Centre for Heritage Collections and Digital Imaging Services and at the Nizami Ganjavi Centre Library in Oxford was enormously appreciated. Last but far from least many thanks to map maker Sebastian Ballard, designer Tora Kelly, and indexer Brenda Stones.

PART 1
War and Diplomacy

Circassia (1820s-1853)

'In England we hear but little of what passes in those distant and mountainous regions' [1]

When the botanist and physician, Robert Lyall, arrived on the eastern Black Sea coast of Circassia from Taman in 1822 on his tour of Crimea and Russia, he found it 'savage and barbarous', inhabited by 'lawless banditti.'[2] It had a history of being unsafe, turbulent and predatory, and its native peoples were considered a threat to neighbouring powers if united with those over the Kuban river, he wrote.[3] Lyall had been employed as a physician in Russia, had graduated as a doctor and surgeon in St Petersburg in 1816 and had already published *The Character of the Russians* (1823), critical of Russia, citing despotism, the police state, corruption and the ignorance of the clergy among its ills. This fed into existing anti-Russian sentiment at home. Lyall knew Russia and its language, but knew the Caucasus only by repute and secondary reading, while being fully aware of the wider discourse on the region at the time. He nevertheless suggested that travel in the mountains would offer a rich harvest and a fine field of research.[4] The 'banditti' trope, partially thrilling for a touring travelogue, was to radically change for those who came to Circassia with very different purposes a decade later.

Circassia at that time was large and much of it independent of Russia, with parts nominally under Ottoman control. It stretched from the region of the Taman peninsula in the north-west down to what was the principality of Abkhazia on the coast (with centres such as Pitsunda, Sukhum-Kale), north to the Black Sea and Kuban river, with its Cossack defensive line, and east approximately to Kabarda. Russia's designs on Circassia were already long standing, as was its fixation on Kabarda (which controlled the Dariel pass and access to Georgia) since the building of Mozdok fortress on Circassian territory in 1763. This unleashed a war that lasted until 1779. As later, divide and conquer was the strategy, and more forts were built to divide the Kabardans from west Circassia.[5] Chechnya, to the east of Kabarda, was waging its own resistance, which spread to west Circassia (under Ottoman control) and Anapa, under Sheikh Mansur. Russia's policy of devastation did not acknowledge boundaries although Russia did not then establish itself in the west. Russia's aims had gained momentum in the second half of the eighteenth century after the subjection of Ukrainian Cossacks, who were moved to establish the Kuban frontier cordon and who founded Yekaterinodar in 1792. The annexation of Crimea in 1783 had opened up the steppe, and pro-Turkish and anti-Russian factions which developed in west Circassia and Kabarda after the annexation helped Russia's aim of dissention. By the late eighteenth century Circassia was thus already divided, with the coast still held by the Ottomans.

In 1816, Aleksei Petrovitch Yermolov, a decorated general of the Napoleonic Wars, popular with his troops and notorious for the brutality of his campaigns against the 'mountaineers' or mountain peoples, became Commander in Chief of the Russian forces in Georgia. He had the task of subduing not only the north, but also the recently acquired Persian provinces in the south. Forts continued to be built from Azov to Mozdok and punitive measures increased, and by the late 1820s, with the co-option of some Kabardan princes and the granting of privileges, Kabarda was considered subject to Russia, as was Balkaria. The Karachay mountain people to the west continued their resistance.[6] Their resentment was doubly fuelled by the behaviour of the Russian troops, who stole, pillaged and raped at will.

In the west, the building of Russian forts along the coast was to increase exponentially after 1829 and the Treaty of Adrianople, concluded after the Russo-Turkish War of 1828-29. This treaty acknowledged Russia's possession of Georgia, including the coastal areas of Mingrelia and Guria (Poti) and the province of Akhaltsik, between Kakheti and Armenia. For coastal Circassians this was the beginning of the end.

Lyall was blunt about Russia's aims in the region and realistic about General Yermolov's 'barbarous' policy towards the 'ferocious' mountain people.[7] His views on Circassia were in keeping with those of Peter Simon Pallas[8] and up to a point the Russian establishment. Russia's policies were clear: Yermolov wanted to consolidate a great and permanent Russian force and army base in Georgia, estimated at c.50,000 in Georgia at the time.[9] (Numbers would be more accurate when given by consuls later, see below.) The goal was to weaken and even destroy the mountain peoples and to extend the 'dominions' of Georgia by encroaching on Persia, and with 'mad ambition' attempt the conquest of Persia itself. Turkey was also in Russia's sights.[10] Fears over Russia's expansion into Persia and thereby threat to Britain's interests in India had been whipped up by the memory of Tsar Paul's expeditionary force sent to India in 1800 (abandoned after a month)[11] and by the likes of Sir Robert Wilson, who had fought against Napoleon and had been familiar with some of his aims and warnings about Russia and India.

Lyall dismisses the possible invasion of India by Russia as a delusion,[12] but acknowledges the strategic position of Georgia for Russia in its movements against Persia and Turkey and the possible dangers of the Russian conquest of Central Asia. His overall conclusion - strange for a man who knew Russia, but perhaps not a for a writer who did not want to be alarmist - was that Russia had already reached the 'zenith' of its glory, and was unlikely to surpass itself but should nevertheless be watched.[13] The British in the east were certainly awake to Russian designs on Erivan, eventually Karabakh and all ports (on both sides of the Caspian) and passes to the west of the Caspian, as reported to Hartford Jones in Baghdad in the early 1800s.[14]

The India question was to be raised by different visitors to the Caucasus and for different motives ten years later.

Sublime Summits

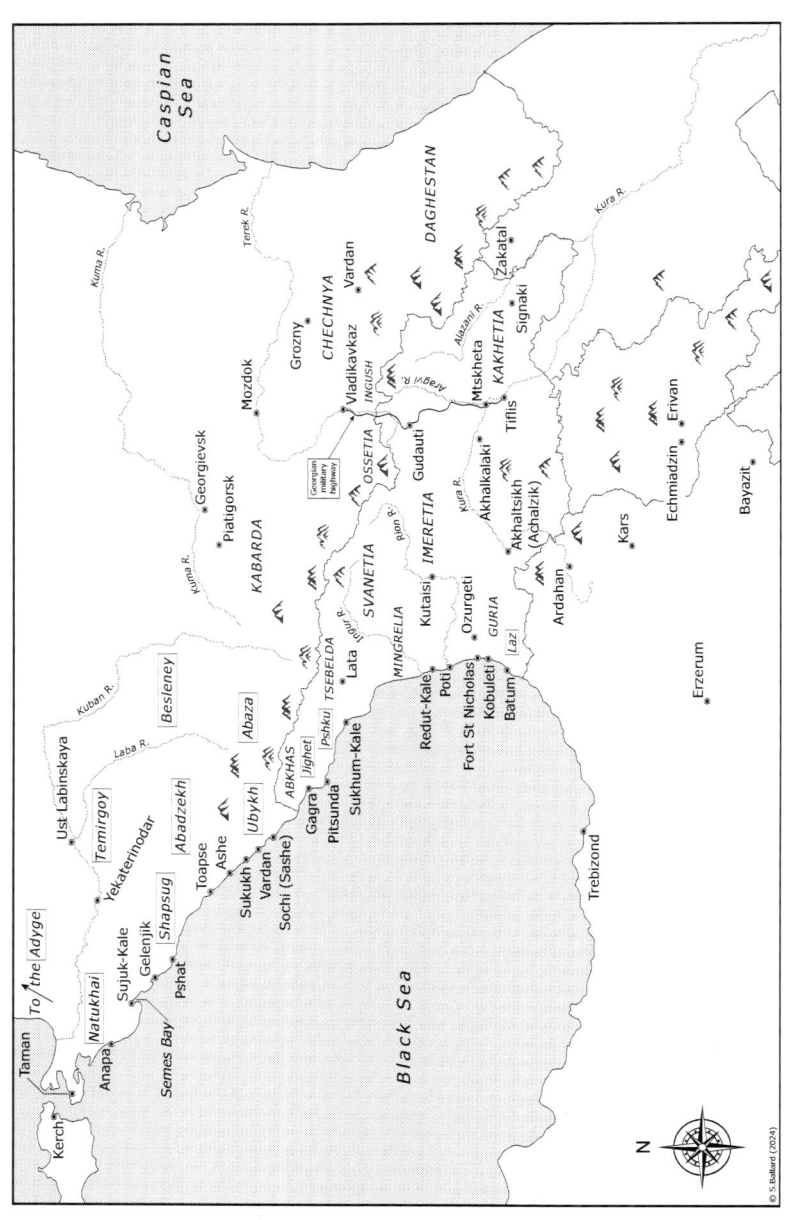

Circassians, or the 'Cherkess' as they were referred to by the Russians, were comprised of several tribes (the main ones being the Chapsugs, Abadzekhs, Natuhais, Ubykh, Bedjuks, Kabardians, Temirgoy, Besleney) then classed as 'friendly' and 'independent'. 'Friendly' (but not true subject) Circassians were to the north of the defensive line of the Kuban patrolled by Black Sea Cossacks and nominally governed by a Cossack *ataman* but actually commanded by the Russians (Yermolov at the time). Lyall emphasizes the vigilance maintained over this border, which he estimated was upwards of 1,000 miles.[15] The two major fortresses at the time were Yekaterinodar and Ust Labinskaya. Both were built to a similar plan: 'an immense square court, included by a deep ditch and an earthen rampart'. Yekaterinodar had about twenty, one-storey, whitewashed houses around the square which consisted of barracks, magazines and workshops. At Ust Labinskaya up to eight battalions, plus corps of 100-200 Cossacks, could be kept to control the mountain people. A large clumsy, unfinished 'cathedral' stood in the square at Yekaterinodar. The town itself, which was the capital of the Black Sea Cossacks, stretched over an immense space, with broad, straight intersecting streets, many without houses. The population was approximately 3,000. Other 'fortresses' or redoubts were weaker, or consisted of pickets and look-out posts. The soldiers' duty was to keep their restless neighbours in check and stop night crossings from one bank to another and raids and attacks on travellers. Serious assaults by independent Circassians were a reality: Lyall describes an event of 1821 when 1,000 men were drowned and 2,000 killed by cannon fire.[16] The prison at Yekaterinodar held Circassian prisoners, while Circassians had taken hostages to be later traded for prisoners (one Circassian to two Russians).[17] Lyall does not see the irony in the touristic show of horsemanship put on for guests (permitted by the local *ataman*) for him by a 'good humoured' Circassian prince and his suite, while native traders (salt in exchange for rye) on the border were poor and plague ridden, as were those on the coast. Such displays were *de rigueur* for travellers in Russian-dominated Circassia and Georgia, and although named, the prince (Prince

Pshi Mahmet Khadjemko) does not appear more than an object of curiosity mainly described for his dress and arms. The image of the Circassian, and other warrior mountain peoples, reduced to a touristic spectacle was part of Russia's colonial propaganda.

The British: Black Sea Fever

Commitment, not curiosity or amusement, forged the accounts of Circassia by the merchant James Bell, the agent, journalist and later consul John Longworth, and the professional travel writer, Edmund Spencer. For the first time reports to the Foreign Office and an audience back home shared original, lived experiences from the coast of Circassia and its interior and assessments of the tribal situation, which had become a matter of preoccupation for the British government.

 The incident that had galvanized the British establishment and the public was the seizure by Russia of a British brig, the *Vixen*, in 1836, owned by the the family of James Bell at the blockaded port of Sujuk-Kale.[18] The Russians were trying to enforce the blockade of their recently acquired (since the Treaty of Adrianople)[19] Black Sea ports. Only two of these, Anapa and Redut-Kale, were open to foreign commercial shipping. The vessel had left England, with the knowledge of the Foreign Office and Embassy at Constantinople, to test the blockade. While it docked at Constantinople, it unloaded some of its cargo (ammunition and gun powder), then continued to the coast of Circassia with salt and other commodities, which probably included illicit ammunition. The seizure was felt to be unlawful and, as some would have it, a provocation and an insult to the British Crown. It became a *cause célèbre* with demands for compensation, long standing repercussions and lengthy parliamentary debates, swathes of correspondence and newspaper articles.[20] Moreover the *Vixen* was not the first vessel to have been seized. The *Lord Charles Spencer* had been detained in 1831.[21] These incidents became inextricably linked to future free access to the coast of Circassia by British shipping and the issue of Circassian freedom.

The cause of Circassian freedom had been raised in Britain by the diplomat and agitator David Urquhart (1805-77), who was attached to the embassy in Constantinople from 1835-37. Urquhart was an ardent nationalist, first in favour of Greece, then of Circassia and a vehement Russophobe with a passion for Turkey and Turkish civilization. He refused to accept the Treaty of Adrianople's concessions over the Circassian coast because he argued that Circassia was an independent country (which it nominally was). He had visited Circassia in 1834 at the request of Lord Ponsonby (the fear at the time being that Russia had set her sights on Turkey).[22] During this visit Urquhart became closely involved with Circassians, who were at time being pummelled by Russia. He designed their flag (three crossed arrows pointing to twelve stars, representing the Circassian tribes), a version of which is in use to this day and was also responsible for their manifesto of independence. In a long letter to, Foreign Secretary Palmerston (1830-41) Urquhart outlines his key arguments for the necessity of British involvement in Circassia and the need for an independent Circassia. Russia was universally hated in the region, even by Christians, he states, and Circassia was Russia's gateway to Turkey and eventually its 'preponderance' in Europe. Russia's army was not as strong as it was reputed to be and mortality high, but nevertheless he foresaw Russian dominance. Circassia was 'de facto' independent, her rights should be defended by Britain and thus it would create a barrier to Russia's interests in Turkey and Persia. Urquhart had been instrumental in providing a manifesto of Circassian independence signed by the tribal chiefs (see below). He also outlines the effect of the loss of Anapa and the blockade of the coast by Russia: the regular trade in hemp, flax, skins, wool, honey and butter was now interrupted, with poverty spreading inland. Even salt had been cut off by the Russians. Arms could only be obtained by smuggling, he writes (the locals were hopeless at trying to extract gunpowder), and the only harbour occupied by the Circassians was now Sungach (and thence to Ghelenjik). The message was clear: Britain should interfere and help; the Circassians would be open to establishing a government if a chief was sent from Britain.[23] Lord Ponsonby (ambassador at Constantinople) was also encouraging British involvement in Circassia, was in touch with Circassian chiefs and recommended the appointment of a permanent British agent in Circassia.[24] Palmerston was intent on keeping the integrity of the Ottoman Empire (also keeping the balance of power) and seems at first to have been impressed by these arguments, but essentially remained cautious and unwilling to act in any significant way. Urquhart developed his arguments (the illegality of the cession of the coast of Circassia to Russia in the Treaty of Adrianople, that Russia was ready to take action against a weak Turkey, that British trade in the Levant would disappear if Russia were to seize the Dardanelles and that all were looking to England for action, and that if she acted France would support her) in numerous publications, including the political, anti-Palmerston journal *Portfolio*, which Urquhart edited, where he was to accuse, with Karl Marx, Palmerston of collaborating with the Russians.[25] Urquhart became hugely influential in fostering the hope of Circassians for British intervention and in encouraging British partisanship and reconnaissance of the area. The fate of independent Circassia became a matter of national debate and disagreement in the government. King has assessed Urquhart's contribution to Circassian or north Caucasus nationalism as both romanticizing the cause and seeing the potential geopolitical value of an as yet unconquered territory on the Black Sea coast.[26]

Petitions from the chiefs of Circassia to the British government came as early as 1835 and continued until 1843, later to be picked up again (see below)[27] and the Proclamation of Circassian Independence addressed to the Courts of Europe was published in *The Times* on 26 December 1836.[28] Thus was indulged the curious, and eventually damaging, British involvement in Circassia. This involvement mostly went unnoticed at the highest level, as Britain had no desire to confront Russia other than diplomatically, but it prompted reconnaissance, limited supplies of ammunition and gunrunning to Circassia. These moves aggravated and agitated Russia but never threatened it. The official British line was that the Circassians should make peace with Russia and encourage trade, knowing that Russia would not relinquish Circassia.[29]

This approach was to frustrate agents such as Dr Riach, sent by John McNeill,[30] the British Envoy at the Court of Persia, to report on the Caucasus (see below and Dagestan). Not all the Circassian provinces, as has been noted, were officially at war with Russia. Russia had already succeeded in co-opting (often nominally only) the provinces east of Shapsug on the Kuban. Some chiefs had made treaties with Russia promising to be neutral, but not fully allied, as they saw their immediate neighbours being laid waste.[31] The Emperor (Nicholas I) had visited the region in September 1837.[32]

Partisans and agents (1835-39)

'...*first comes Daoud Bey, then Kutchuk Bey, then Yakoob Bey, and lastly yourself...[Alciade Bey] all to keep the pot boiling over... but whether [it] will turn out ditch-water, porridge or good mutton soup, Allah alone can tell.*'[33]

Spencer, passing in 1836 via Crimea and Moldavia from Trebizond, 'inundated with Russian agents',[34] was on the bandwagon that Circassia was becoming. The 'theatre' of his 'wanderings', he writes, had been invested in the commercial and political events of the last few years. Spencer was strongly influenced by Urquhart: the frontispiece of his *Travels in Circassia* shows the Circassian flag and he includes the text of the Circassian Declaration of Independence in the book.[35] There was never a more favourable moment for 'our government' to 'acknowledge the independence of Circassia' not only for commercial and political reasons, he writes, but for the sake of rational justice and truth.[36] The state of the Russian navy was weak and the army inferior and both would be unable to carry out a successful war against the European powers, he argues.[37] Moreover, the Circassian 'was not slothful not fanatic' and by inference would make a worthy partner.[38]

He continued the partisan Circassian theme in his *Travels in the Western Caucasus* (several editions), where he goes into far greater detail about the geopolitical 'prize' that would be Circassia. He devotes several didactic chapters to this idea (IV-VII), with one chapter wholly dedicated to the threat posed by Russia to England's Indian dominions.[39] Yet he was aware that time has passed, the crisis of 1837 was over, and the mood had altered. Her Majesty's advisers 'have become fettered' with the 'no war' party or entangled in Muscovite intrigue, he comments derisively.[40]

Bell and Longworth were to stay in Circassia for extensive periods of time. Bell felt he was owed reparation for the seizure of the family vessel, and while ostensibly staying for trading purposes, also took an 'enthusiastic interest' in arresting the progress of the 'cruel and unprincipled' warfare in the country.[41] He arrived from Sinope (one of the ports, with Samsun, most frequented by the Circassians) and stayed from 1837-39. Longworth came first and foremost as an official observer from His Majesty's Government 'as a volunteer in the cause of my country' and out of excitement for the cause of Circassia. He stayed for a year (1837) and came fully prepared, via Constantinople and Sinope, to meet Circassian chiefs and assess the situation.[42] He arrived with gifts (pistols, swords, needles, work boxes and 1,400lb of lead for bullets).[43] Bell and Longworth (Alciade Bey) met up and also encountered others: a Mr Knight (Nadir Bey) and a Mr S(tewart),[44] who came for a short time only, ready to 'storm castles'[45] and Spencer, not named. Bell, with others (certainly Longworth), reported back to London.[46]

All felt the danger of arriving in Circassia, as Russian and local spies were everywhere; Russians disguised as Circassians, Armenians spying for Russia. Other partisans, French and Poles, were also in the mix. Landing either at Pschat (Longworth) or Subesh (Bell), where the 'natives rushed down hills… streaming along the beach' to welcome the boat, they were greeted by local notables, and were taken inland, or as with Bell, sailed and rode along the coast from Subesh south then as far north as they could get to, with forays inland. The result of Bell's voyage down the coast was an extremely useful and detailed coastal map (from Anapa to Poti but focusing on the northern Circassian coast) which named most landing places and inland rivers flowing south from the Kuban. The experience had shown him how many vessels from Turkey escaped the Russian trade blockade. This was corroborated from the Constantinople side by the number of boats arriving there from coastal Circassia. This knowledge was also to fuel Bell's enthusiasm for potential British trade along this coastline. Spencer also takes up the matter of a commercial alliance between Great Britain and Circassia in his *Travels in the Western Caucasus*.[47]

Inland, Bell and Longworth spent time with local chiefs in the mountains, valleys and river banks of Shapsug territory, up to the Kuban. They reconnoitred the area, spied on Russian forts, witnessed Russian and Circassian attacks and, perhaps more importantly, attended tribal council meetings (*medjilis*), held to discuss the war, consider alliances, allot gunpowder and resolve local matters. Bell in particular took on the role of adviser in matters of military tactics and promoter of British involvement. Spencer spent less time in Circassia, and focuses more on ethnographic detail rather than political or military reporting when writing about Circassia (see Part 3), although he did encounter the Tubians and Ubikians (Ubykh) on the way to assist the Temirgoy in one battle.[48] The Englishmen were not automatically trusted by all and alternately exhibited, argued about or escorted with a guard of honour.[49] The Russians were also after them: a reward of 2,000 roubles had been set for Bell's capture.[50] Towards the end of their trip there were threats that the men would be hanged if caught.[51]

Urquhart (Daoud Bey) had tried to introduce an oath of fidelity and brotherhood sworn on the Koran to the tribes, which he hoped would bring about unity and effective government. Unity was not straightforward in the elitist and separately headed Circassian tribal system and the issue was compounded by real difficulties, as some tribes might be on temporary good terms with the Russians (because they were so exposed, such as the Bey of Zadoog province),[52] while also wanting to side with their compatriots. As a result, not all provinces were united[53] and taking the oath proved divisive. It became necessary to enforce the oath on some recruits, such the *Tokavs* (or freemen), who were often richer than the nobles and were at odds with them. The latter's power was nevertheless on the wane.[54] Yet Bell and Longworth still hoped that a 'national movement' might come about.[55] Spencer, in support of his arguments and for literary purposes, emphasizes 'the closest bonds of fellowship' between the tribes.[56]

For the Circassians what was pressing was the Russian advance and whether British help would be forthcoming. This was issue on which Bell and Longworth also waited for clarification. Bell referred to the 'tergiversation' of the Foreign Secretary with regards to Circassia as reported in *The Times* of 19 December 1837.[57] Amidst petitions, correspondence and envoys, rumours in Circassia were rife, including that of the arrival of a British fleet.[58]

The number of Circassian chiefs and notables encountered by the Englishmen on their quest illustrated the complexity of the situation. The most unifying and dominant figure was 'the best leader in battle' Mansur Hawduko (of the Natukhai tribe, Semes or Novorossisk region).[59] There was also the elderly but still hugely respected 'Lion of Circassia, a Shapsug leader, Ghezil/Ghuz Beg, given a full frontispiece by Bell (front cover). Others were Shamuz, a noble of the Tshupako tribe (who accused the English of being spies, but later regretted it),[60] and Atshaigag-oku Pshugui (of the Psadug). The Ubykh to the south were led by Ismail Berzeg. Spencer mentions an Aitek Tcherei of the Temirgoy tribe, with whom he travelled a while.[61] There were other more local chiefs, such as Kalabat-Oku Hatukwoi, the chief of Ghelenjik, or Achmet of Vardan. Not all were worthy of respect or trustworthy: Hadji Oli Effendi was 'a master of humbug',[62] Shimaf Bey (Prince of Semes)[63] was only interested in plunder, and the daredevil dandy known as The Wolf (Churuk Oglu Tungus), who always insisted on wearing full Circassian regalia, was someone over whom the ladies swooned, but who was known to have become too close to a Russian officer.[64] Other notables included judges, such as Mehmet Effendi and Hadji Ismael, from Adugum. A key figure was Sefer Bey, the envoy and ambassador of the Circassians to Constantinople. He had been recommended to the British Crown by Urquhart (generally supported by Russian and western observer thinking, see Part 3).⁶⁵

Further complicating the local situation was the attempted influence of Shamil's envoys from Dagestan in the late 1830s, who were preaching a strict form of Islam and a disciplined 'jihad' (see below). Islam was at time 'but slightly cultivated' by the Circassians,⁶⁶ who preferred their traditional 'pagan' ways. Longworth elaborates on this in a later report on Circassia to the Foreign Office prior to his second trip there in 1855.

The *medjilis*, held in open air clearings or groves, were rife with rumours, counter rumours, spy mania and local jealousies. They could be extremely volatile. Out of the plethora of the costly (to the tribal host) *medjilis* attended by Bell and Longworth, one of the most consequential took place in May 1837, when the nobles, elders and judges of the Shapsug and Natukhvitch (Natukhai) assembled near Semes.⁶⁷ Mansur opened the meeting, speaking in Circassian: he enquired after Daoud Bey (Urquhart) and asked what hopes Britain could give them. He wanted to know the truth. A document (i.e. the petition) had been taken to England years ago (1834) and they were still waiting for a proper response. The Turks, they felt, had deserted them. Longworth qualifies this account by stating that they were at the mercy of their interpreters (a Georgian, and Mehmet Hadji Oli, the 'humbug' judge),⁶⁸ as in the hands of interpreters such communications were always prone to editing and embellishment. Bell and Longworth felt obliged to give encouragement but said that they were there not there as official representatives of the government but in a private capacity.⁶⁹ Bell added, however, that Lord Ponsonby had charged him to tell them that a message that would satisfy them would be forthcoming from the government.⁷⁰ This was contained in despatches from Constantinople and Adrianople which had arrived via Sefer Bey and were opened in a separate area of the council. Both Bell and Longworth showed their commitment to the cause by offering to join in battle and Longworth shared the lead he had brought with him.⁷¹

Circassian frustration and distrust of foreigners was perfectly legitimate as the communications between their envoy, Lord

Ponsonby and the British government never seemed to yield anything substantial.[72] Yet the now opened round of despatches on the part of the ambassador excited the judge: peace terms were to be agreed with the Russians, the Russians were to retire beyond the Kuban and evacuate fortresses in Circassia, the Circassians were to abstain from crossing the Kuban line, and Britain was to be their guarantor. The message conveyed to the Russian General Veliaminov by a delegation served only to enrage the Russians. Veliaminov disparaged Britain and the 'adventurers', derided the Circassians and proclaimed that only total surrender to the emperor would be acceptable.[73] In accordance with the official British request, heralds were sent a second and a third time to the Russians, who remained implacable. The Circassians, seeing they had nothing to hope from negotiation, prepared for action.[74] Bell usefully prints the key documents about this debacle in his Appendices.

Knowing that it would never relinquish Circassia, Britain's actions in this case were surely aimed only at badgering Russia (ultimately at the expense of the Circassians). The 'incessant' war then being waged did not consist of outright battles but raids and forays (on both sides, and on 'peaceful' Circassians) to capture cattle and take hostages, skirmishes and ambushes. Major attacks had to be timed to take place after the harvest (August), as this was crucial to the Circassians,[75] and were best at night. The Russian strategy was to send annually a large expedition to the north-east shore of the Black Sea from Georgia and to defend the Kuban. The Kabardians and Shapsugs had been targeted in 1835-36 and the western Akhasians had been chiefly aimed at in 1837. The eastern Abkhazians, 'who served Russia' under the local Bey or Prince Michael, had recently returned from exile in Siberia and had fallen out with his brother.[76] Generals Wilheminoff and Sass (the latter with a reputation for extreme savagery) systematically destroyed crops and villages in the push to build forts inland as they tried to occupy or retain the coast. They might come from sea and valley simultaneously, as was the case in the assault at Subesh and Sukhum-Kale, which the Circassians lost, reported

Bell.[77] Things on the coast could also work against the cause, as some the Circassians, who were better off, were more likely to come to terms with the Russians and fighting had then to be conducted both against the Russians and their own compatriots, as at Sukhum-Kale.[78] Some immediate advantages could be had when the Russians retreated without completing an attack because of the condition of the army, as happened in 1836 when Veliaminov retreated to the Kuban from attempting to hold Sujuk-Kale (near Semes).[79] Situations could also be turned: an assault on the Russian fort of Sashe which failed at first was later successful.[80] Keeping up with Russian movements was essential, and Bell and Longworth took part in much reconnoitring from high ground: they spied on Ghelenjik fortress, wanting to see its fortifications,[81] on Pshat,[82] noted the completion of Shapseen fortress[83] and observed the isolation and misery of Aboon, 'more like an encampment' than a fortress, where soldiers died of disease and poor conditions as much as from the enemy.[84] Desertion from these forts was a common problem, as was that by recently imported coastal 'military' colonists, who found the conditions intolerable.[85] Riach lists the posts held by the Russian forces (c.1836-37) from Anapa southwards: Anapa, Gelenjek (Ghelenjik) Pshaad, Gagra, Peetsoonda, Bzeel, Bombore, Sukhum-Kale, Drandra, Eelore, Redou-Kul (Redut-Kale) Pote (Poti) and Fort St Nicolai, on the frontier between Russia and Turkey. Some of these posts, he reports, were old Turkish fortresses (Anapa, Sukhum-Kale, Poti). But these were not secure: in all posts north of Soukhoum-Kul the 'power of the emperor is said to be in most places entirely confined to the space within the walls of the redoubts, and there seems to be no exaggeration in the statement that so closely are the garrisons besieged, that a man who goes only a few yards from the walls runs a great risk of being shot or carried off, while armed men and even guns, it is said, have to be sent with along with the parties who are obliged to go for forage or firewood, or to feed and bring cattle belonging to the garrison.'[86]

The numbers of Circassian fighters were difficult to assess at any one time. A fairly large muster was considered to be c.5,000, but Bell was told (and believed) that up to ten times that number could be mustered.[87] Indeed, Riach's figures, taken from official Russian sources, record four 'clans' of Circassians to be over 500,000 in 1833 or 1834. These outnumbered the Russian army, estimated at the time to be c.45.000 in the Caucasus, a 'ruinous drag' on the Russian purse.[88] These were 'not a few thousand wretched highlanders' who, due to geography, feuds and social custom were unable to combine their power, despite their hatred of Russia, reported Riach.[89]

'Gathering of the Circassians'

Bell records the situation as he found it locally: one chief was able to bring 5-6,000 men to the field but numbers could be scaled up to 15,000 with volunteers, who nevertheless had to support themselves and could not always be relied on. Up to 15,000 could be assembled at a *medjilis*. New districts joining forces could add new numbers.[90]

To the difficulty of disunity was added the perpetual problem of lack of gunpowder and firearms. Spencer describes one group, descending from the mountains, armed only with shields, bows and arrows as well as light guns.⁹¹ They depended on what was brought to them (by Longworth and other foreigners, for example), from raids on forts, booty and shipwrecks. Inability to produce their own materiel has already been mentioned. Spencer refers to the wealth of other trophies taken from the Russians apart from firearms: articles of dress, gold watches, snuff-boxes.⁹² British gunpowder was found in 'Circassian flasks' in 1835-37, writes Riach, but Britain should not be content to smuggle a few flasks but should give aid and instruction to this 'most interesting and suffering' people. War between Russia and Britain would be favoured by all in Tiflis, he notes, but while deriding British apathy, he concludes not by encouraging war, but by reflecting on what kind of government would be set up if the Russians were driven out (by means of a fleet on the Black Sea, support from Turkey and Persia, although the latter was not likely). Would it be a native government, and would the European powers allow it?⁹³ Riach's analysis was clear and realistic, but London continued to toy with the idea of partial aid and giving encouragement to the Circassians to the detriment of the Circassian cause.

When Longworth and Bell felt it was time to leave it was with a heavy heart: they realized things were not going well for the Circassians. Longworth stated that he could no longer be instrumental in deceiving them with 'expectations that were wholly fallacious', and as his 'single arm' could not 'avail them in their struggles', he went first.⁹⁴ Bell nevertheless prints a letter (March 1840) from Hassan Bey listing recent attacks on Russian forts and the fall of Waia, Shapsug and Toapse, an event reported in *The Times* of 1840 as well as the *Morning Herald* (Longworth's paper) and others.⁹⁵ 'We are gathering again,' concludes Hassan.

These victories were to galvanize the Chechens into action.⁹⁶

A Neutral Traveller (early 1840s)

'… On whose right to the disputed territory [of the Caucasus] I offer no opinion…' So wrote George Poulett Cameron, East India Company officer, in the preface to his *Personal Adventures and Excursions in Georgia, Circassia, and Russia* (1845). Cameron had had a varied carrier, including a stint in Portugal, commander of the garrison in Tabriz between 1836-38 and as agent in Arcot and later Madras. His biographers mention his visiting Russian garrisons in Circassia in 1838 (but this is not mentioned in his *Personal Adventures*).[97] A letter to Lord Palmerston of November 1839 (en route via Turkey to Baghdad), however, describes his meeting with Circassians (on board a steamer to Sinope and beyond) including The Lion (the elderly Kizbech Bey), who had been to Constantinople to garner support for an attack on Russians that did not take place, and who was now returning to Circassia to mount an offensive. In the same letter Cameron refers to having been in the Kuban provinces in 1838-39 and having come across Longworth (who appeared surprised to find him there, he wrote peevishly).

His aim in writing the travel book (addressed to the Whig Marquis of Lansdowne, Lord President of the Council) was to redress the acrimony against Russia displayed by the press and elsewhere in Britain. He points to Britain's own 'acts of oppression' and suggests that Russia was not the only acquisitive power. But he continues, somewhat tongue in cheek, if Russia were really a threat to the British Empire, then a flotilla of warships in the Baltic or Euxine (Black Sea) would surely send the appropriate signal.[98]

The book is very much a travelogue: Cameron travels from Tabriz via Tiflis to Kharkov, Moscow and St Petersburg in the company of Russian officers and enjoying elite hospitality. His section on the Caucasus does not provide much new information, although he does correct a detail of one account by Longworth, accusing him of exaggeration in his telling of mistreatment by the Russians of a captive chieftain.[99] He assesses the aggregate forces of the western Caucasian tribes as 120,000-130,000 plus 12-15,000 foot soldiers, which if led properly would have been 'insurmountable'.[100] Otherwise, as an army man, he relishes descriptions of the ongoing 'fierce and sanguinary conflict' and guerrilla warfare on the Kuban line and elsewhere, acknowledging the weakness of Russian infantry. He notes the 'beleaguered' port of Anapa and the lack of trade. He meets the envoy Omar

Bey, who offers him much information on the geography and customs of Circassians.[101] He gives a dramatic turn to some of the Circassians he encounters, such as a seasoned and cosmopolitan warrior named 'My Friend of the Mountain', who was unrivalled as a partisan, and writes of the 'ugly affair' which left hardly any Cossack alive[102] and of a venerable old chief, who laments, in theatrical prose, the betrayal of his country and the devastation of war.[103]

Cameron thus joins the list of writers contributing to the tropes that were being created about Circassia and its leaders (see Part 3).

Dagestan and Chechnya

Although part of the same swathe of mountains, those in the southeast, Dagestan and parts of what is now Azerbaijan, were different worlds from the west: they faced east and south (to the Caspian and Central Asia and Iran) as well as looking to the Ottoman west. Multiple ethnic groups, speaking multiple languages and dialects (which fascinated ethnographers and linguists to the point of extravagant speculation, see Part 3) inhabited the mountainous areas of Dagestan. The main ethnic groups were the Avars (west-central), the Lezgi (south, towards Azerbaijan), the Laks or Qazi-Kumuks (small, central) and the Dargins (between the Laks and the Tabarasans).[104] Russians and Europeans tended to refer to these groups as the 'Lesgees'. The Kumyks were on the north piedmont towards Kalmykia, and a small group, the Tabarasans, lived by the Caspian, south of Derbend. The mountain people, some who lived in high natural fortresses, were essentially independent, tribal and clan-based. The east coast was composed of principalities ruled by khans, sultans or *shamkals*. The geography of the area had produced different influences, traditions and histories. For example, the Laks, ruled by a *shamkal* from Tarki, were traditionally the first to be converted to Islam.[105]

Chechnya, on the northern flank of the great range, with the Argun as its main river, was also formed by the piedmont with the Terek and Sunzha rivers and the steppe to the north. It was enclosed by Kabarda and Ingushetia to the west, Georgia, north Ossetia, and Dagestan to the south and the piedmont by the Caspian. The Chechens were the largest, arguably one of the oldest and most remote ethnic groups in the area, with a long martial tradition. They were clan (*taip*) based, but not feudal, and considered themselves 'free', in contrast, for example to the Circassians.[106]

Dagestan had had an early introduction to Islam, first from Arab conquerors in the mid-seventh century. then from sheikhs from Central Asia spreading a Sufi *tariqa* or path of Sunni (Sufi) Islam, known as the Naqshbandiyya, founded in the thirteenth century. named after Sheikh Muhammad al-Din Naqshbandi (1318-89).[107] Ordained sheikhs were to spread the movement through deputies, and it reached Shirvan and the influential Sheikh Ismail al Kurdumiri in the early nineteenth century. The movement was temporarily halted there by the Russians when they annexed the area in 1820, but it took hold again under Sheikh Muhammad al-Shirvani, who spread the movement to Dagestan. A succession of ordained sheikhs ensued with Sheikh Ghazi Muhammed proclaimed Imam of Dagestan in 1829-30 (killed in action). He was followed by Hamza Bek in 1832, and after he was murdered, Shamil, the most legendary of them all, was ordained the third imam in 1834.[108]

Chechnya had historic contacts with Christianity and Islam, but native traditions remained at its core until Islam was forced upon the region by Dagestani sheikhs, as part of the resistance, first under Sheikh Mansur in the eighteenth century, then notably under the Naqshbandiyya and Shamil. In 1840, spurred on by the fall of Russian coastal forts in Circassia, the Chechens asked Shamil to lead them.[109]

Both areas had long lived with Russian intervention. Fortified Russian lines were established in the north in the course of the second half on the eighteenth century: the Kizliar-Mozdok, which became the Terek defensive line, in 1763, the Azov-Mozdok in 1777-78. They were to join the north-western lines of the Kuban (1792) and the Black Sea (1793).[110] In the early nineteenth century the north-eastern line was extended southwards (the Sunzha), which extended into the then Shamkalte of Tarki on the Caspian. A line was also built due south, effectively separating Ossetia from Chechnya. The major fort of Groznaya (Grozny) was built in 1817-18. The campaigns against the mountain peoples were directed by many military commanders but were associated with Yermolov from 1816 onwards, whose primary aim was to subdue the Chechens and then tackle Dagestan. His and his successors' tactics (raiding, destroying, building forts, coercion, co-option, elimination) were to define these campaigns until the mid-1860s and beyond.

The south had suffered from the fall-out between the Russo-Persian wars and the treaties that disrupted their border, and the initiative for consistent, organized rebellion against the Russians had traditionally been taken from Dagestan. The Treaty of Gulistan (1813) proved definitive in this context: Persia ceded the territories north of the River Aras (Dagestan, Derbend, Baku, Shirvan and local khanates and statelets, such as Shaki, Quba, Karabakh, Ganja), rights to the Caspian, and parts of Georgia to Russia. In the 1828 Treaty of Turkmenchay, the khanates of Erivan, Talesh and Nakhichevan were ceded. Politically these areas were piecemeal: Tarki on the coast, for example, had been a Shamkalate (from the title *shamkal*, ruler), with other centres (Shaki, Kiura, Qazi-Kumuk) being khanates. These were all eventually abolished.

The co-option of elites, the advent of Russian administration and dues expected from the populations (troops, horses, taxes) in ceded territories were not only unacceptable but highly damaging to a local way of life and economy. The deliberate introduction of alcohol, for example, had a major detrimental effect.

The khanates turned against each other and/or intrigued with Persia, but also turned towards each other. Those statelets that had originally feuded with each other or had strong loyalty to their own leaders slowly succumbed (by force or otherwise) to the Naqshbandiyya movement.

The Naqshbandiyya goal was unification, loyalty and obedience, the implementation of the right path of Islam and sharia (Muslim religious law) as a way of life. Jihad or resistance against the Russians was essentially in reaction to Russia aggression and Christian proselytization, and was at times pragmatic, with a readiness to negotiate for peace.[111]

The order was gradually built into a state, notably by Shamil. It had not been a simple endeavour. It had required duress, punishment and persuasion. The imams also had rivals, such as Hajj Muhammed Efendi, who belonged to an influential Chechen family[112] and objected when Shamil was asked to lead the Chechens. What emerged was a privy council (*diwan*) with deputy administrators and military commanders (*naibs*). A treasury and taxation were established, so was a regular standing force with cavalry recruited from villages, whose duties were only to the armed conflict. The implementation of sharia was serious: there were strict rules forbidding customary law (which included blood feuds) and severe punishments for anything such as drunkenness or theft, dancing and smoking, as well as for clearing wood or using Russian coin.[113] Such rule, which broke with previous feudal structures and norms, could be considered as equally, if not more, oppressive.[114]

Unlike the Circassians the mountain people here did produce gunpowder, but most artillery was captured from the Russians and managed by Poles. With unequalled knowledge of the terrain, roads were built where necessary, with one engineer Yusuf al Misri ('the Egyptian', i.e. returning from Egypt) helping to build fortification works.[115] A reference to this chief engineer ('Pasha from Egypt') is found in Vice-Consul Cameron's 1860 report from Poti.[116]

The British: '*A state of near open revolt*'[117]

The British were not (yet) attracted to the region *per se* but were alert, via diplomats and agents, to its turmoil; consequences with regards to British relations with Persia and possible threats to India were being assessed.

From the start of the century they witnessed Russians moving troops in preparation of occupation of the provinces of Shirvan down to Baku, and predicted that the Russians meant to possess every port on both sides of the Caspian, and observed that embassies from Shaki and Shirvan were seeking assistance against Russia, and that Armenian merchants were fleeing from area in anticipation of conflict.[118] They noted the flight of native princes from conquered territories and that 'none remains which are strictly dependent on Russia'.[119] Reports on the second war with Persia (1826-28) mention the ill-preparedness and reluctance of the shah to wage war and resulting confusion, but also that the war would end Russia's possible conquest of Persia and threat to India. Yet it would also place Britain in a difficult position vis à vis Persia if the Circassians and others wanted help against Russian aggression. The disaffection of the Muslim inhabitants of Dagestan, Shirvan and Karabagh (who had contacts with their families and followers in Persia) was noted, they were only waiting for a revolt instigated by Mustafa Khan (the Khan of Talysh). However, revenues coming to Russia from these lands were considerable.[120] With regards to the Dagestani mountaineers or Lezgins, the Russians were subduing them prior to Yermolov (1801-02) and by 1823-24 Yermolov had curtailed the power of the Chechens. Riach, reporting in 1837, shows that nothing had quietened down: the provinces recently taken from Persia after the Treaty of Gulistan, 1813, 'watched...for any opportunity... that might...give them a prospect of changing their masters.' The whole region of Quba, Lower Dagestan and Shirvan was in a state of near open revolt, he continued. In Dagestan things had also started to move again after the death of Cazee Mullah (Ghazi Mullah, d.1832) but it was a local chief from Deedos in Dagestan who had done the most damage. He had come down from Toosh in Kakheti, slaughtering many, including a colonel, and seizing large amounts of booty.

Figures Riach obtained from an official Russian document of 1833-34, numbered ten Caucasian groups at 1,535, with the seven ex Persian provinces at 471,046.[121]

These reports show how closely Russian and local activities were being followed, but interference by the British among the mountain peoples of the ex-Persian statelets was not yet directly sanctioned. The report also highlights the growing political and economic importance of Tiflis (Tbilisi) and that the French had already installed a consul, M. Gamba, there. This was perhaps a hint, but the British were not to appoint a consul in Tiflis until after the Crimean War, and then for a short time only.

The Crimean War (1853-56): Circassia and Dagestan

A war came; perhaps it was not the one the mountain peoples wished for, but it came nevertheless, with opportunities both for them and the allies.

The cause of the Crimean War, initiated by Russia and Turkey, was ostensibly over concessions granted by the sultan to the Catholics over the holy places in Palestine and Russia's demands to protect Orthodox rights in Ottoman lands. Deeper reasons were the interests of the Great Powers (Britain, France, Austria, Prussia and Russia) in parts of the shrinking Ottoman Empire, the extent of Russia's demands from the Ottomans and her desired monopoly of the Black Sea. The Turks declared war in 1853 after Russia had invaded the Danubian Principalities (Moldavia and Wallachia). Britain and France joined in 1854 as the defence of Turkey was required against Russian aggression. Palmerston also saw extravagant opportunities: an opened Black Sea, Crimea and Georgia back in Turkish hands and a free Poland.[122] There was high rhetoric over this prospect.[123] The focus for Britain (and France) now fell with greater force on the uses of the mountain people (in Dagestan and Circassia) in this conflict. The thought was that they would unite and fight alongside Turkey and the allies.

The theatre of war in the Caucasus was mostly the southern border with Turkey (with the Russian aim to capture Kars, Ardahan and Bayazit, with Kars a major prize) and the eastern coast of the Black Sea, approximately from Sukhum-Kale to Poti with inroads southwards from the mountain communities into Georgia. The key Ottoman fortresses on the south and east coast were Trebizond and Batum.

The British: *'A Superior Man'* and Others

From 1854-56 there were no shortage of volunteers to assist with intelligence gathering and the supply of arms to the Caucasus. These dates show that Britain's tentative attempts to involve itself in this aspect of the war was comparatively late; the French had started earlier.[124] A Captain Francis Hughes is known to have had orders to talk to chiefs and visit Circassia with rifles in 1854-55 as well as ascertaining the practicality of obtaining supplies of cattle for the army in Circassia,[125] and an ex-consul to Bolivia, J.A. Lloyd presented his services to Lord Clarendon the same year as a 'geographer, scientific officer and engineer'.[126] One man, however, was recommended to Lord Clarendon (the Whig Foreign Secretary) as a suitable envoy to Circassia: John Longworth. Since leaving Circassia in 1837 or 1838 he had fought and distinguished himself in the Hungarian war of 1848-49 and had become consul at Monastir (Tunisia). He was a 'superior man', wrote H.D. Seymour (diplomat) from Constantinople. Longworth had had a Jesuit education (later changing his religion), could understand Turkish, knew Circassia, knew the manners of the East and had been a correspondent for the *Morning Herald* on eastern matters.[127]

When closer to their objectives the agents were soon confronted by the political and other realities of the situation. Between June and August 1854 Lloyd spent his time in and around Constantinople (Pera, Tarabya, Buyukada) and Varna gathering information on and from Circassian chiefs politicking in Constantinople, outlining ambitious plans for the war effort (based on map information only) and demanding ammunition, ordnance, gifts (including a chainmail suit for Shamil) and better support.[128] By this time the allies were already engaged, and he had the extra complication of having to communicate via Lord Raglan and others such as Admiral Bryant. Lloyd was clear from the start about Turkish intrigues vis-à-vis the Circassians, with the Circassians' being bought by the Turks, and he noted that the sultan was obsessed with sovereignty over Circassia. His reports on the chiefs and 'the Naib' (Shamil's envoy) whom he encountered at Varna, together with Lord Raglan, and at Akseray (chaperoned at first by Turkish interpreters) are telling. Many of the chiefs he met were old and sick, pressured by the Ottomans (the Naib was in thrall to the Porte), he wrote, but still hoping for French (of which Lloyd was suspicious) and British support. He wanted to have the chiefs conveyed to Varna under British protection, away from Constantinople, and thence to Circassia, where they could be rallied into battle. Lloyd sent a long list of names of chiefs from Dagestan (the Naib's) and others from villages of Circassia. Raglan refused. No British ship was available. After three months' 'idleness' and despite Raglan's wishes it seems that due to 'circumstances' Lloyd had been unable to enter Circassia, partly because he had not the support he needed from His Majesty's Government, he complained. Lloyd never made it to Circassia; he died in January 1855.[129]

Longworth's record put him in a strong position to ask for proper support: £1,000 (with an added £500) would be necessary to recruit an interpreter, servants and for other necessities, he wrote to Lord Canning (British Ambassador at Constantinople).[130] Palmerston's orders for his mission were clear: he was not to give 'a political character' nor pledges to the mountain people, but to give encouragement for co-operation with the allies. Accurate information on this possible co-operation was needed. He should enquire how much Circassian cavalry might be put at the British government's disposal (it was difficult to ship horses from England). He should bring presents of lead and gunpowder, and rifles and mountain guns would also be made available; he was to attempt to communicate with Shamil in Dagestan and learn of his plans; he was to realistically ascertain what the state of the tribes was; could they be united despite their feuds and under what sort of government; what sort of assistance and protection would the tribes require from the allies? He was to point out that assisting the allies would be the best option for them; French envoys were also being sent. Longworth was to act in concert with the French agent in Batoum (M Champoiseau). Further, Lord Clarendon demanded that Longworth should carry a disclaimer from the Ottoman Porte that they had no designs on the sovereignty of Circassia themselves. A *firman* (royal mandate) in favour of

Circassian independence after the Russians had been expelled was obtained from the Porte in June 1855.[131] This was not to prove solid, and the ambiguity of the wording, which stressed that 'the rights and privileges' of the Circassians should be maintained (but not by whom) was noted at the time.[132] Reassurances were asked for and given via Lord Stratford de Redcliffe (Statford Canning, ambassador at Constantinople), to London.[133] The Embassy then learnt that Mustafa Pasha had been appointed Governor-General of Circassia.[134]

Longworth was ready but not naive: he had outlined the pitfalls of dealing with the tribes in a memorandum on Circassia written for the Foreign Office in preparation for his mission while still at Monastir. He states at the very beginning that the power and resources of the Circassians were very overrated and the nature of the tribes misunderstood. They were good at defence and raids but had not the discipline to maintain an offensive. The chiefs had limited control over external matters, were liable to false promises and could be bought. The uses of a 'political agent' conversant with the system 'might be of use' as would be the protection of the British flag, material assistance and the benefits of trade. If the allies were to take the strategically important, but weak, fort of Anapa a land offensive would be needed. Better landing places would be the bays of Sujuk-Kale and Ghelenjik to the south. He assesses that links (leading to co-operation) between Circassia and Shamil in Dagestan were 'fallacious', pointing out, correctly, the differences in race, language, customs and type of Islamic practices between these tribes (Lezgins, Chechens) and the Circassians. Not only was the type of Islam preached different from that in most of Circassia but the submissive, levelling teachings of the Koran was totally at odds with the aristocratic social structure and government of the Circassians. As discussed below, this assessment was fairly correct, if not accurate in detail. The former (Dagestanis) had become far more disciplined, obedient and united under their chiefs than the latter. The Dagestanis' 'emissaries' relative lack of success was due to 'theological hatred', Longworth concluded. In this again he was only partially right (see below for Longworth's encounter with the most notorious emissary of them all 'the Naib'). He was also clear on the aims of Russia: far from any 'civilizing' mission, all it wanted were lines of communication from the Black Sea to the trans-Caucasian provinces and to maintain the supremacy of the Black Sea. He also points out, in a long tirade against the slave trade, that it was in Turkey's interest to re-activate the slave trade on the coast.[135]

On sea and land

By 10 June 1855 Longworth was on board the *Caradoc* off the Sea of Azov, waiting to be taken to Anapa and Soudja (Sujak). He had received his money, rifles and Minié rifles. From now until the end of July he was to send valuable intelligence to Foreign Secretary Lord Clarendon.

Once off the coast at Anapa Longworth signalled (having received intelligence from Captain Hughes) that the Russians had evacuated Anapa, having deliberately ruined the fortress, leaving it open to Turkish aims and interference from the Circassian envoy, Sefer Bey. The Turks arrived in June to occupy the fortress, which Longworth argued with them would be a waste of time. Sefer Bey proclaimed that he had a mandate to be governor of the Circassian provinces. Then Mustafa Pasha, Commander of the Turkish forces, arrived and addressed some 300 Circassian notables with the news that he had been appointed Governor-General of the Circassian provinces. This was evidence of the projected Turkish conquest being underway despite assurances to the contrary. Further, no cavalry would be available for foreign service. The Circassians were the first to resent this Turkish takeover, added Longworth.[136] From now on Longworth's (British) objections and presence became an increasing irritant to the Turkish authorities, and the *firman* he had been issued of no value. Hughes had experienced the same hostility from the Turks in May when landing at Varna (on his way to meet the Naib), with the local Turkish official refusing to allow the arms and ammunition Hughes had brought to be brought ashore.[137]

As regards the Circassian tribes, Longworth explained that Sefer Bey was out of touch with the area, much of which had been

Russianized. The districts bordering the Laba and the Kuban (Bzhedug, Khatukai, Demigoi, Beslenoi and Karachai) and the Kabardas, being on the plains and contiguous with Russia, had become either subject or neutral. The situation was not stable, however. The Russians feared that, given the circumstances, the tribes would cross the Kuban *en masse*; Longworth thought there was little chance of this despite Sefer Bey's assurances to the contrary. The only way to ascertain the truth was to visit the provinces of Shapsook (Shapsug) and Natauoich (Natukhai) in person, wrote Longworth. After a twelve-day expedition (accompanied by a Polish Colonel Yordan and a Mr Alfred Sandison) he reported that these provinces had ceased to be interested in negotiating with foreign powers. Whole populations had been bought, with the erosion of the nobles' powers and their rift with the commoners part of the problem. Whole sectors of the once volatile Kuban and Laba lines had been pacified, with families emigrating across the Kuban to land allotted to them - but they were still distrusted and asked to remove themselves further inland in times of trouble. Just as he anticipated going to Bzhedug and other Kuban provinces where the chiefs were more amenable, a 'social revolution', or revolt by the commoners against the nobles, fomented by the Naib at the head of 500 horsemen, broke out in Bzhedug. The Naib had proclaimed that class distinctions were against the precepts of the Koran that all Muslims were equal in the sight of God.[138]

Shamil and the Naib

Shamil had repeatedly appealed to the Ottomans for help and support against the Russians, but the Ottomans, keen to keep the peace with Russia, had not been responsive in any meaningful way. When war loomed, however, co-operation with Shamil was explored, both by the Ottomans and the allies (France and Britain). The former failed due to poor logistics and no precedent, even when Shamil had written to the sultan stating his disastrous position in 1853.[139] Lack of co-ordination or co-operation between the two forces was proven, when Shamil, taking advantage of the enemy's troop dispersal during the war, made two attempts to march in the direction of Tiflis. In 1853 Shamil marched south to attack Zakatali (east of Tiflis, unsuccessfully) then moved northwards attacking the post of Meseldereg and retreated.[140] A link up with the Ottoman army (from the coast) would have been a possibility around this time, but Shamil either did not wait nor had accurate information. Russian interception of communications between Shamil and the Ottomans also played its part in this war. Omer Pasha's troop deployment on the west coast was piecemeal, however (as the occupation of Sukhum-Kale showed), and considered too late to have any significant impact on the enemy there. As discussed above, the Circassian question and allied interference were also something the Ottomans had to deal with.

Shamil's resistance had caught the public imagination in Europe and in Islamic lands long before his due to accounts such as August Haxthausen's *Tribes of the Caucasus, with an Account of Shamyl and the Murids*, London, 1855.[141] In 1854 he became even more renowned because, in the course of his second campaign towards Tiflis, put off by a rebellion in Kakheti (pro-Russian) and beaten off at Shilda, he followed the retreating Russian army to Tsinandali (the estate of the Princes Chavchavadzes), where he captured the Princesses Chavtchavadze,[142] their children and governess (Anna Drancey) at Tsinandali (sacking the estate) and held them in captivity in his camp in the mountains (across the Alazan, by the tower of Pohali) for eight months. This was not a mindless act on the part of Shamil, but both opportunistic and calculated to shock the Russians into action; his first son (Jamal al Din), kept hostage by the Russians since 1839, was returned to him in exchange, plus 40,000 roubles in ransom and a mutual exchange of prisoners.[143] This became a *cause célèbre*, which generated a flurry of accounts and a memoir.[144] It has been argued that the incident had a negative impact on the western and Ottoman powers' desire to co-operate with Shamil. Clarendon and Stratford de Redcliffe were said to be outraged, calling Shamil 'fanatic and barbarian'.[145] In Shamil's courteous response to a letter from Colonel Williams (British Commander to the Ottoman Forces in Anatolia) about releasing the hostages, he responds as an equal: he congratulates Williams on victories over the enemy, states that the women had been liberated before his letter arrived, and that all knew they (Shamil's army) were humane, and that if Williams had known of the circumstances he would have done the same.[146] Cooperation with the allies eventually proved futile due to mutual distrust, although ammunition for Shamil was supplied (or was intended to be supplied) by the allies in Constantinople, and contact via his envoy was achieved.

'Swelling the ranks of Islam'

As well as searching for volunteers from Ottoman centres such as Batum and gathering reinforcements from neighbouring Sunni Muslim populations of the Caucasus, in his quest for support Shamil also had had contacts with the Qajar court, had hosted two Englishmen ('the name of one is said to be Elliott', well supplied with money, see above) and was bringing captives and defectors into the fold, [147] Co-opting Circassia was a major objective. Hajj Muhammed had been sent as Shamil's envoy in 1843 (killed 1844), followed by Suleiman Effendi. The Circassian response at the time was varied but generally failed to produce what Shamil hoped for.[148] Interestingly, the Georgian mountain tribes do not seem to have been brought into the resistance movement. Mohammed Amin, the Naib, sent in 1848, was able, however, to establish a base and a following in the Abzakhs/Abadzekh region (north slope of Adygea range, Krasnodar). But his relations with the Ottomans were troubled. In a letter to the Grand Vizier in 1854, essentially asking for support for the work he had done and less interference from Ottoman officials after the start of the Crimean War, the Naib describes some of the measures he has taken 'to unify' the tribes. This had not been easy as some had 'been bought' by the Russians and some areas had to be taken by force. In three years, 150,000 families had submitted, he wrote. He had obliged them to take a sacred oath, he had burnt to the ground 'the objects of their ancient adoration' and sacred groves, mosques were raised where none had been before, he had appointed judges, muftis and imams, all according to the precepts of Islam. It is not difficult to see how this extreme enforcement of Naqshbandiyya Islam would have been contrary to some of the Circassian social structure and way of life, particularly the nobles', as indicated by Longworth and others. Now the agents of the Porte each sought to establish their own administration, the Naib wrote, thus dividing the tribes again, creating a new schism and making him waste nine years of work. He considered himself leader of the Circassians, and wanted recognition for his work, but Sefer Pasha, promoted by the Ottomans, had been declared Civil Governor of the Circassian Provinces (between the Black Sea and the Kuban). The Naib went to Istanbul where he was nominated pasha to appease him. The Russians, who had been in fear of the Naib, had promoted and backed opposition leaders in Abadzekh. This led to chaos and pitched battles between the two Muslim armies as well as with the Russians.[149]

In the presence of the Naib

Given Clarendon's instructions about making contact with Shamil, it was imperative that the British envoys should make an effort with his deputy, the Naib. Hughes and Longworth went out of their way to meet him although by this time the Naib's powers were already waning. Their reports reveal the volatile situation of the times.

In May 1855 Hughes pointed out to Rear Admiral Bryant the Naib's considerable influence in the Abadzekh district, and how this would be useful against the enemy on the Laba line. He suggested that some of howitzers waiting to be shipped to Circassia at Scutari might be brought up for service on the Laba with a few intelligent artillery men to train the natives. Hughes disembarked at the tiny Turkish-held hamlet of Vardan (not being allowed to land the arms and ammunition) and after a march of five days reached the Naib's lodgings in the Abadzekh district, near the Russian frontier of the Laba. He was greeted with a drumbeat, a rifle volley and about 300 riflemen. In a private meeting with the Naib (who revealed himself to be fluent in Turkish even though he did not admit so publicly) Hughes asked where on the coast he could deliver the arms. The Naib answered that this was not possible at the moment as the Turks controlled the coast and had 'neutralized' him. They had fostered dissent among the Shapsug tribes and blocked communication (almost as badly as the Russians had). He spoke of a certain 'Keir Hajj Ismail', 'an instrument of the Porte', who was particularly influential. There had been news of Shamil, who was constantly harassing the enemy and even if not victorious, was still responsible for curtailing its power. Hughes took leave of the Naib, with mission unaccomplished, while the Naib set out on a tour of the Abadzekh district.[150]

Unlike Hughes, who did not give his personal opinion of the Naib nor of his movement (at least in official despatches), Longworth did not restrain himself. Even though there were many reprehensible things about the Circassian social order, the 'theocratic principle' proclaimed by the Naib was the most objectionable, he wrote. The 'reactionary movement' headed by the Naib, whose brutal methods (fines, confiscation, even death) towards those who did not comply had turned people to the Russians, but then back again to Sefer Pasha when the war broke out. Anarchy was afoot. While witnessing the 'social revolution' between nobles and commoners of Bzhedug, in which the Turks also participated, Longworth felt it his duty to give support to the cause of the nobles (in line with the *firman* that dictated that he should not interfere with the traditions of the Circassians) as they were the only ones who offered a chance to raise a fighting force. Some 200 men rallied to him immediately. Hearing that the Naib was in the vicinity, Longworth invited him to a 'conference' on 6 July. In contrast to the festive reception afforded to Hughes, the Naib snubbed Longworth and refused to come out and meet him. The reasons given were that the Porte and Mustafa Pasha had 'incurred serious displeasure' at the Naib's meeting His Majesty's Ambassador and others in Constantinople, and would do so again if he received Captain Hughes. His pay and a sword of honour had been withheld. The Naib was clearly ready to play on the tension between the Turks and the British. Longworth advocated the recall of the Naib by the Porte (which effectively happened). In a second attempted meeting in a 'popular assembly of arms' the Naib again refused to talk politics, and the chiefs of the Abassakhs (Abadzekhs) were also intractable. They would only listen to Mustafa Pasha, Longworth's *firman* proving useless. Each went their separate way, with Longworth still hopeful that his intervention had not been in vain. He optimistically suggested that if the cooperation with the nobles proved to be fruitful, they might prove useful and provide irregular cavalry. Their assistance would be chiefly valuable against the communications of Russia with her trans-Caucasian provinces, either on the line of the Kuban, or from the south-east coast of the Black Sea, through Abkhazia and Mingrelia.

After these meetings Longworth felt that the Naib's scheme of 'forming a new Empire in the Caucasus' based on the principles of Mohammedan fanaticism had been merely adjourned. The Naib was trying unsuccessfully to curry favour with the court at Constantinople, and Longworth understood why His Majesty's Ambassador had formed a poor opinion of him, given the proud, cunning, ignorant, artful, dangerous and fanatical character of the individual. If the allies were to choose between the cooperation of the Porte or of the Naib, they should choose the former. Longworth now realized that a large part of the problem was the Turkish leadership in the area: Mustafa Pasha proclaimed solidarity with the allies, while undermining them at every opportunity, and Sefer Bey was incompetent and negative. Longworth rated only one leader, Beshet Pasha. He concludes his despatch by writing that unless a completely new policy was adopted regarding the Turkish functionaries (and waiting for a response from Constantinople to this effect), he had decided, with his French counterpart, Champoiseau, to suspend negotiations with the Circassians.[151]

Thus ended Longworth's mission on Circassian land. By the end of July he was back in Trebizond. It is not known what immediate effect these letters, which were considered important enough to have been printed by the Foreign Office, had on policy but they cannot have been very encouraging. The Foreign Office had also needed reminding of the previous treaties and debates over Circassia.[152]

Back to the war

There were several engagements in Transcaucasia during 1853 and 1854, mostly concentrated on the border with Turkey. The Russian Fort St Nicholas on the coast fell in 1853 with the Russians vacating Redut-Kale[153] as a result and the Turks were defeated in Akhaltsik inland. The main battle of the region that year took place at Bashgedikler (near Kars) with a major Turkish defeat.[154] The Ottoman army was not in good shape: it had gradually dwindled from c.120,000 to c.54.000 men by 1855. This was not only due to losses in battle, but to desertions, rivalry among leaders and ill health. It had needed reinforcements on the Turkish frontier, but this was delayed as the allies were concentrated on Crimea and Sebastopol.[155]

The Russian aim for 1855 was to deal with the town of Kars. Having first started a siege in September, they then unsuccessfully stormed the fortress, then besieged it again until the Nova Scotia-born commander of the Turkish troops General Williams surrendered on 26 November. By this time the inhabitants and troops were dying of starvation and disease. This was a temporary victory for the Russians, and from the losers and captives it spurred a spate of explanatory publications, and a tourist trail (see below). General Williams' valiant resistance made him renowned in the Caucasus.

After the end of the 1855-56 campaign, Russian troops began to move back and the French wanted the war to end. Britain would have liked in theory to continue in Crimea and the Caucasus, but this was unrealistic since a major campaign in Europe involving all the allies would have been needed to properly defeat Russia.[156] As things stood, France was the dominant military partner and Austria had the upper hand with Russia. Austria gave an ultimatum to Russia for armistice, which was agreed upon; peace negotiations started in 1855 and the peace protocol was signed in Vienna in February 1856.

In March 1856, however, envisaging a continuation of the war, or the prospect of another one, Major Cathcart was on a mission to investigate the 54-mile route from Batum to Ardvin (inland from the Black Sea) to see to what extent it was passable for guns and to assess the available ground for military places and posts. He provided a detailed description (and map) of the terrain, sea levels, rivers, weather, resources, local people (Kurds and Laz, see below), as well as describing the port of Batum (much depleted by the Turkish occupation) and Ardvin.[157] The country was not secure, reported Colonel Williams in a military report of 1857 (see note 157). He refers to the undefended nature of Tiflis and Erivan and the aim of facilitating resources between these 'important lines of operation'. Around 60,000 Molokans (Eastern Orthodox sect) had been settled along the frontiers of Turkey and Persia and in the Province of Erivan to increase provisions and transport. The roads between the two were still terrible and impassable in winter, he concludes. Given the volatility of this frontier, such reports would always have been useful.

The terms of the Treaty of Paris, signed on 30 March, a day before the armistice was going to finish, were not fully satisfactory to all but tackled the main issues such as the Christian populations of the Ottoman lands, Bessarabia, Danubian navigation and - crucially - the demilitarization and opening up of the Black Sea to merchant vessels.[158]

For Britain this was to prove not quite the opportunity it might have anticipated, but sheds light on its real interest in the Circassian coast and its nominal investment in Circassian independence (see below).

Shamil's surrender

The peace treaty scuppered many plans, but above all it dealt the final blow to Shamil's resistance in Dagestan, and later to the Circassians. By 1856 the Russians had decided to crush Shamil definitively. They reorganized the Caucasian Army and relocated units so that each would concentrate on a specific area with a clear chain of command. A report from Col. John Simmons to Lord Clarendon on the state of the Army in 1857 numbers it as 201,000 men (on paper 300,000 plus 'valueless' irregulars), with the Lezgin corps consisting of 50.000 men with its headquarters at Zakatali. There were 165 battalions of regular infantry (1,000 men each) plus irregular infantry, 28 squadrons of cavalry, 120 squadrons of Cossacks, 380 field guns and 16 field mortars.¹⁵⁹ The campaigns became savage, taking possession of strategic defiles, moving populations, storming forts, clearing forests. Shamil's forces were exhausted, and refusing negotiations with the Russians, desperate and against his better judgement, Shamil asked for help from the British and the French. He was rebuffed. By now the British were washing their hands of their direct venture with the mountain peoples. The Russians had learnt strategy, and 'well planned' tactical movements and bribery were to contribute to the final defeat of the mountain people. The Russians encircled Mount Gunib, where Shamil had taken refuge with his family and followers, and on 6 September 1859, Shamil surrendered. The Russians were keen to have him alive, aware of the kudos of this success after so long. Shamil was treated with honour, moved to several places within Russia, including Kiev, whence he was allowed to perform the hajj to Mecca. He died in Medina in 1871 and was buried there.¹⁶⁰

Given Shamil's lack of proper support, the length of the resistance was exceptional and proof of his organizational powers. Having been duly lionized, his surrender made headlines and was widely illustrated. Gunib became incorporated into a tourist trail (see Parts 3 and 4).

'Shamyl'

The Naib was recalled to Constantinople at the request of the Russians in 1857,[161] and on the way in Trebizond he reported to Consul Stevens on the state of the ongoing war in Circassia. There had been monthly engagements during late 1856-1857, involving not only the Naib's troops, but those of local chiefs from different villages taking matters into their own hands (including some who had reneged on their oath to Russia) as well those of Sefer Pasha and a Polish contingent. A chief from Sochi had raided Sukhum-Kale in the old-fashioned way and taken 400 into slavery, the Naib reported, and there had been a major battle between his troops and the Russians around an upper Laba fort (Russians retreated, inhabitants from surrounding villages taken captive). This conveys the chaos of the situation. The Naib was imprisoned on his return to Constantinople, escaped, came back to Circassia, and finally surrendered in 1859, having accepted bribes (it was rumoured) and moving to Turkey.[162]

'Prospects for Circassia all but desperate'

In 1856-57 communications by Stratford de Redcliffe to Lord Clarendon and between the British and the Russians showed that the Circassian question had not gone away. The British, with their eye on free trade with the Circassian coast, continued to debate the legitimacy of the Russian monopoly and ownership of the coast. But the Russians were adamant: they possessed the coast, they objected to direct trade with the Circassians, and the Circassians had nothing to offer (except slaves), and had no ports, no traders. Britain urged the Russians to 'civilize' the Circassians with trade rather than continue with attrition. In order to deflect the question, the Russians, in a scenario already familiar from the affair of the *Vixen*, accused the British of violating Russian regulations and possibly being engaged in the slave trade. This was vehemently denied, but the Russians took advantage of the chaos in response to the Circassians, who were again 'beating about the bush' in seeking assistance from foreign sources, both governments and individuals, of whom many of 'different nations' had volunteered to go and fight.

An English steam vessel, the *Kangaroo*, carrying a 'number of adventurers' including Poles and other officers, arms and ammunition and towing another vessel with salt, had been chartered from a merchant named Weare, for the sum of 70,000 piastres, to go to Wardum (Vardan between Anapa and Sukhum-Kale). It had been chased by the Russians, it was rumoured. Boys and girls had certainly been landed at Constantinople from the *Kangaroo*, but the captain had assumed they were passengers. Another steamer *Enchantress* had also been chartered by the Turks, and later the *African* was also implicated.[163] Taking advantage of forts abandoned since the war there was clearly money in the slave trade. The British were not responsible for individuals' actions nor for those of the Turks, they told the Russians, but they agreed to do what they could not to encourage the slave trade. It was clear to the British that the Russians were against any foreign trade on the coastline of Circassia (also forbidding Circassians to trade), despite assurances that the Black Sea was to be opened to foreign trading as stipulated by the Paris Peace Treaty. Meanwhile English merchants were worried in case their legitimate trade would be disrupted by the Russians. In October 1857 the Russians issued an official notice regarding trade: only three ports - Anapa, Sukhum-Kale and Redut-Kale - were to be open to foreign trade and under regulations regarding quarantine, customs and police. There would be consequences if these regulations were ignored elsewhere.[164]

Stratford de Redcliffe was realistic about the Circassians' fate; their prospects were desperate, he wrote. They had again submitted a petition to Queen Victoria asking for protection. Clarendon's replies were unequivocal: given their inaction during the late war and their lack of assistance to the allies, any help given to the Circassians by British subjects would be at their own risk, and that given this inaction the Circassians had forfeited their rights to negotiations. Finally, Britain was not prepared to go to war against Russia for the sake of Circassia.[165]

This marked the end of Britain's dubious venture with Circassian independence. The resistance was not over, however.

Consuls

Circassia: *'A nation driven out of their ancestral seats'* [166]

The post-Crimean War period was a watershed moment for Britain's relations with Russia: competition and guarded conciliation were the order of the day. The establishment in 1858 of the first consuls on the eastern Black Sea coast at Sukhum-Kale (Charles Hammer Dickson) and at Poti (Captain Duncan Cameron) put the English on new (for them) Abkhazian and Mingrelian ground. It was a precarious position in the case of the former: Sukhum-Kale was a garrison town bordering insurgent mountain peoples.

Abkhazia, on the north-eastern coast of the Black Sea, is defined by a narrow strip of coastline, with foothills rising to highly forested mountains (despite clearances) and high peaks. The climate is subtropical. Abkhazia emerged as a principality in the fifteenth and sixteenth centuries ruled by the Chachba or Shervashidze dynasty after a tangled relation with Georgian kings. Pragmatic allegiances and religious affiliations fluctuated between Islam during Ottoman and Orthodoxy during Russian occupations. The fort at Sukhum-Kale had been in Ottoman hands since the later sixteenth century but was taken by the Russians in 1810 as part of the Russo-Turkish War of 1806-12 (the Ottomans had retained Poti).

The ruling Prince of Abkhazia (1822-66) during the period discussed here was Michael Shervashidze, who had turned Orthodox (see further below). The west of Abkhazia was used as a buffer zone between the Russian Empire and the independent tribes of Circassia, with the prince put in the difficult position of being a mediator. However, he played all parties, profiting at the same time from the smuggling and slave trafficking that defined this section of the coast, while accepting large sums from Russia to prevent such practices.[167]

Mingrelia is geographically and climatically similar to Abkhazia, but with the disadvantage of marshes on the coastline. It was originally part of Georgia when it was a kingdom (eleventh-fifteenth centuries), then became a principality under the house of Dadiani. Like Abkhazia it was under Ottoman occupation, was seized by the Russians, returned to the Ottomans, then finally retaken by the Russians in 1828.

Both the Shervashidze and the Dadiani families went back generations, and were cousins.

'I have the honour to report'

The majority of consuls were moveable, assigned from post to post, compliant or not. Some stayed a long time, others moved on quickly depending on circumstances (illness, political changes, war). They were far from insignificant men, many with military and intelligence experience. Thus Charles Hanmer Dickson, before his appointment at Sukhum-Kale and Redut-Kale, had been Vice-Consul at Bengazi and Ghadames, had fought at Alma, Balaklava and Inkerman, had received the Crimean medal and had been interpreter and private secretary to the commander of Her Majesty's troops in the Bosphorus and Dardanelles. He was a member of both the Royal Geographic and Royal Asiatic societies.[168] Dickson was briefly followed in 1866 by William Gifford Palgrave (before he went to Trebizond in 1867), the great traveller, agent and author He had served in India, travelled extensively in Arabia (receiving the Gold Medal of the French Geographical Society), went on special mission to Abyssinia, and returning from Egypt was appointed to Sukhum-Kale. After Trebizond he was consul for the Caribbean islands of St Thomas and St Croix and consul in the Philippines. After several other postings he finished as Consul-General to Uruguay, where he died in 1888.[169] Captain Charles Duncan Cameron (appointed to Redut-Kale in 1858, then moved to Poti in 1858-59) had served in the Kaffir wars of 1852-53, receiving the Kaffir war medal, acted as Her Majesty's Commissioner to the Turkish Army in Armenia, superintended the fortifications of Erzerum during the Crimean War and was on special mission in Trebizond. After Poti he was appointed Consul at Massawa.[170] His four-part report on the Caucasus, seemingly the first of its kind from an English source, stays hidden in the archives, but informed by historical and local sources, it has much valuable information on the politics, military, ethnography, transport, commerce and topography of the Caucasus.[171] It was regrettably never printed by the Foreign Office.

Other consuls such as St Vincent Lloyd and Robert Wilkinson had less stellar careers. The former had a mostly consular career from Bucharest, Ismail and Sulina in the Balkans, Sinope, back to Sulina, thence to Poti in 1860 (or late 1850s until replaced by Wilkinson).[172] Wilkinson (vice-consul at Poti 1858-61) had been an unpaid consul at Tinos and vice-consul and acting consul at Syra.[173]

The post of consul was inevitably full of challenges and potential opportunities but was tightly controlled by London. Circulars with instructions were periodically sent out; consuls and vice-consuls could not be seen to be breaking the law, nor at the time trade or do business and had to report every quarter on everything from shipping to births and deaths, trade returns, repatriations, fees received, expenses etc. They were involved in miscellaneous activities, from sending and receiving agricultural samples, to filling in questionnaires sent by learned societies such as, for example, the Acclimatisation of Local Species. Dickson would be happy to oblige, he responded, when the country was 'quieter'. More importantly, they had to promote all interests of Her Majesty's service,[174] providing intelligence in confidential despatches, sent by 'flying seal to Constantinople' via Trebizond, to avoid Russian eyes.

Consuls were responsible for finding their own accommodation (£35 per annum at Sukhum-Kale), clerks and interpreters, for looking after the archives and transferring them if need be. Pay and allowances varied according to posting. In 1866 the Consul at Poti (Palgrave) received an annual salary of £500, with office allowances of £100, and £170 for an outfit.[175] At Sukhum-Kale the office allowance had been £50 plus the annual rent of £35 in 1860-61.[176] Some were unpaid (see below). In later periods there was much correspondence about money and leaves of absence due to illness and exhaustion, even death, because of the sub-tropical conditions they lived in.

'Under flying seal to Constantinople' (1860-67)

The confidential reports of Dickson (mostly), Wilkinson and Palgrave to Lord John Russell, Foreign Secretary, chart not only the crucial turning point in Russia's war against the mountain peoples in the west, but the ethnic cleansing and resulting decimation of the coast. The reports also address the effect of Alexander II's Manifesto on the Emancipation of the Serfs (1861), relations with the Prince of Abkhazia and local nobles as well as important administrative changes and troop movements.

The language used in these reports is objective, formal and never partisan, although a sentence or two or some adjectives occasionally convey contempt and outrage at some events.

The following essentially paraphrases the voices and content of these reports (with added commentary) to give a flavour of the consuls' lived military and political context.

The war intensifies

The target of the Russian offensive was against the still 'independent' tribes (the Jighett, the Ubykh, the Shapsug and Abadzeks), whose resistance was far from finished: they doubted Shamil's defeat, as well as being inspired by the ongoing Polish insurrection. The Russians' main aim was to subjugate the Ubykh, who were considered 'eminently distinguished for their bravery and unity of purpose; the latter a rare virtue among Asiatics in general and one that is seldom proof against Russian gold in the Caucasus,' wrote Dickson (31 March 1860).[177] To this end dogged expeditionary forces were sent in the direction of the Ubykh (slightly inland south of Tuapse, north of Sukhumi) in conditions that were unforgiving: approach from the coast put the Russians at a disadvantage as the mountains immediately rose up giving their adversaries an excellent viewpoint, while by land a thick mass of forest and jungle had to be fought through. A major expeditionary force by sea in May 1860 was repelled by a line of waiting Circassians, with the Russians' only prize a Turkish *sandal* (sailing ship) containing a few live turkeys. A second objective in 1860 was to cut a road through to Psh'oo (Pshku) a strategic crossroads for access to the tribes, to make a topographical survey and eventually erect a fort there.[178] An expedition under General Karganoff set off from Dzebelda, with an advance party of engineers. Such expeditions were massive: 23,000 infantry, a detachment of engineers, mounted Cossacks and 480 Abkhazian militia. The engineers, guided by an Abkhazian chief, were completely misled after they had executed works (which turned out to be of no use to the army). The army, due to a delay in supplies, had no food for two days except a little Indian corn, purchased from the natives 'at fabulous prices'. When the confrontation occurred, the Abkhazian militia, led by Abkhazian princes, were ordered to go first, fired in the air and retreated. The Russians eventually dislodged the mountain fighters, forced a declaration of submission, took hostages and retreated having no more ammunition. As usual in such battles, the Russian loss was the heavier (70 versus 20).

In 1861 another expedition (mounted Cossacks, battalions of infantry, sharpshooters, sappers, artillerymen and four field pieces, a total of 4,500 men) to Pshku was attempted. This time it was secret: they set out without informing Prince Michael of Abkhazia and with no native help. In the ensuing battle in the Goumitsa valley the Russians again retreated (with a loss of 92 to 30-40) as the Jighett and Ubykh approached to lend a hand, losing all their supplies, forage and engineering tools.[179]

These details indicate the lack of proper planning, prior knowledge and intelligence, and up to a point the naiveté of the Russian commanders and incompetence of some in charge. The first Pshku expedition had cost 16,000 roubles.[180] The right flank of the Army of the Caucasus at the time, based at Stavropol under General Evdikimov, amounted to c.50,000, rising to 60,000 troops.[181] Thus there was no shortage of men nor readiness to spend. Mountain troop numbers, on the other hand, are barely reported in these despatches, as numbers fluctuated depending on who was assisting whom, and who was leaving. In 1861 the Ubykh were said to consist of 60,000 men, and another despatch mentions that 100,000 men from the Jighett and Ubykh tribes could be mustered in an emergency.[182]

Russian troops always seemed to be on the move, and a pattern of tactics (or circumstance) emerged: assault, exchange fire and retreat under 'harassing fire', as well as assault from several sides, for example firing rockets from the coastline to alarm the Ubykh. Offensives and retreats were taking place elsewhere: to Ghelenjik (1861) to Dal (on the border with the natives of Dzebelda, 'notorious freebooters'), to Vardaneh (1862).[183]

The hope of another European war to distract the Russians was still present in the mind of Circassians, and there was even nostalgia for the British and the French. But a continuing weakness in the Circassian movement, wrote Dickson, which considerably aided the Russian cause, was feuding between clans and feuds within clans, between those who cooperated with the Russians and others, such as within the powerful Marshani clan (nominally subject to the Russians but bearing them little good will) and the Battal Beys. The Russians took advantage of these feuds, setting one group against another, offering seductive gifts and positions in the military.[184] Lack of cohesion was another problem, Dickson later wrote.

By 1862 the advance to Pshku was deferred (owing to Prince Michael's objection) although a reconnaissance party was sent, wearing Circassian dress, but returned, having met Russian deserters and Poles (now serfs) at Pshku, but with no observations or other information given by natives.[185] The war moved to the Abadzekhs, with whom the Ubykh were cooperating. By 1863 the Army of the Caucasus was making advances around the two Labas. With each advance and despite the tribes fighting off the Russians - the Grand Duke had been captured by the Circassians as his escort was attacked (30 March 1863) - the net was closing around Russia's enemies: emigration, thus weakening the resistance, seemed the only option. In 1864 it was decided to prosecute the war 'with renewed energy'[186] and to force natives to go to the Kuban or emigrate to Turkey. Officers, 'committing excesses', scoured the country ordering the mountain peoples to quit their communities.[187] The attack on Sochi, which was to be the definitive move in the conquest of the Ubykh, was supposed to be in the Grand Duke

Michael's 'honour' and reserved for him. It was in fact forestalled by General Evdikimov, who ordered Major General Heyman to advance on Vardan and Sochi, which were occupied without further resistance after an engagement at Subachi in April.[188] The Ubykh had been considerably weakened by the emigration of the Abadzekh, followed by the Shapsug, famine and livestock disease. Dickson saw no future for 'these people', whom he deemed unfit to govern themselves, and the result 'of the present cruel war', he wrote, could not be better illustrated than by a local saying: 'even a woman might nowadays travel alone from Sukhum-Kale to Anapa without fear of meeting a single person.'[189]

The defeat of the Ubykh was considered an achievement on a par with the defeat of Shamil, and symbolized the final conquest of the Caucasus, east and west. No more forts were to be built on the coast.[190] With their land 'laid waste by fire and sword', the Ubykh and Jighett tribes were fast embarking for Trebizond, refusing to go to the Kuban. Dickson writes of their distress: 'In the hurry of departure, the overcrowding of their boats is so little heeded as to lead to frequent disasters; and such of their horses and cattle as war and famine have spared are being sold for a few paper roubles. In some instances the emigrants sooner than see their weapons, maybe heir-looms in the family for centuries, exchange hands with the enemy have flung them into the sea.'[191]

The land was to be offered to Azov Cossacks and government employees having served ten years. The idea was to have Orthodox Russians settle there.[192]

But it was not yet over. In May 1864 an expeditionary force of two divisions each with a battery of four-pounder pieces (total 1,900 men) was despatched towards Cape Adler by sea and land. One division was under General Schatyloff; the other headed by the Grand Duke and Count Evdikimov, was to march towards Ackipsoo and Pshku on two sides. The aim was to drive the remnants of the tribes away. The necessity of this sledgehammer force when there were no more than 1,000 families there, dwelling 'on most inaccessible rocks', is questionable, unless the Russians actually did not know how many were there, or they wanted to terrify by sheer force of arms. In the event the natives defended themselves by hurling rocks from above on the storming troops with some ammunition supposed to have been provided by the Prince of Abkhazia. The Russians took the day. A *Te Deum* was chanted, and crosses and orders distributed by the Grand Duke.[193]

A beleaguered prince

These events were to have a catastrophic impact on the position of the semi-independent Prince of Abkhazia. The prince had long walked a tight rope between his own interests, his people' interests and Russian demands. He was distrusted and increasingly ignored by the military, yet still expected to mediate, and he found excuses to stay away. One particular grievance, adding to the constant pressure of the war, was the extent to which the forthcoming emancipation of the serfs would infringe on the noble families' rights. Immemorial rules governed the mutually dependent master and serf relations among the nobles, and these were not like the Russian serf master relationship,[194] but more like a clan structure. On the occasion of the Emperor Alexander II' s visit to Sukhum-Kale and Kutaisi in October 1861 (partly to verify claims of corruption and systemic abuses by the general administration), the prince and Prince Eristoff (a senior Georgian noble) as the nobles' spokespersons assembled with the nobles of Mingrelia, asking for pecuniary compensation for serf-holders. Without letting the prince speak the emperor pinned the Order of Alexander Nevsky on his chest and walked away.[195] He also bestowed 1,000 roubles on Prince George Shervashidze (the prince's brother), and corresponding 'emoluments' on other influential locals. The prince was careful not to show his eldest son to the emperor, lest he should be taken to St Petersburg, but by 1864 the prince's heir was permanently attached to the staff of the Grand Duke Michael, and forced to serve in a detachment against the Abadzekh, contrary to his father's wishes.[196] When in 1861 the command of the troops was temporarily offered to Prince Michael in an atmosphere of conciliation, the prince declined, citing ill health and a desire to go to Constantinople to seek 'skilful medical practitioners'.[197] This last request, Dickson believed, was a feeler to alarm the Imperial government. In the event the emperor refused to exempt the nobles from taxes and imposts, with no exceptions. The nobles were still clamouring for indemnification in 1864.

The tsars's visits were major events accompanied by fanfare, marking territory, displaying Russian power and supposedly part of their civilizing mission. As argued by Jahn, they were also meant to demonstrate the union between the tsar and his people. This image did not resonate.[198]

The writing on the wall for Abkhazia had been clear since 1861, when major changes were affected in the administration, both military and civil. Georgian nobles, like Erisoff, the Provincial Governor of Kutaisi, Abkhazia, Mingrelia and Akhaltsik, known for his liberal tendencies, was removed from post and Major General Karganoff (an Armeno-Georgian), the Governor of Sukhum-Kale, was dismissed. Both, and others, were replaced by Orthodox Russians: Colonel Shatylov became Governor of Sukhum-Kale. The expected disruption expected over the emancipation of the serfs, 'the national movement' in Poland and discussions about the rights of Georgians to a 'separate nationality' were the reason behind this move, understood Dickson.[199]

In November 1864 Prince Michael was arrested at his residence and accused of disloyalty thus forfeiting all 'claims to the possession and government of Abkhazia'. He had been ordered to come to Tiflis but refused leaving the Russians suspicious that he would depart for Constantinople. The prince was led to believe he was to go to Poti and Tiflis, but was secretly conveyed to Kerch, whence he was exiled to Russia. The prince died in exile and his body was returned to his family residence in 1866.[200]

Expulsion

Complementary to the relentless military onslaught was the weapon that the Russian had planned for and knew would assist in the conquest: emigration. Deportation as a strategy (for the Muslim and semi-Muslim population) had apparently been proposed as early as 1857 and only officially sanctioned in 1862,[201] but was ongoing by 1860: 25,000 Circassian families and another 500 from the inland Caucasian line arrived at Sukhum-Kale to be transported to Trebizond.[202] The process became more accentuated in the mid-860s. There were many ways of brutalizing the natives, even pacific ones. For example, tribes who had tendered their submission (such as the Abadzekh) were compelled to move away from the mountains and relocate to the Kuban, with troops setting fire to their crops.[203] These acts would lead to retaliations and/or emigration. The consuls' despatches reveal emigration to have been piecemeal and continuous as tribes were cornered and ordered to quit; numbers varied and the number of whole tribes emigrating at one time was unrecorded and nor were overall estimates given in the despatches.

The May 1864 Akhipsoo and Pshku defeat provoked another wave of emigration: the number of Jighett and Akhipsoo leaving was estimated to be 22,000.[204] The Pshku were again ordered to quit: 5,000 families were assembled at Bombori, amidst an epidemic of smallpox.[205] In the meantime emigration from the southern Caucasus was also ongoing (twenty Lezgin families embarked then at Poti on the French Messageries Impériales line), but circumstances and the location of the tribes in Dagestan prevented the movement becoming more general, wrote Palgrave.[206] All remaining natives were now forbidden to carry arms, and had to renounce allegiance to their feudal princes.[207]

Still clinging to hope of assistance from Britain, petitions were sent from Circassian refugees to Britain (1864) asking for safe passage and in 1867 regarding the detention of Abkhazian refugees by Russia. Help came but it was infrequent and not enough.[208]

The evacuation process was chaotic and desperate, with inadequate vessels, even though the Russian Steam Navigation Company, the Messageries Impériales, chartered English vessels and Turkish ships of all sizes made money out of it. People sold their vessels, cattle, all goods. They offered themselves or their children as slaves to obtain passage. Some were in a state of famine and disease and filth and many vessels did not want them.

Over half died on board. Once arrived at an Ottoman seaport (Trebizond and Samsun, later Sinop, Varna and Kustendji), many died, or were put in camps until they were moved on again. Heart-rending accounts of mortality and suffering (at the rate of 500-700 per day) experienced by emigrants who were reaching the coast were reported in *The Times* of 31 August 1864.[209] This human tragedy had a pernicious effect on these ports (see below).[210]

In these last moments the Grand Duke ordered that the exodus should be regulated in order to avoid the misery and danger of overloaded Turkish boats. Rations of biscuit and flour were given, with the Grand Duchess dispensing tea, sugar and other comforts. The price of selling cattle was also regulated. These regulations were local.[211] By 1867 the situation had become generally more efficient.

'The prostration of Abkhazia'

The removal of the prince meant the annexation of Abkhazia. The prince's lands (three-quarters of Abkhazia) were confiscated as were those of the Dadianis and of the nobles of Guria. The sons of Prince Michael were detained, his brother (inculpated in the 1866 insurrection without proof) was put to death in prison. The Marchiani family was banished to Russia.[212] Besides these confiscations, timber cutting, a source of employment and profit for the region, was forbidden. This left the estates, laden with fruit trees, uncultivated and fast turning to wilderness.

Unrestrained from consular officialdom, Consul Palgrave was to write 'of where violence has turned to desolation' and observed that 'the loss of Russia is Turkey's gain' in *Essays on the Eastern Question* (1872).[213] Other travellers were to witness this desolation. Even the obsessive mountaineer, Douglas Freshfield, was to ask, 'What is the future of this earthly paradise'? in his essay 'The Solitude of Abkhazia' (from *The Exploration of the Caucasus*, 1896): 'Its ancient and primaeval inhabitants are gone. They have been exiled for a quarter of a century; their dwellings and their tombs are alike lost in the glorious vegetation that feeds nothing but bears and mosquitoes and fevers… The Abkhazians have vanished.'[214]

Although no doubt sincere, travel writers exploited this tragedy, and the decimation of Abkhazia became a trope (variously used) of the Caucasian war.

After Abkhazia's annexation 'entire emigration' now remained the only resolve of the Abkhazians, wrote Dickson, who thought this was fuelled by 'distrust of their new rulers', not from 'a spirit of fanaticism'.[215] Those who converted had a chance to remain. In 1864 the population of Abkhazia was about 60,000,[216] fast reduced to 30.000 with between 20-30.000 leaving in 1867.[217] This mass emigration ruined the country, yet more was to follow during the 1877-78 Russo-Ottoman War.

'An outbreak of despair': the 1866 Abkhazian insurrection

In the summer of 1866, a Royal Commission arrived at Sukhum-Kale from Tiflis to take a census of the population. It fixed itself at Goudavouta, north of Sukhum-Kale. Here the native chiefs were so insulted by a General Cognaid that the incident provoked a mutiny conducted by the son of Hassan Morgana (aide de camp to Cognaid) and his brother, Mustafa. About 100 Cossacks, along with Cognaid and his staff, the Commissioners, and Colonel Ismailov (the Military Governor of Sukhum-Kale) were put to death, 'the last it is reported with…aggravated cruelty'. Mustafa Morgana escaped to Trebizond. The insurrection spread through all of Abkhazia and a few days later, 1,000 (Palgrave writes 2,000) armed natives descended on Sukhum-Kale, plundered and set fire to the barracks, the hospital, a Catholic Church and other buildings. The inhabitants, 'having received intelligence', retreated to Russian ships of war. The troops of the garrison withdrew into the port, then support came from Poti and the mountain people retreated on 15 August 1866. 'It was an outbreak of despair, a last struggle of hatred,' wrote Palgrave.[218]

In retaliation, the measures taken by the military tribunal for the insurrection were originally capital punishment for all; this was commuted to capital punishment for three insurgents, with others who had surrendered exiled to Siberia for seven to fifteen years. The death sentences were kept secret in fear of reprisals.

The men were led to their stakes still thinking they were to be exiled. 'When stripped... they made one last request, that their clothes might be sent to their families, in remembrance.' One of the condemned belonged to a noble family (the Ma'ans), the other was a landowner, and the last a peasant under twenty years of age: pointing to one purposefully chosen from each class.[219]

Meanwhile in the mountains a tribe related to the Ubykh, 'defying all efforts ...to dislodge them, continued in arms' (November 1866).[220] Emigration was ongoing, but now in detail rather than in mass, and not through Russian ports.

The period 1864-66 was disastrous for Sukhum-Kale; it had been flourishing before mass emigration, but now the Naval Station was closed, there was no commerce and shops were disappearing as there was no more custom from troops who were leaving after the end of the 1866 insurrection. There was no work due to the confiscation of the nobles' estates, which were being ruined by Russian soldiery. Poor Turkish Muslims, mostly fishermen, 'still lingering' about the coast were systematically harassed or imprisoned, and badly treated as there was no longer a Turkish consul at Sukhum-Kale to represent them because of the port's decline.[221] By 1867 the consulship had closed, with Poti given priority.

Administrative changes

Major administrative changes took place in the conquered regions from 1865 onwards. Kuban province was divided into five districts. After its annexation the principality of Abkhazia became 'Sukhum Territory' (with three *otdel* or districts) under the authority of the Province (*Oblast*) of Kutaisi. In Dagestan Province the districts mostly retained their traditional entities, but were grouped into north, middle, west and south, with the Shamkalate of Tarki replaced by Temir-Khan Shura district (which also included the Khanate of Mekhtuli and Naibate of Sulak). The mountainous areas of Chechnya were, however, defined by the resettlement of natives and the establishment of Cossack settlements. For example, some Ingush were regrouped around Nazran so that the Sunzha defensive line could be completed. It also divided Ingushetia. Ethnically diverse but otherwise integrated groups, such as the Kumyk and Nogai districts, were broken down into smaller, ethnically homogeneous sub-units (*uchatsocks*). The Military Government of Abkhazia was modified to a civil tribunal (four members, one a president) to reside at Sukhum-Kale. It was to oversee all cases except political ones according to the Russian Code, with Kutaisi having the last word. In the sub-provinces of Abkhazia subordinate tribunals were established (three members from among the natives and presided over by the Military Governor, which was to address minor offences (theft, quarrels etc.); and this was to follow the 'native' (or military-native, *voenno-narodnoe upravlenie*) established usage, until Russian law could be applied.[222] Such 'military-native' law was also implemented in the Terek province (which included the Ossetians, Chechens, Ingush, Lezgins, Avars) and Dagestan.[223]

Ethnic cleansing

It is clear that the consuls in post at Sukhum-Kale and Poti did not have access to information, or were circumspect about reporting (within Russia), about the true extent of the emigration locally and in the wider Caucasus region, and equally about what was happening at the receiving end in Turkey.

Russian sources from the time gave a number of 400-500,000 Circassian emigrants, whereas Turkish sources give 595,000 as an estimate. And that was only Circassians. In the re-organization of the provinces, 22,000 Chechens and 3,000 Kabardians and Ossetians were expelled to Turkey.[224] Ingush and Karabulaks also left.[225] Others in these parts considered troublemakers were executed or sent to penal settlements.[226] The overall numbers are still being debated today. Owen (2007) cites other scholarly sources: 600,000 (McCarthy), up to a million (Henze) Circassians, with a total of two million Caucasians (Karpat), with only 1.5 million reaching their destination.[227] Nobody disputes that this was ethnic cleansing and genocide.

Ports of call

The Black Sea Ottoman ports of Trebizond, Samsun and Varna were the first ports of call and witnessed the misery that ensued as refugees flooded in.

Refugees were put in camps around the port towns or hung about the shore waiting for room to be found. At Samsun, some 40,000-50,000 'individuals… preyed upon by disease, decimated by death were cast there [in a camp] in the most abject state of destitution… without shelter, without bread and without sepulchre,' wrote Consul Stevens in 1864.[228] A letter to *The Times* in June 1864 by Dr Barozzi describes how Circassians impacted the towns; they 'encumber the squares, obstruct the streets, invade enclosed grounds, penetrate everywhere, remain stationed there during the whole day and retire only late after sunset.'[229] Local governors abused the refugees[230] and crimes must have committed on both sides. The consuls themselves were also stretched to their limit: Consul Stevens had a mental breakdown and was replaced by Gifford Palgrave, who witnessed the panic in Trebizond with the ill and dying, the lack of burial places, the unburied bodies, the spread of typhus and contamination. Almost 550 perished in two months (1864).[231]

In Istanbul the consuls had to work closely with their Ottoman colleagues to try to balance everyone's needs and help find solutions for a disaster in which the British had been complicit for so long. Personal involvement and doggedness by officials attempted to ease the situation. Palgrave, for example, mediated a petition drawn up by Abkhazian refugees in 1867 presented to the Governor of Trebizond to be passed on to the Russian government, while the British Ambassador in Constantinople, Sir Henry Bulmer, sought a loan of £1.5 million to aid the Ottomans over the refugee crisis. This did not materialize and the government sent £500, which was used to provide tons of biscuits.[232] Bulmer also suggested that British steamers should be chartered for the express purpose of transporting the refugees, but this did not come about officially. It appears that some British transport was provided at various points, presumably from Trebizond.[233] This is not mentioned in the Sukhum-Kale or Poti despatches. It was also a drop in the ocean:

once in Turkey, with little support, and an increasingly hostile reception as numbers increased, many refugees were resettled in Anatolia. Some went to the Balkans. In Istanbul the Circassian Aid Committee was formed in 1864 to collect donations from the British public (headed by Viscount Stratford de Redcliffe). Laurence Oliphant, a member of the Committee, believed that Britain shouldered part of the responsibility for the Circassian exodus by allowing the Russians to rebuild their fortresses after the Crimean War.[234] It can be argued that the responsibility went farther back than the war: the British had an historic debt to pay to the Circassians for having so long encouraged and fuelled their belief in independence. In the event, the Committee was not successful and only raised £2.067, spent on bedding and clothing.[235]

In Britain the flurry of newspaper reports[236] on these events had aroused sympathy for the Circassians and against Russia. There was public lobbying, after a Circassian delegation visited in 1862 in the hope of assistance. Particular sympathy was generated in Scotland, stirred by the memory of the Highland Clearances.[237]

Looking to the Future

As emigration and land grabbing continued, other factors occupied the Russian military and civil administration: local disquiet over the official declaration of serf emancipation, discontent in Georgia concerning military conscription and, crucially, sabre rattling on the south-east border with Turkey. This was to foreshadow the 1877-78 Russo-Ottoman War. Four divisions (32,000 men) were sent to the ports of Suram, Gori, Kutaisi and Achalzik, points which commanded Georgia, the west coast, Gouriel and the Turkish frontier. These were supposedly strategically important as regards the interior of the Transcaucasus (Abkhazia, Samurghkhan, Mingrelia, Gouria and Georgia), although it was thought the Turkish frontier and coastline were the main focus. Some 5,000 troops were sent to the area around Kars, where offensive and defensive works of 'gigantic' proportions at Alexandropol and fortifications at Achalzik were underway.[238]

British enterprise

On the ground in Abkhazia amidst the mayhem, development involving the British was in motion, but not on a large scale. British shipping at Sukhum-Kale seems to have been non-existent and the high hopes of the likes of Bell for a thriving trade with the coast of Circassia did not materialize. Reports show that no British shipping cleared or entered the port in 1861: Sukhum-Kale was no longer a coal depot (now left at Batum).[239] Nevertheless a lighthouse (made of British cast iron) was erected at Sukhum-Kale.[240] As mentioned above, by 1866 there was hardly any commerce at all at Sukhum-Kale. In contrast, in 1862 eight British vessels arrived at Poti, three loaded with sugar, en route to Azov, and five loaded (in ballast) with Indian corn for Britain. Here the shipping was overwhelmingly Russian and Turkish, followed by one vessel each from Austria, Italy, France and Prussia.[241] The Russians also tried to limit the Turkish coastal trade, by not authorizing ships of over eighteen tons to trade.[242] What British imports there were came through Trebizond and included ale and porter, crockery, pickles, long cloths, cotton prints and 'dryssatteries'.[243] Commercial agents at Trebizond would send on British goods to Persia. Prime boxwood hewn into blocks was the most valuable asset of this part of the Caucasus, and this was shipped in Turkish bottoms from Constantinople to Liverpool.[244] Sumac, fustic and marten skins were also shipped. Dickson hoped that cotton would be grown one day and 'become an important' product, but the climate interfered and the roads, he concluded, were so bad that they shackled commerce.[245] Trade would grow on the coast when troops were around and correspondingly declined otherwise,[246] yet the coast was still swarming with contraband trade and Turkish smugglers.

Poti was becoming a hub: by 1864, besides steamers from the Russian Steam Navigation Company, the French Messageries Impériales established a weekly line of steamers serving different Turkish ports (Inebolu, Sinope, Samsun, Kerasonda, Trebizond and Batum). In addition, a 'very fine [revolving] lighthouse' with white and red lights costing 60.000 roubles was erected.[247] By 1863 English engineers (called Belgians locally) were at Poti, led by a

Mr Gabb, considering whether Poti would make a good harbour. All the Russian engineers were against his plan.[248] Money was a problem, yet the plan went ahead. In 1864, eight British vessels came to Poti, two with British machinery for the harbour works and one with sugar; the other five were chartered to take sleepers to Marseille. 'The prospects of Poti look brighter owing to the Harbour works and to the projected railroad from Poti to Tiflis,' wrote Wilkinson, and the line was eventually to reach Baku, with work due to begin in 1865.[249] The British were also involved in the railway: Mr Chapman, contractor, and Mr Gabb the engineer were attached to a Mr Baly, employed for the undertaking. The route was considered to be invaluable for the transit trade to and from Persia, the value of which was up to £1 million annually. In 1865 a hydraulic press by Peel, Williams & Peel of Manchester was installed by the Russian Steam Navigation Company for pressing bales.[250]

Travellers' Voices (1865-77)

The war was officially over, and parts of Abkhazia and Mingrelia were considered reasonably safe from 1864-65 onwards: there was a surge of visitors and new travellers. The touring travellers in question (John Ussher RGS on a tour to Persepolis, the mountaineers Douglas Freshfield and Florence Craufurd Grove, the writer Mrs Annie Jane Harvey, the military men Arthur Thurlow Cunynghame, and Capt Buchan Telfer R.N. and the jurist and historian James Bryce), whether en route to Tiflis, the north or the south-east, passed through and docked at Sukhum-Kale or Poti, often both, leaving their impressions.

Descriptions of Sukhum-Kale show it to have been far more pleasant than Poti. Ussher found it clean and neat, the streets 'had a pleasing aspect' and he took a walk with Consul Dickson.[251] It had an alluring prospect from anchorage, wrote Telfer in 1876.[252] Its fortress was dilapidated, but was a seat of garrison with a parade ground, surrounded by the 'best houses', a military hospital, otherwise 'low, pretty houses', with broad verandas covered with creepers and gardens.²⁵³ Mrs Harvey met a Prince of Abkhazia and his Muscovite wife (Princess Constantine) living in a very cheerless, modest house, but hung with the 'magnificent arms' and 'accoutrements' of gorgeous Abkhazian saddles. The ladies of the house (but not the prince's wife), although nominally Christian, retained 'Mahommedan' habits, spoke no languages except their own, never appeared in public unveiled, and spent their time smoking, arranging their dress and eating sweet-meats.²⁵⁴ Here Mrs Harvey is hinting at the life of harems, which as the titillating title of her book suggests (*Turkish Harems and Circassian Homes*) was probably meant to evoke Lady Mary Wortley Montague's famous *Letters from Turkey* (1763). Serfs still seemed to be part of the household.²⁵⁵ Members of the Abkhazian ruling family were still in exile, in 'honourable captivity', she writes, and the Abkhazians' sympathies lay with 'their highland brethren' although nominally Russian subjects. The hatred between them and the Russians was mutual with the Abkhazians still helping the mountain people. Mrs Harvey concludes that Circassia, 'like a lovely wild animal', had to be tamed rather than beaten, and that roads and harbours would subjugate the land far more than 'the presence of a vast standing army'.²⁵⁶

Flat and swampy, Poti on the Rion river was considered dismal by all and did not seem to improve. A 'most miserable place', wrote Freshfield in 1869.²⁵⁷ Bryce went further: arriving by rail from Tiflis through a 'sea of mud' he spent one night in 'the miserable inn of the most miserable town that ever a traveller was condemned to halt in'.²⁵⁸ Arrival from the sea was by small boat, then by a flat-bottomed boat to the shore. All houses were wooden on stilts driven into the mud with fetid water underneath, on a single long, narrow street. Ussher saw the house of Mr Cameron (he names him as consul still, who was away): a hut of two rooms, one with a bench, another with a table.²⁵⁹ The settlement (rather than the town it was hoped it would become) consisted mostly of small hotels, lodging houses, inns and a garrison of about 1,000 men of mixed nationality (Mingrelians, Gurians, Greeks, Armenians and Turks). The atmosphere was not helped by the incessant croaking of frogs and the occasional wandering jackal.²⁶⁰ There was only transit trade (exports were Indian corn, silk, walnut and box-wood and cotton). Imports were mostly manufactured goods. It was considered the headquarters of usurers, chiefly Armenians, Telfer wrote, who were taking over the properties of the nobles, who with extravagant pensions from the Russians to placate them, had been indulged in excesses (encouraged by the Russians). This ruined what remained of their estates and put them into the hands of the money lenders.²⁶¹ The railway, which 'was first undertaken by an English company, then a French one, then again an English one', was almost complete (completed 1872) and being worked on by both British and native labour. The latter's work was inferior wrote Cunynghame. He also speculated on whether the railway would be profitable as an investment: the terrain was too difficult and the Persian transit trade might prefer the Erzerum to Trebizond route, avoiding Russian territory.²⁶² Cunynghame was right about the terrain: the Russians had objected to digging a tunnel through the mountain ridge to reach Tiflis (as had been suggested by the British) and to save money had decided to go over the top of the ridge. This was likely to prove more costly in the future, wrote Bryce.²⁶³ By 1875-76 a bridge was being built to span the Rion to reach the railway (otherwise reached by boat) on the northern shore.²⁶⁴ Grove, who took the expensive railway to Tiflis (via Kutaisi, Gori, Mshkheta), speculated that when railways spread in the Transcaucasus, 'hordes' of tourists would come.²⁶⁵ Bryce comments that the opening of the railway had made 'intercourse with the mother country easier and more frequent and strengthens the unity of sentiment between Holy Russia and her children in these outlying provinces.'²⁶⁶ By 1875-6 a new harbour was also being built.²⁶⁷

Despite the area's recent turbulent past and uncertain prospects there are only scant references to this situation, despite the abandonment and neglect seen by all and the press reports in Britain. It was almost as if it had all been part of the area's ancient history. John Ussher, the closest in date to the troubled times (1865), had met on his journey from Odessa to Kerch both emigrating

Circassians and a Circassian noble and his retinue travelling to Mecca. He comments on the 'sad state of dirt and wretchedness' of the refugees. The ship's captain, who was used to such cargoes, said that he often fed the refugees and had to disinfect the decks after a passage. The emigrants, writes Ussher, had bigoted and intolerant reasons for leaving, it was due to 'fanaticism' (not patriotism or self-sacrifice, nor because the Russians were alien in race, language and customs) and a 'hatred of the cross'.[268] Furthermore, the 'appalling suffering' of the 'miserable fanatics', he suggests, was unnecessary and self-inflicted, for would they prefer the rule of the Pasha to that of the Russian government coupled with civilization? he asks.[269] It is evident that all travellers depended hugely on Russian official support in their travels, but this viewpoint resembles hyperbole (with an increased use of the term 'fanatic') addressed to a certain anti-Turkish audience at home. Ussher nevertheless repeats the tropes of the fine-looking Circassian nobleman and his weapons, the veiled wife and the haggard women servants (old before their age because of hard work).[270] Mrs Harvey (1871) uses every available trope when speaking of Circassians: many 'wild looking Circassians' (and Russians) greeted her yacht, the *Claymore*, when it arrived at Sukhum-Kale; the Circassian males were nevertheless bold and proud, preserving their idea of liberty (despite their nominal submission to Russia); the secluded veiled women were 'decidedly plain'; banditti or 'hostile Circassians' would have taken them prisoner if they had gone on shore further north. The last may have been true for, as she soberly writes later, Circassia 'was still in a very disturbed state' as random shootings showed and it was not safe to go beyond Russian forts and pickets.[271] She attributes the neglect of Abkhazia to the 'pride and indolence' of the natives.[272] Freshfield, in his 1869 (in contrast to his later 1896) publication, writes nothing about Circassia, except searching for Circassian cream to bring back home,[273] and Cunynghame (published 1872) only mentions Circassia from anecdotes of combat recounted to him.[274]

All refer to the punishing climate in these still remote places; according to Bryce, Poti was 'a perpetual vapour bath' and 'the most fever smitten den in all Asia'.[275] This brings to mind the fortitude and endurance of Consuls Cameron, Dickson, Wilkinson and Palgrave, who had no opportunities to go touring for pleasure.

The Russo-Ottoman War (1877-78)

The war and its aftermath were momentous: its territorial gains, ethnic conflict and vast displacements of Christians and Muslims laid the foundations for the demise of the Ottoman Empire and for the future instability of Europe, Russia and the region.

There had been a growth since the 1860s of ethnic and religious mobilization in the Ottoman Empire's mixed communities; the Maronite and Druze massacres in Lebanon 1860, Christians and Muslims in Syria, the Cretan revolt (1866), and in the Balkans from 1875-76 Herzegovina, Bosnia and Bulgaria. These were partly sparked by agrarian unrest, the non-implementation of promised reforms, Christian nationalism (a movement to which the traveller Bryce belonged) and/or a desire for self-determination. The Ottomans intervened in Bulgaria in a particularly brutal way with Russia supporting the Bulgarians with pan-Orthodox Slavic rhetoric. In 1876 Serbia and Montenegro declared war on the Ottomans. When diplomacy failed, Russia (having assured Austrian neutrality) declared war in April 1877, setting its sights on valuable Ottoman assets such as the port of Batum and the fortress of Kars. The potential involvement of Britain in the war (on the side of the Ottomans) was a real fear for the Russians, who were much relieved when Britain declared neutrality in May 1877.[276] This did not prevent the active hostility to Britain demonstrated by Russia. There was 'disquietude' in commercial and financial circles; they were afraid that if Britain joined the war, Russia, because of hopeless finances and the 'exhaustion' of the male population (due to the war) 'will not be able to accomplish her political destiny in the East,' wrote John Mitchell from St Petersburg in December 1877. He continued: they try to pacify the 'public mind' by stressing the isolation of Britain and disagreement within the British Cabinet, claiming that the Liberal

Party and commercial classes were against the war.²⁷⁷ Extracts from the Russian press, which had a field day both before and after the armistice, were sent to the Foreign Office, partly to show 'the way public opinion is acted upon in Russia'. The Russian press would not tolerate Russophobia in the British press (they correctly list the *Daily Telegraph*, the *Morning Press*, the *Pall Mall Gazette* etc.); it would retaliate, wrote the *Westnik*. After all Britain only existed because of her conquest of India, 'whose blood and sweat feed that little European country'. Despite stating her non-intervention, 'she (Britain) is highly influential at the Ottoman court', wrote the *Crop Almanack*, suggesting that Britain had supported the 'fanatical' Michal Pasha who had caused the atrocities in Bulgaria. Such non-intervention gave licence to the Ottomans to commit general atrocities in Bulgaria, Serbia and Montenegro. If the Turks win, 'all Europe will be against Lord Derby (Secretary of State for Foreign affairs) and England.'²⁷⁸ These sentiments were to have an economic impact, particularly on shipping (see below).

Widespread insurrections in the Caucasus by various groups (Circassians, Abkhazians, Chechens, Avars, Ossetians, Svanetians, Dagestanis, Kurds and others) were to be major diversions for the Russian campaigns.

A proselytising advocate

The jurist, historian, and future politician James Bryce travelled in the Caucasus before the war but revised his book (*Transcaucasia and Ararat*, 1877) after it had broken out. Disgusted by the Bulgarian massacres and with a strong pro-Armenian bias,²⁷⁹ his Christian proselytising pervades the whole book (which is otherwise very informative). The main theme lies in the four central chapters on the history, language, literature, people and monuments of Armenia, and the emotive centre surrounds his partial ascent of Ararat. As stated in the Introduction, Armenia is only marginally the remit of this book, but Bryce's weighty political reflections need to be considered as they address the geopolitical preoccupations and attitudes (the future of Turkey and its minorities) of the day, including thoughts on Russia and the future of Transcaucasia.

Bryce was critical of Russia in Transcaucasia; it was not well governed and over- and ill-administered; other European countries would have achieved more in seventy years of occupation. Yet he argued the 'fortunes' of Georgia and Mingrelia were nevertheless better off under Russia than under 'their own Princes', or under the Sultan or the Shah.[280] Bryce was not afraid to demonstrate his ignorance and dislike of the east. Muslims were not without good qualities, but they had no capable military leaders, they had no administration, no poets, no artists, and had never made any contribution to the thought or wealth of the world.[281] Things were as bad at the periphery as at the centre. His attitudes to Circassia and Circassians (only ten years after the genocide) was completely coloured by the atrocities in Bulgaria (to which the Circassians, among others, had contributed): there was nothing in their history to deserve sympathy, he wrote, despite being 'a nation driven out of its ancestral home': they lived from robbery and from the sale of their children, fuelled by 'hideous' examples of ferocity (as in Bulgaria).[282] The Abkhazians were now few, 'inert', fickle and cowardly,[283] and the Georgians' spirit had been broken. He compared the latter to a semi-civilized race enslaved by foreigners.[284]

The Armenians on the other hand were the most vigorous people, envied, ill-spoken of, thrifty and stuck 'wonderfully together'.[285] They were persons of learning and ability. Given the current climate of war, partition and self-determination, what could their future be, asked Bryce. Armenian nationalism was hugely on the rise in the late 1870s (see below) but had been preceded by patriotic demands for reform going back to the 1860s and the establishment in 1863 of the National Constitution (or regulations, a code of articles defining the powers of the Patriarch and condition of the Armenians) and the establishment of the Armenian National Assembly. The latter acted as a focus for progressive ideas.[286] Promised Ottoman reforms had not materialized and the Russo-Ottoman War fuelled nationalist thoughts not only among the Armenians. Were these people ready for self-determination? asked Bryce. He concluded that the Armenians were too dispersed and downtrodden, and that the Muslims and Kurds among them were an obstacle, pointing to the demographic and geopolitical headache that was eastern Turkey. Besides Russia would be against it, because it wanted to make Armenia 'her own creature'.[287]

Here, as argued by Laycock, Bryce was tapping into the prevailing British ambivalence towards the Armenians: they were eastern peoples, they had been flawed and tainted by the effects of Turkish government, they had absorbed the degeneration of the Turkish Empire.[288] In fact prejudice against the Armenians was longstanding and equal to if not worse than that shown towards Jews.[289] Despite an Armenian cultural renaissance from the late eighteenth century (in education, in the press through which ideas of freedom were disseminated, and in the promotion of history and culture, literature and the arts) it was in essence a small bubble concentrated in Constantinople, some monasteries, and Tiflis, remote from the ordinary people of the east,[290] for whom the Armenians often remained merchants and unpopular moneylenders.

Could the problem in Ottoman lands be resolved in other ways by influence from the Great Powers and Britain in particular, whose prestige was still great, Bryce wondered.[291] The Ottomans had lost authority within their own empire, and whereas too much involvement would not be a good thing, in Lebanon some reforms had been achieved through European intervention.[292] Britain could not avoid the decay of the Ottoman government and it had to be prepared for it: Christian communities already there, and others who offered 'a more hopeful prospect' than Muslims should be established and encouraged to live and settle in current and lost Ottoman lands under proper reforms assuring them of their rights. Muslim jurisdiction should be confined to civil courts (not the ecclesiastical, *sharia* law), and Christians should be admitted to the police and the army and be permitted to carry arms.[293] Some reforming ordinances existed but were not carried out.

What of the future of Transcaucasia? Bryce was not optimistic. The people were not united, nor did they have national feeling, although fanaticism had cooled down since Shamil's day.[294] The people, divided by language and manners from the Russians, had no prospects under Russia, which itself was barely civilized. The area was held together by despotism and the army. It was unlikely that Transcaucasia would become independent, he stated.[295] (The future of Georgia was to be taken up by a later, highly influential traveller, Oliver Wardrop, with different ideas, see Part 2.) What about British interests in the east? continued Bryce. If Russia were the mistress of the Bosphorus and Constantinople (a great fear in British circles), it would be unfortunate but not a massive loss to trade. The route to India was of greater importance. How would the loss of Constantinople affect the Suez Canal? It would only mean increasing the British naval fleet, for Russia had no real naval power.[296] How would the annexation of Armenia or the taking of Erzerum affect India? Would it mean the conquest of Baghdad or Damascus, would Russia want to attack Persia, which would be a quicker route to India? There were huge distances, no transport and these acquisitions were so far of no benefit to Russia's power nor had she showed any desire of acquiring Persia.[297] The present war, he concluded, would not affect Britain's interests in India, although its prestige might be damaged in the Levant and the Euxine (the Black Sea). Bryce was seeking to dismiss old, reiterated fears about Russia and India, which were now being eclipsed by the perceived threat of Russia's advance towards Constantinople. Surprisingly, Bryce does not mention the potential consequences of the ongoing Russian conquest of Central Asia, which was of interest to the British Foreign Office.

Bryce concluded his deliberations by returning to his argument that the only solution to the present situation of Christian minorities in Ottoman lands (and perhaps by implication in Russia) was to build up western institutions which would regain and maintain Britain's 'legitimate' influence in the east.[298]

A panicked communication from Austen Henry Layard (the British Ambassador in Constantinople) to Lord Derby in December 1877 highlighted the threat to British interests in the east if Russia were to annex Armenia as a result of the war. Russia would command the valleys of the Euphrates and Tigris and deprive Britain of alternative routes to India; Russia would command the whole of western Asia and Mesopotamia; the Black Sea would be turned into a Russian lake, thus destroying British power in the east.[299] These matters were to be later resolved in the Treaty of San Stefano (see below), including greater Ottoman protection and reforms regarding the Armenians.

New Consuls (1876-88)

Despatches continued from Poti, now under Vice-Consul Thomas Gardner (appointed in April 1877), but the main source of information came from the major centre in Transcaucasia, Tiflis, where a consulate had been opened in 1876. George Thorne Ricketts served here, followed by Walter Tschudi Lyall from 1878-81, when the post was abolished. Both Ricketts and Lyall had had army careers, with the former having served as consul and on special service posts from Belgrade to Borneo, having also been at one time private secretary to Mr Longworth ('the superior man') at Monastir.[300] Lyall had served in the Bengal cavalry and had been involved in the Indian mutiny, but little is otherwise known about him.[301] His despatches are among the more outspoken and he ended up being ousted from Tiflis.

Poti continued to be a dismal posting, only more so as since 1875 there was no salary (probably linked to savings to cover the opening of Tiflis) and only an allowance (£200 raised to £400), which Gardner nevertheless accepted, eliciting complaints about incidental expenses, such a support for an English widow left destitute, or the purchase of a consular flag.[302] Tiflis, having more cachet and whose jurisdiction extended over the whole province governed by Prince Michael, was better remunerated. The salary was £1200, with an office allowance estimated at anything from £270-350. Here expenses included a guard, servants, an interpreter, newspapers such as the *Journal de St Petersburg*, the *Bombay Gazette*, Russian newspapers (extracts of which were sent to the Foreign Office) and the Russian Almanack. Regulations were strict: there were to be no commercial pursuits.[303]

Instructions at this time were clear: reports were expected on the movement of the Army of the Caucasus in general and on both sides of the Caspian, on native disturbances and on Central Asia. For the latter future consul Ricketts was to inform himself by visiting the topographical department of the Foreign Office.[304] Consuls were to be especially careful in relaying matters of a political nature and not to attract the attention or suspicion of the Russians. No letters were to be sent by the Russian post for they risked being compromised. They were to be sent by a trustworthy person to Poti then by steamer to Constantinople.[305] Despatches on military matters were to be sent by telegram via the Indo-European Company[306] and in compressed cypher when important. Vice-Consul Ricketts was admonished for deluging the FO with cypher messages, which were either of no use or contradictory or repetitive.[307] In the climate of constantly changing events and intermittent information this was to prove difficult. The consuls' communication with the FO did pose a problem for the Russians for in April 1877 they refused to forward telegrams, and they had reason to be worried since it was clear that embedded in the messages was advice to be passed on to the Ottomans.[308]

Reporting the war

The Russians 'are bent on war', wrote Ricketts to Earl Edward Stanley (Secretary of State for Foreign Affairs 1866-68, 1874-78) as troops were arriving in Poti and Tiflis in 1876.[309] In fact plans for a Russian advance towards Erzerum had already been made in 1874, but subsequently abandoned.[310]

The almost daily consular despatches and telegrams during 1877 follow the course of the war, but as information was received from a variety of sources, through military men, other consuls, locals, interpreters sent on missions, it was piecemeal and sometimes confusing. The letters and despatches address significant military engagements, shifting troop and reserve numbers and deployments, advice on specific routes and the building of defences. They convey the vast, time-consuming logistical effort both in preparation and during the war: ships and steamers had to be chartered, railways and camels[311] commandeered for troops, fodder and war materiel assembled, hospitals built, forts and batteries erected. In 1876 war materiel amounted to 500 tons of vodka, flour and powder.[312] The despatches also convey much collateral information: time spent waiting for troop reinforcements, atrocities, the insurgency, bribery of Turkish officials, atrocious weather, the suffering of the troops and the mood of the country.

Russian troops in January were estimated by Consul Ricketts to be from 80,000 to 90,000; by February the estimate was 129,200. The Ottomans (Turks) were said to have 160,000 men at Kars and Erzerum. In March local militia amounted to 107.950, 23,000 infantry and 13 batteries en route, with 15,000 troops set for Dagestan.[313] Numbers were extremely fluid not only because troops kept being added or lost as the war progressed, but due to misinformation. The Russian army had been reorganized, with newly formed divisions and numbers on their side,[314] yet there were problems of transport and disagreements at the command level. The Turkish army, despite having modern Peabody-Martini and Prussian guns (manufactured by Krupps) and Prussian advice, had transport, storage and supply problems as well as inadequacies at the top command.[315] This placed it at a disadvantage despite early victories.

The war in the Caucasus was essentially fought inland in the south-east, with lesser coastal action around Abkhazia and Batum. The aim was to take Kars, Erzerum and Batum. Troops were deployed at the key points of Alexandropol (where jewellery was sent to be distributed to spies and others in Turkish territory,[316] Akhaltsik, Erivan and Kobuleti). The war was mainly fought in 1877, with a spill-over into 1878. The following summary gives the bare bones of what were very difficult offensive and defensive campaigns in often unforgiving terrain.[317]

The war started on 24 April 1877, with the Russians crossing the Turkish frontier in the direction of Ardahan, which was taken by the Russians in May after apparently having been bribed to surrender.[318] A massacre ensued - 800 dead - attributed by the Russians to the Karakalpaks. They 'fell upon the place like dogs upon dead bodies, it was not our troops,' wrote the *Westnik*,[319] but information suggested it was the work of irregular Lezgin troops in the pay of Russia. 'If this happens in such an army at the beginning of the war, what will follow?' asked Ricketts.[320] He was right, other atrocities followed.

The taking of Ardahan was followed by an attempt to seize Batum in May with a failed siege ('a farce' according to Ricketts, with useless siege guns, discord among the generals, the fortress undamaged, but with the loss of 5,000 men) which was aborted in July.[321] In May the Turks had landed at Gudauti to the north of Sukhum-Kale, which was bombarded and evacuated (May 1877). It fuelled a local insurgency around the Kodor valley. Sukhum-Kale had already been looted in 1876 at a time when peasants in Mingrelia rebelled against giving 25 per cent of their crops to proprietors.[322] Moves against Batum were diverted by the ongoing Abkhazian insurgency: the Russians advanced towards Sukhum-Kale and Gudauti and the Turks withdrew their forces from the former.[323] There was another massacre around this time at Ozurgeti. In retaliation for Turkish soldiers firing at Russian soldiers (who had tried to bribe them) the Russians were ordered to bayonet the women and children and burn their villages to the ground.[324] Such sanctioned killing was *de rigueur*: Kurdish women in the Turkish army who had been taken prisoner were murdered. 'It is lamentable to hear that prisoners are treated thus…by a power that calls itself civilized,' wrote Ricketts.[325]

There was no quarter for the insurgents either. Ricketts had thought that the insurgency would only start if the Turks 'were victorious',[326] but how wrong he was. By May-June the insurgency, fought both to divert Russian troops and for the insurgents' own causes, was spreading to Svaneti,[327] Christian Ossetia (5 June)[328] and Chechnya south of Grozny.[329] In Chechnya villages were burnt because they had refused to quarter Russian soldiers at their own expense and to contribute recruits when they were told they would have to fight outside their territory.[330] The Grand-Duke was afraid to leave Tiflis, it was reported.[331]

The war against the Ottomans picked up pace in June. In the far south-east, east of Erzerum and south from Erivan, Bayazit, which had been partly taken by the Russians but poorly defended, was blockaded by the Kurds. A massacre of the local population by Kurds, Cossacks and irregulars ensued.[332] After actions at Tahir (heavy Turkish losses),[333] the first major battle in the east ensued. This was at Zivin Dag (June 1877, *en route* to Erzerum); with fighting on very high ground the militia ran away and the Russians were repulsed with heavy losses. An operation was mounted to relieve Bayazit.[334] The next major engagement in the east was at Kizil Tepe in August-September, which was finally won by the Turks at the end of August (with approximately equal losses on either side) partly due to confused handling of the day's fighting by the Russians.[335] Time was now given for the exhausted armies to recoup and wait for reinforcements.[336]

In October 1877 there was a Russian push towards Kars and Erzerum (which was being fortified). The Russian lines, covering Alexandropol, ran north-west and south-east. There was panic at Kars, but the attack was deferred, partly due to bad weather.[337] The battle of Camel's Neck (or Deve-Boyu col) of November was a decisive one for the Russian push towards Erzerum. The Turkish losses were huge (3,000 killed, 4,000 deserters, against 1,200 Russian casualties).[338] The Russians demanded the surrender of Erzerum, but this was refused. A Russian night attack was repelled, and the Russians decided to wait for the fall of Kars rather than storming Erzerum there and then.[339] With each Russian success or encroachment in the Turkish east the Armenian population would head for the Russian border.[340] In 1877 Consul Lyall used his brother Henry W. Lyall, to hand in a report on the campaign up to October to the Foreign Office.[341]

Meanwhile the insurrection was spreading. By August and September confidential memos stated that no sooner was the revolt stopped in one place than it started up in another. It had now moved to around Gunib in Dagestan and encompassed not only Chechnya, but most of Dagestan and the districts of Zakatali and Signaki ('a hundred "versts" from Tiflis').[342] General Franchini had been sent to Dagestan with 80,000 roubles to keep the chiefs quiet, but the money had been used to engage Lezgin fighters, who later revolted against the Russians at Erivan.[343] After severe Russian reprisals in Chechnya (killing of women and children, exile to Siberia) and arresting the chief of the rebellion Ali Bey (now looked upon locally as a saint), Dagestan had 'common cause' with the Chechens.[344] In the west, the insurrection by the Abkhaze (which was hopeless as they only had about 5,000 men from thirty villages), joined by remaining Circassians and Avars, continued to be bloody. In August Ricketts reported that whenever the Russians approached a village in Abkhazia it was burnt. The soldiers had been ordered to bayonet all women and children and to spare no prisoners. This was carried out to the letter. Ricketts foresaw that even more rigorous measures would be taken in winter when the inhabitants would come down from the mountains. 'They will either be exterminated or driven into exile,' he wrote. He suggested that women and children should be removed from Abkhazia and that in the event of peace, steps should be taken to offer an amnesty for the people of the Caucasus; but given the timidity of the people of Tiflis and the plains, and the lack of unity, especially among the mountain people, he was pessimistic about the outcome. Meanwhile the *St Petersburg Gazette* insisted on the state of tranquillity in the Caucasus.[345]

Panicked estimates in May imagined that up to 840,000 mountain fighters could be gathered, but in fact numbers were highly fluid.[346] Local insurgencies were joined by Kurds, Poles, Russian deserters and enrolled native troops who turned against the Russian military. By October the insurgency had spread to the Caspian provinces (telegraph wires were cut), and it was feared it would spread to Baku, Derbend and Shemakha, where refugees were already heading to Astrachan.[347] The insurrection also stirred up brigandage. Bands (led by Tatars Mir Ali and Deli Agha, the former stealing from the rich and seemingly a local hero) were roaming around Tiflis stealing cattle, murdering and raping.[348]

The penultimate chapter of the war was the siege and storming of Kars (November 1877-January 1878). Since the Crimean War, Kars had been reinforced by a ring of forts, but the garrison was not huge (15,000) and the resistance of the defensive forts was weak.

The population was said to be in favour of capitulation. As forts were taken defenders fled and the line fell. The final attack was on the moonlit night of 17 November and by dawn the Russians had taken the citadel and the town. It was difficult to know whether bribery had been involved, wrote Ricketts, but presents (such as tobacco boxes set in diamonds) had been distributed in advance. Turkish losses were estimated at 2,500, with 17,000 prisoners including 800 officers and five pashas. The fall of Kars completed the 1877 campaign. It would help calm the insurrection and augment Russian prestige, assessed Ricketts.[349] By December and January, reprisals, Turkish losses and the phasing out of the war had pacified much of the insurrection.

Two objectives remained for the Russians: Erzerum and Batum. The first was blockaded, but an epidemic of typhus and freezing temperatures ravaged troops on both sides. The Russians entered Erzerum in February 1878 after an armistice had been agreed at the end of January. The operation against Batum had begun before the armistice; here the defence was strong. But the armistice intervened and Batum surrendered. In August the Russians took possession of Batum with no particular incident, except for a mullah endeavouring to incite the people from a minaret. He was arrested. The town was almost empty anyway with 'no food, man or beast' and the bazaar burnt by the inhabitants. There was a twenty-gun salute and the Turkish flag lowered.[350] Batum was retained by Russia at the Congress of Berlin (see below).[351]

The End of the War and its Aftermath

The armistice led to the Treaty of San Stefano between the Russians and the Ottomans in March 1878. Here Ardahan, Batum, Kars and Beyazit were ceded to the Russians, and Erzerum was returned to the Turks. Major changes were also made to borders and political status in the Balkans: Bulgaria was declared an autonomous principality, with greatly extended borders. Montenegro also increased in size and Serbia became autonomous. The Straits (Bosphorus, Dardanelles) were to be open to neutral ships of war in peacetime. A number of objections from the Great Powers and local actors to this expansion (particularly of Bulgaria, which it was feared would be unduly influenced by Russia) demanded revisions and this led to the Treaty of Berlin (July 1888), in which Britain, Austria-Hungary, France, Germany and Italy participated. The result was a much smaller autonomous principality in Bulgaria, the autonomy of eastern Rumelia, and the Austro-Hungarian occupation of Bosnia and Herzegovina. The Ottomans, at British insistence, retained some jurisdiction over Bulgaria and eastern Rumelia, and Batum was to be a free port. In 1878 the Ottomans had ceded Cyprus to the British in exchange for its support.

The Russians were left dissatisfied by the Treaty. They were not the only ones: numerous Georgians and Armenians had previously entertained hopes that with a European war they might obtain equal privileges with the Bulgarians 'to whom they consider themselves superior,' wrote Gardner.[352] In 1880 the Armenians sent Mkrtich Khrimian, the future Catholicos, to Berlin to argue their case for autonomy, but he was excluded from the talks. The rights of Armenians in the Treaty of Berlin (Article 61) put the onus, once more, on the Ottomans, who were to undertake improvements in the provinces inhabited by the Armenians without delay and to guarantee their security against the Circassians and Kurds. Even if the Ottomans had wanted reforms, they were bankrupt and in debt because of colossal war reparations.[353] Exchanges between Christian and Muslim communities in Kars, Erzerum, Akhalkalak and Akhalstike were agreed but it has been argued that Russia was not keen to incorporate so many into the newly formed Armenian *guverniia*.[354]

The Treaty of Berlin's conclusions precipitated radicalism, and by 1890 a revolutionary movement had been founded at Tiflis. Following local anti-Kurdish and anti-fiscal peasant revolts in Sassun (mountains just east of Lake Van) and Zeitun, the first systematic, deliberate wave of genocide of the Armenians in the east took place in 1894-96. This was followed by anti-Armenian pogroms in Sassun in 1904 (also in Baku) and elsewhere, widespread massacres in 1909 and finally, in the context of a Pan-Turkish climate in the east, the start of the war in 1915 and accusations against the Armenians of betrayal, the ultimate expulsion of 1915-16.[355] The treatment of Armenians became war propaganda, when Britain turned the subject into a national concern.[356] As Forsyth has stated, such genocides were not without precedent, as the fate of the Circassians showed.[357]

Post-war Poti, Batum and Kars

British shipping interests in Poti were already affected by the high duties placed on all imports in 1877, when Russia, short of money, demanded payment in gold. These measures affected everyone, as Armenian merchants who controlled the principal trade in the Caucasus, were forced to go to Nighzy Novgorod and Warsaw for supplies, which were of low quality.[358]

British trade picked up after the peace, but with difficulties at every turn: steamers were obstructed, kept in detention, fined with trivial penalties. This was deliberate, an official openly stated to Gardner. Poti became the least favourite shipping port on the Black Sea coast, Captains were offered cargoes, but refused them or refused to come near the place. When the consulate was abolished, merchants complained that there was no-one to help them.[359] Nevertheless, development of the port (bought by Russian capitalists) continued despite the rise of Batum.[360]

The transition to Russian possession of Batum was unsurprisingly not an easy one. The district was a disaster, wrote Lyall from Tiflis. As the local population wanted to emigrate (c.60,000), there was a land grab in the district, reducing the population to beggary. The government alone authorized and sanctioned the land sold by the inhabitants but original buyers had to wait so long for this to materialize that they withdrew, and civil and military employees formed a cartel and 'swooped in', buying everything at nominal prices. Armenian government employees made life difficult for the Muslim inhabitants, harassing them, 'screwing' money out of them and refusing passports. It was spoliation and extortion, Lyall concluded.[361] The Turkish government sent weekly steamers for the local Laz population to leave gratis with their cattle for Trebizond, Samsun, Amastra and Constantinople.[362] In 1880, 1,100 Abkhazian emigrants with no passports turned up on the beach at Batum (170 dying of exposure). With the younger men escaping into the interior, the rest were embarked on a Russian steamer heading for the coast of Anatolia. The Grand Duke had been adamant he did not want them, but neither did the Turks nor the Laz at Kappa, so they were re-embarked and left on an uninhabited part of what used to be the coast of Circassia beyond the Russian frontier. They had been given two days' provisions at Batum and many of them, women, children and old men, would die of starvation, wrote Lyall. In effect, two hundred died,[363] and subsequently some were allowed to proceed to Sukhum-Kale. The captain of the Greek brig, sailing under a British flag, was arrested for the expenses claimed for feeding the migrants and re-landing them. He asked Gardner for help over in having his boat released.[364] The Russian press, continuing its anti-British campaign, blamed the unprincipled speculation of an English merchant captain, who had previously been the original contractor for the railway between Tiflis and Baku (but had resold it to a Reinholt of St Peterburg).[365]

Migration remained a policy: those who did not want to leave had to sell and emigrate within three years or become Russian subjects.[366] But Batum was a semi-free port of great potential and many projects were afoot: the semi-circular railway along the coast (Batum, Poti, Tiflis), strengthening fortifications, draining swamps, the development of the harbour.[367] The town itself received little improvement except two new streets and forty brick houses (with Marseille tiles). Prices were high, as no maize, fruit or vegetables were now grown: everything had to be imported, whether from Trebizond, Odessa, Kerch or Poti. Yet small merchants and shopkeepers from all over the Caucasus came as the terms were better than elsewhere and shops and magazines were well stocked with English and French goods.[368]

In 1881 Demetrius Rudolph Peacock, married to a Russian woman, was appointed as British Consul (of whom very little is known).[369] The Governor of Batum, General Komaroff, was removed on grounds of negligence, intoxication and the requisition of women from villages. By this time most Muslim inhabitants had left, with houses, vineyards and orchards left abandoned.[370]

From the 1880s and 1890s the city took off, with a focus on petroleum and the development of this trade with India, China and Japan. The journalist and author Charles Marvin visited Batum in 1893 while researching the Russian oil industry and found the city 'under rapid development'. Builders were at work everywhere, hovels were being knocked down to make way for wide streets and residences of several storeys, trenches and canals were being put in place for draining marshes. There were canning factories, oil reservoirs and piers for a port that was destined to be splendid. Marvin envisaged fleets of cistern-oil steamers conveying Baku petroleum from its harbour to 'every part of the West and East'. Other trade was already booming (Batum was then a free port, ceasing to be in 1886), with much contraband and evasion of duty payments.[371] By the later 1880s the focus was on petroleum. In 1888, 108,971 tons of kerosene was exported, and the trade in caustic soda used for refining at Baku boomed. The majority of foreign oil carriers were British (18 in 1888 compared to one German and one Belgian). Kerosene was conveyed in tin plates (made in Swansea) and wooden crates, already threatened by the introduction of tank steamers for the Far East and India. Besides petroleum, grain, wool, manganese were major exports, but were dependent on availability, market fluctuations and transport. Imports were iron, machinery, cement, caustic soda and eventually tanks for petroleum.[372] The poorer classes did not profit from this growth. A severe winter in 1889 left people dying of cold and foot passengers frozen on the spot.[373]

Kars presented more intractable problems. The traditional multi-ethnic and denominational populations (Muslims both Sunni and Shia, Christians of various denominations, Kurds, Yezidis) and their way of life in this region of south-eastern Turkey had been severely disrupted by longstanding Russian and Ottoman centralizing interference.[374] Tensions between Muslims and Christians and within religious groups (such as between Armenian Catholics and Armenian Orthodox) were exacerbated by each border reorganization, which brought about population movements and settlers. The 1877-78 war resulted in a massive exchange of populations: about 100,000 Armenians crossed from Kars and Ardahan into Russian Transcaucasia and 110,000 or more Muslims, Kurds and Laz crossed into Ottoman territory. These were not single events but continuous, and the result of pressure as much as the desire to leave. For example, in 1892 a large Muslim population from Akhaltsik district left because it was feared Russian soldiers would insult and attack their wives and children (probably false information, wrote Murray).[375]

Such emigration caused existing social and economic structures to collapse. Not everyone wanted the migrants. Many Muslims settled in Erzerum but were later resettled in Sivas, Amasya, Tokat, Istanbul and the wider Ottoman empire (Damascus and Aleppo). In Istanbul they crowded public buildings as there was no space for them, and in Anatolia, where there had already been a wave of Circassians, they were not welcome, as the local population did not want to share land. Disputes ensued. There were also cultural differences. Some wanted to return, and despite some re-allocation support, many did not want to become Ottoman subjects, pay taxes or be conscripted.[376] Russia threatened Siberian exile for those who returned.[377]

In Kars there was local grief because the governor did not want Armenians there and it had been decided to settle German and Russian colonists in the area.[378] Kars itself was virtually ruined, and to add insult to injury, the local mosque (which had once been an Armenian church) was being converted into a Russian Orthodox church. 'They are behaving like the Turks,' commented the Armenians. The Armenians themselves were a massive problem in Kars, according to Lyall, whose antipathy may have been the result of traditional prejudice, although his report makes clear that (as at Batum) scandals, disorders and criminal behaviour such as extortion were emanating from the mostly ill-educated Armenian government officials. The chief of police had been suspended for theft, extortion, and using *maisons publiques* without paying. No principled Russian or German official wanted to serve there.[379] However, such scandals also seem to have been characteristic of the state of the whole Caucasian administration at the time, which Lyall described as 'an Augean stable'.[380]

Revolution in the air

The war not only had a massive effect on the geopolitics of Europe and what had been eastern Turkey but also precipitated events in Russia as well. In 1879 Lyall was beginning to mention plots against the emperor (probably referring to an assassination attempt in 1879) and socialist sedition inciting peasants to revolt. A trial and execution of officers related to socialist movements in 1879 had been a serious source of discontent. The Empire attributed radicalization to British agency.[381] Activity against the emperor and the state had, however, also manifested itself in the early 1860s and had culminated in an assassination attempt in 1866. The successful assassination of Tsar Alexander II in 1881 brought to the fore once more the existence of violent revolutionary feeling in Russia. The assassination did not create the sensation such an event would have done in Europe, wrote Lyall, as people of all classes looked upon it as a 'fatal necessity'.[382] After the war, low wages in public works (with all money spent on munitions) and consequent strikes, taxation, corruption and hatred of the emperor's and the grand duke's entourage, together with resentment of misgovernment - 'an universal system detested by all' - had led to social demoralization and anger. Georgia and Armenia applauded the assassination, wrote Lyall. It had not been a palace coup, as some people thought, but was carried out by a revolutionary movement (*Narodnaya Volia* or The People's Will) and the educated classes, with both socialists and nihilists approving the revolutionary movement.[383] Alexander III (1845-94) succeeded his father. Autocratic and a believer in Russian nationalism and the supremacy of Orthodoxy, he cancelled his father's reforms and clamped down hard (all public amusements were forbidden). Lyall foresaw the probability of a 'severely repressive regime' being instituted and thought it 'rash and ill-advised' to cancel the reforms. People were now expecting summary executions, and the trial of the ten conspirators and assassins, who were looked upon as heroes and martyrs from mixed social backgrounds (graduates and working-class, one of noble descent), resulted in the hanging of the majority (including Sophia Petrovskaya, the first woman to be hanged in Russia for political reasons).[384] Two other women were sent to prison, one man committed suicide and another died from one of the explosions. The photo of Sophia Petrovskaya was favoured above that of the late emperor lying in state, Lyall noted.[385]

Lyall gives a frank assessment of Russia's attitude to war and the social situation. As 'the existence of the Empire depended on its military prestige', no expense was spared for the army,[386] which in addition provided needed employment. The military feared revolutionary feeling if defeated (strangely ignoring what was happening around them) and would be inclined to go to war if they could be successful.[387] Civilized and honest officials realized that the present situation was dangerous and were upset that 'the Foreign Powers' seemed to acquiesce with the social unrest and were duped.[388] Lyall hints that bankrupting wars always loomed without referring to the one that was perpetually in the news: Russia's in Central Asia. However, he does state that Britain could not remain inactive if Russia advanced further into Central Asia.[389] Yet despite the Foreign Office's request to Consul Ricketts to inform himself on Central Asia, there are very few reports on this area from Tiflis, until the sensational and savage conquest of Geok Tepe in Turkmenistan in 1881. Clearly Tiflis was not a major source of information on Central Asia.

Russia had been engaged in its advance in Central Asia since the 1840s and 1850s when it endeavoured to create a new frontier along the Syr Darya (east of the Aral Sea). This was followed by the conquest of Kokand and Bukhara (1864-85), Khiva (1873), Turkmenistan (1879-85) and finally the eastern mountains (1872-1895). Morrison has shown how Russian sources reveal the messy process of this advance, which in contrast to its aims in the

Caucasus (also messy), had no strategic and economic purpose, but was fuelled chiefly by the desire for prestige and by military ambition.[390] Morrison also argues that the famous 'Great Game' between Russia and Britain was a myth and the result of paranoia from India.[391] The threat to India was nevertheless widely used as a political goad and trope by the press, consuls' reports and travellers in the region. Russia was fairly certain that the British would not venture into Central Asia, and where they did (in Afghanistan), the advance was settled by the definition of the north Afghan border in 1919.[392]

Lyall's Geok Tepe reports show Russia's crushing and bloody victory and its huge expenditure (up to £3 million). It panicked Lyall that the 'division of Russian and British dominions in Asia will menace India' and might be used to 'coerce Britain'. The British had missed their chance in Afghanistan, he added, without elaborating.[393] Neither the First Afghan War (1839-42) nor the Second (1879-81) were military successes for Britain.

By spring and early summer of 1881, Lyall was writing that Turkmenistan had accepted the Russians (perhaps in the sense of accepting military defeat), place names were being changed from Turkmen to Russian, and officers were purchasing arms, carpets and curiosities locally.[394]

On the Russian social front, Lyall assesses that there were delays in forming a viable middle class; the choice was between corrupt officials and peasants, with the latter kept in fear of the outside world, agreeing to wars because they thought they made Russia formidable.

Lyall's depressing and prescient assessment was that there would be either a new war or revolution.[395] In fact, perhaps a little later than he anticipated, both occurred.

1. Lyall 1825, 1 53
2. Lyall 1825, 1 390-1
3. idem 1 397, 390, 423
4. idem 1 42
5. Forsyth 2013. I am hugely indebted to this publication.
6. Forsyth 2013, 284-289
7. Lyall 1825 1, 448-9
8. Teissier 2014, 79
9. Lyall 1825, 2 54-55
10. Lyall 2, 57-76
11. Schimmelpenninck van der Oye 2014, 143-152
12. Lyall 1825 2, 65
13. Lyall 1825 1, 415
14. IOR/L/PS/9/76/214
15. Lyall 1825 1 ,411
16. Lyall 1, 397-8
17. Lyall 1, 405
18. FO 881/618, 39
19. 1829 peace treaty between Russia and the Ottomans whereby the Dardanelles were opened up to commercial shipping, and Russia gained control of Anapa and Poti, and access to Akhaltsik and Akhalkalaki.
20. Urquhart (An Old Diplomat) 1839 (third edition) including the correspondence between George Bell (brother of the traveller), Lord Ponsonby and Lord Palmerston over this affair. FO 881/618, 1-32, and ff.; for references to *The Times* see King 2007, note 40; see also e.g. *Blackwood's Edinburgh Magazine* 1837/42, 636-647
21. FO 881/68, 34, 40
22. MSS FO 97/344 Letter from Lord Ponsonby to Lord Palmerston 1834
23. MSS FO 97/344 Letter from Lord Ponsonby to Lord Palmerston, 1834
24. MSS FO 97/344, 1836
25. Marx in *The Story of the Life of Lord Palmerston* (1853) seems to have adapted his views on Palmerston and Urquhart, marxistnkrumaistforum.word.press.com
26. King, C. 2007, 238-255, esp. 254-255
27. FO 881/618, 12-14
28. Also referred to in the regional press: e.g. Western Times Jan 9, 1836, and in subsequent years as the petitions came in e.g. The Era, June 25, 1939. See also King 2007 with full references to the Circassian question.
29. FO 881/681, 41
30. Later Sir, author of *The Progress and Present Position of Russia in the East* 1836, several editions, London: John Murray
31. Bell 1, 199-200, 277
32. Bell 1, 275-276
33. Longworth 1, 23
34. Spencer 1837, 1 197
35. Idem 2, 339-346
36. Idem 1, xvi
37. Idem 1, 59
38. Idem 1, xvii
39. Spencer 1838,1, 55-56, 61, 62-76

40 Idem 138, 55-56, 61-76.
41 Bell 1, vi-viii
42 Longworth 1 15-16
43 Ibid 60-61, see also Bell 1 235
44 Bell 1, 56, 119-20
45 Longworth 2, 162, 198
46 FO MSS 97/344, Letter of Ponsonby to Palmerston, including a copy of Bell's report, no.7. 1837. A Colonel Macintosh had already been sent in 1834 FO MSS 97/344 Dec. 16.
47 Spencer 1838,1 29
48 Spencer 1838 1, 95-97
49 Longworth 1, 108, 128,151
50 Bell 2, 20
51 Longworth 2, 323
52 Longworth 1, 133
53 Bell 1, 357-358, 2, 368
54 Bell 2, 316, 325, 335, 358
55 Bell 1, 200
56 Spencer 1837, 1 271
57 Bell 2 , 164
58 Bell 1, 216
59 Bell 2, 119
60 Bell 1, 435, 442
61 Spencer 1838, 1 93ff.
62 Longworth 2, 128
63 Longworth 2, 128
64 Longworth 1 258-260, 294-293
65 On Sefer Bey and London FO 881/618 37-38 and passim
66 Longworth 2, 198
67 Longworth 1, 104
68 Longworth 1, 106, 117
69 Bell 1, 120-126; Longworth 1, 117
70 Longworth 1, 121-122
71 Longworth 1, 120-123
72 For the protracted correspondence and FO thinking over this at the time see FO 881/618, 1- 61
73 Bell 1, 100-127; Bell 2, Appendix 2, 431-432
74 Longworth 1, 163
75 Bell 1, 381
76 FO 881/510 no.3, Riach 1837 9-29
77 Bell 2, 325-327
78 Bell 2, 328
79 Bell 1, 92
80 Longworth 2, 327; Bell 2, 387-90,422
81 Longworth 1 ,186
82 Bell 1, 154
83 Bell 2, 152-153
84 Longworth 1, 192
85 Bell 1, 236-237
86 FO 881/510 no.3, Riach 1837, 19

87 Bell 1, 397-398
88 FO 881/510 no.3, Riach 1837,19,29
89 FO 881/510 no.3, Riach 1837, 20
90 Bell 1, 93, 168, 389, 394
91 Spencer 1838, 1, 96-98
92 Spencer 1838, 1, 160
93 FO 881/510 no.3, Riach 1837, 20,21, 23
94 Longworth 2, 333
95 Cameron 1845, 310-314
96 Gammer 1994, 117
97 Arbuthnot, revised by James Lunt, Oxdnb/4441
98 Cameron 1845, xiv-xvi
99 Ibid 290-291, note 1
100 Ibid 275-276
101 Ibid 250-251
102 Ibid 245, 257, 270, 293
103 Ibid 266 ff.
104 Tsiutsev 2014, Map 18
105 Forsyth 2015, 170
106 Gammer 1994, 20-21
107 Gammer 2004, 39-40. Shamil's spiritual path was associated with the Mujaddidi-Khalidi branch of the Naqshbandi order: Zelkina 2002, 251-260. Ibid for the different branches of the Naqshbandi order and Shamil's legacy.
108 Gammer 1994, xiv, 49-80
109 Ibid 113-129. See also Gammer ed. 2009
110 Tsiutsev 2014, Map 5
111 Gammer 1994, 44
112 Ibid 44
113 Ibid 232-238
114 Mahomedov 2002, 246-248
115 Musayev and Alkhasova 2009, 51
116 FO 65/569, 190
117 FO 881/510 no.3, Riach 1837, 16
118 IOR/L/PS/9/76/214, no.1 1801-2 Letter to Hartford Jones (British Resident in Baghdad) from Samuel Manesty and Robert Rickarts
119 IOR/L/PS/9/69/140, Letter from Henry Willock, Chargé d'Affaires in Persia (Tabriz) to George Canning (Secretary of State for Foreign affairs) and the Secret Committee
120 IOR/L/PS/9/69/140 (1824); as above; IOR/L/PS/9/70/132 (1826) Letter of Lft. Col. MacDonald Kinneir to the Government of India
121 FO 881/510 no.3, Riach 1837, 19. Caucasian divisions: Circassians (the most numerous with the Lesghees), Abazeks, Nagatai, Kabardians, Koomekee (Kumykhs), Chechenses, Aphazians. Swanetees, Osseteens). Ex Persian provinces: Karrabagh, Shaki, Shirvan, Talish, Quba, Baku, Derbent.
122 Baumgart 2020, 32-33; Ponting 2005, 227
123 Ponting 2005, 227
124 Ponting 2005, 227-228
125 National Army Museum 6807/377/3 Bundle 1 (Raglan papers, May

1855); 6807/303 (1854) Report on Circassia
126 National Army Museum 6807/303, 10 June 1854; see also FO MSS 195/443
127 FO MSS 97/350 Memorandum on Circassia
128 National Army Museum 6807/303 Reports by Mr. Lloyd nos1-6 re. 11 despatches
129 National Army Museum 6807/303 letter of 28 January 1855 from Sir J. Burgoyne to Lord Raglan
130 FO MSS 195/443 Letter from Longworth to Lord Canning, June 2 1855
131 FO 881/1443, 3-4 Correspondence Regarding Circassia 1855-57; FO 881/618, 63-64, Memorandum relative to Circassia 1839-1857
132 FO 881/618 , 64-66
133 FO 881/618, 66
134 FO 881/618, 66
135 FO MSS 195/443 Longworth's Memorandum relative to the military resources, political position and relations in Circassia.
136 FO 881/618, 65-66
137 National War Museum MSS 6807/303, Memoir respecting a visit to the Naib of Shamil, 1955
138 FO 881/1443, no.12
139 Gammer 1994, 267
140 Ponting 2005, 226
141 My thanks to Alexander Morrison for this reference.
142 Princess Anna Chavchavadze, the wife of Prince Chavchavadze and Princess Varvara Orbeliani, his sister in law.
143 Gammer 2004 ,277
144 E.g. Evgeni Verderevski (editor of Kavkaz) *Captivity of Two Russian Princesses in the Caucasus: including a seven months' residence in Shamil's seraglio*, London: Smith and Elder Co. 1857 (translated by H. Sutherland Edwards); Anna Drancey *Les Princesses russes prisonieres an Caucase (souvenir d'une Francaise captive de Chamyl* , Paris: Sartorius 1857.
145 FO MSS 78/1243, 6th October 1855
146 Atwell Lake, *Kars and Our Captivity in Russia*, 1856 340-341
147 Gammer 2004, 250-251, 274 n.66.
148 Gammer 2004, 163
149 FO MSS 195/443 Report of Mehmet Emin, Naib of Sheikh Shamil, to the Grand Vizier, August 15, 1854
150 National Army Museum 6807/303 Report of May 27, 1855
151 FO 881/1443 nos. 6-14, no. 14 re the Naib
152 FO881/545 compiled by Longworth, 1856
153 Ponting 2005, 226
154 Ponting 2005, 227
155 Ponting 2005, 228
156 Baumgart 2020, 311-312; Ponting 2005 316-317, 328-329
157 FO 881/661 Report from Major Cathcart to Brigadier General Mansfield, 1856
158 For the text of the Treaty: FO 881/618, 68-88
159 FO MSS 65/654, no 26 from Akhalkalati Camp, south Georgia
160 Gammer 1994, 285-294
161 FO 881/618, 101

162 FO 881/1443 no.18
163 FO 8881/618, FO MSS 65/654 Report by Robert Casolari to Lord Stanford
164 FO 881/618, 104-108
165 FO 881/1443 no. 19, Letter of July 6, 1857 from the Earl of Clarendon to Lord Canning
166 Bryce 1877, 59
167 Cameron 1860, FO MSS 65/569-70, Report on the Caucasus, 1, Political and Statistical, Division into Districts, Protectorate of Abkhasia (no page numbers).
168 Foreign Office List 1859, 59; Jason Thompson, online Oxford DNB 2004, William Palgrave 1826-1888
169 https://doi-org.ezproxy-prd.bodleian.ox.ac.uk/10.1093/ref:odnb/21159
170 FO 1859, 59-60; FO MSS 65/590, 16 April 1861
171 FO 65/590 Report on the Caucasus 1860, Parts 1-2: Political, Statistical, Military; FO 65/570 Parts 3-4: Topography, Commerce
172 Foreign Office List 1861, 105
173 Foreign Office List 1862, 159
174 FO MSS 65/613, February 25, 1863 Letter from Dickson to Earl Russel at the Foreign Office; for general duties see files passim FO MSS 65/590, 1861 and yearly
175 FO MSS 65/712, Letter of July 31 1866, Copy of Palgrave's commission
176 FO MSS 65/590 Letter of April 6, 1861
177 FO MSS 258/4 March 31, 1860 Dickson to Lord Russell at the FO, Confidential 2
178 FO MSS 258/4, May 8, 1860 Dickson to Russell, Confidential 3
179 FO MSS 258/4 July 22, 1861, Dickson to Russell, Confidential 3
180 Idem
181 FO MSS 258/4, July 16 1862, Dickson to Russell, Confidential 2
182 FO MSS 258/4, Nov.16 1861, Dickson to Russell, Confidential 6; idem May 15, 1863, idem April 12, 1862, Confidential 2
183 FO MSS 258/4 July 16, 1861, Dickson to Russell, Confidential 2; idem April 12, 1862, idem Confidential 2, May 29, 1862, Confidential 3, July 5 1862, Confidential 4
184 FO MSS 258/4, Dickson to Russell, April 12 1862, Confidential 2
185 FO MSS 258/4 Dickson to Russell, May 29 1862, Confidential 2
186 FO MSS 258/4 Dickson to Russell, March 17, 1864, Confidential 2
187 FO MSS 258/4 Dickson to Russell, June 29, Confidential 6
188 FO MSS 258/4 Dickson to Russell, April 18 1864, Confidential 3
189 FO MSS 258/4 Dickson to Russell, February 22, 1864 Confidential 1
190 FO MSS 258/4, February 22 1864, Dickson to Russell Confidential 4
191 FO MSS 258/4 April 13, 1864, Confidential 3
192 FO MSS 258/4 June 29, 1864, Dickson to Russell, Confidential 6
193 FO MSS 258/4, June 29 1867, Dickson to Russell, Confidential 6
194 FO MSS 258/4 October 9, 1861 Dickson to Russell, Confidential 4
195 FO MSS 258/4 November 15, 1861, Dickson to Russell, Confidential 5
196 FO MSS 258/4 February 22, Dickson to Russell 1864 Confidential 1
197 FO MSS 258/4 December 31, 1861 Dickson to Russell , Confidential 7
198 Jahn 2020 , 184
199 FO MSS 258/4, May 4 1861, Dickson to Russell, Confidential 1

200 FO MSS 258/4 November 2 1866, Palgrave to Lord Stanley Confidential 1; FO MSS 258/4 November 22, 1864, Palgrave to Stanley, Confidential 10
201 Rosser-Owen 2007, 16
202 Rosser-Owen 2007, 20 re. FO MSS 97/4247, November 17, 1860 from Dickson
203 FO MSS 258/4 July 11, 1861, Dickson-Russell, Confidential 2
204 FO MSS 258/4 June 29, Dickson to Russell, 1864, Confidential 6
205 FO MSS 258/4 June 29, 1864, Dickson to Russell, Confidential 6; epidemic ref. FO MSS 258/4 August 12, 1864, Dickson to Russell, Confidential 8
206 FO MSS January 22 1867, Palgrave to Stanley (from Poti), Confidential 1
207 FO MSS 258/4 June 29, 1864 Dickson to Russell, Confidential 6
208 Rosser-Owen 2007, 49 and Appendices 1 and 2 for full text of the petitions
209 Rosser-Owen 2007, 30, note 2
210 Rosser-Owen 2007, 24, 30
211 FO MSS 258/4, July 4 1864, Dickson to Russell, Confidential 7
212 FO MSS 258/4, 1864, December 29 1866, Palgrave to Stanley, Confidential 2
213 Palgrave 1872, VIII : The Abkhasian Insurrection
214 Freshfield 1896 Vol 2, 191-220
215 FO MSS November 22, 1864, Dickson to Russell, Confidential 10
216 FO MSS 258/4 August 12, 1864 Dickson to Russell, Confidential 8
217 Rosser-Owen 2007, 21
218 FO MSS 258/4, November 2 1866, Palgrave to Stanley, Confidential 1; also in Palgrave 1872
219 FO MSS December 28, 1866 Palgrave to Stanley, Confidential 2
220 FO MSS 258/4 November 4, 1866, Palgrave to Stanley, Confidential 11
221 FO MSS 258/4 December 1866, Palgrave to Stanley, Confidential 3
222 FO MSS 258/4 December 29, 1866, Palgrave to Stanley, Confidential 2
223 Tsiutsev 2014, 27-28, Table 11
224 Forsyth 2015, 295
225 Tsiutsev 2014, 25
226 Forsyth 2015, 295
227 Rosser-Owen 2007, 21-22
228 Rosser-Owen 2007, 30-31 note 1
229 Rosser-Owen 2007, 31, note 53
230 Rosser-Owen 20027, 50
231 Rosser-Owen 2007, 31-32
232 Rosser-Owen 2007,, 50
233 Rosser-Owen 2007, 23
234 Rosser-Owen 2007, 47-48
235 Rosser-Owen 2007 , 46-47
236 Rosser-Owen, list of reports by the British Press, 59
237 Rosser-Owen 2007, 46-47
238 FO MSS 258/4 January 22, Palgrave to Stanley, Confidential 1; Palgrave to Stanley March 10, 1867, Confidential 2
239 FO MSS 65/590, January 24, 1861
240 FO MSS 65/590, February 2 and 11, Dickson to Russell
241 FO MSS 65/649 , March 10, 1863, Wilkinson to Russell, Statement of

trade
242 FO MSS 65/590, January 30 , 1863 Dickson to Russell
243 FO MSS 65/590 January 15, 1861 Dickson to Russell
244 FO MSS 65/590 January 15, 1861, Dickson to Russell
245 FO MSS 65/590, January 21, 1863 Dickson to Russell
246 FO MSS 65/590 February 18, 1865 Dickson to Russell
247 FO 65/590 February 8, 1865, Wilkinson to Russell
248 FO MSS 65/649 May 8 1863, Dickson and Wilkinson via Russell
249 FO MSS 65/590, February 8 1865, Wilkinson to Russell
250 FO 65/649, February 18, 1865 , Dickson to Russell
251 Ussher 1865, 65
252 Telfer 1876, 1, 120
253 Harvey 1871, 214-218
254 Harvey 1871, 244-245
255 Harvey 1871, 245
256 Harvey 1871, 249
257 Freshfield 1869, 97
258 Bryce 1877, 348
259 Ussher 1865, 67
260 Telfer 1876, 2, 130
261 Telfer 1876, 2, 126, 131
262 Cunynghame 1872, 314-316
263 Bryce 1877, 345
264 Grove 1875, 18
265 Grove 1875, 18-19
266 Bryce 1877, 13
267 Telfer 1876, 2, 126
268 Ussher 1865, 61-62, 671-672
269 Ussher 1865, 672
270 Ussher 1865, 63
271 Harvey 1871, 249
272 Harvey 1871, 220-221
273 Freshfield 1869, 84
274 Cunynghame 1872, 213, 225-226
275 Bryce 1877, 92
276 Yavuz and Sluglett 2011 1-2, for an overview
277 FO MSS 65/977, Memorandum 31 December 1877, John Mitchell (St Petersburg) to Lord Derby
278 FO MSS 65/977 18 January 1877, Extracts from the Crop Almanac, Political 11, Ricketts to Derby ; FO MSS 65/977,31 December 1977, Extracts from the Russian Press translated by John Mitchell, John Mitchell to Derby
279 Bryce was to author with Arnold J. Toynbee *The Treatment of the Armenians in the Ottoman Empire 1815-1916*, Joseph Causton and Sons 1916
280 Bryce 1877, 130
281 Bryce 1877, 404
282 Bryce 1877, 59
283 Bryce 1877, 59-60
284 Bryce 1877, 142
285 Bryce 1877, 142

286 Mouradian 1995, 44-45
287 Bryce 1877, 408
288 Laycock 2009, 73
289 Teissier 2011, 80,141
290 Mouradian 1995, 43-44
291 Bryce 1877, 418, 420
292 Bryce 1877, 412
293 Bryce 1877, 409
294 Bryce 1877, 126
295 Bryce 1877, 129
296 Bryce 1877, 414
297 Bryce 1877, 415-16
298 Bryce 1877, 420
299 FO 881/3410 Layard to Derby December 16, 1877. For a discussion of Russian peace terms see FO 881/3214
300 FO List 1878, 172-3
301 FO List Lyall 1881, 137
302 FO MSS 65/982, 28 December 1876, Gardner to Derby
303 FO MSS 65/950, 24 April 1876, Foreign Office to Ricketts
304 FO MSS 65/950 12 September 1876, Confidential, War Office to Ricketts
305 FO MSS 65/977, 3 January 1877, no.2, Ricketts to Derby
306 FO MSS 65/977 15 May 1877, no. 5 (draft) India Office to Ricketts
307 FO MSS 65/977 20 May 1877, War Office to Ricketts; also internal FO to Tentuden by a P. x?
308 FO MSS 65/978, 17 November 1877, Telegram War Office to Ricketts
309 FO MSS 65/950, 9 December, Ricketts to Derby
310 Allen and Muratoff 1953, 114
311 FO MSS 65/977 12 May, Ricketts to War Office (decyphered)
312 FO MSS 65/951 12 July 1876, no.11, Gardner to Derby; FO MSS 12 February 1977, no.24, Ricketts to Derby
313 FO MSS 65/977 16 January, Ricketts to Derby; ibid February 1, 1877; ibid March 29, 1877; see also ibid printed assessment of 26 February 1877, no.278
314 Allen and Muratoff 1953, 108
315 Allen and Muratoff 1953, 112-113
316 FO MSS 65/977, 14 April 1877 Ricketts to Derby
317 For maps and terrain see Allen and Muratoff 1953, Maps 7-16
318 FO MSS 65/977 21 May 1877, Ricketts to Derby (deciphered); ibid May 1877, Decypher 83; FO MSS 65/1092, August 17, 1877, Confidential 112, Ricketts to Derby
319 FO MSS 65/977 14 May 1877, translation from the Westnik in 10 June 1877, Ricketts to Derby
320 FO MSS 65/977, 10 June 1877, Ricketts to Derby; 65/1092 no.112, Memorandum, Ricketts to Derby
321 FO 65/978, 6 July 1877, Telegram, Ricketts to Derby; FO MSS 65/977 , 19 June 1877, Ricketts to Derby
322 FO MSS 65/951, 12 July 1876 Jos Carroll (acting vice consul at Poti) to Derby; FO Mss 65/951 26 July, Carroll to Derby
323 Allen and Muratoff 1953, 147
324 FO MSS 65/977 20 May 1877, Ricketts to Derby

325 FO MSS 65/978, 26 July 1877 no.105
326 FO MSS, 1 February 1877, Political, Ricketts to Derby
327 FO MSS 65/977, 26 May 1877, no.83 (deciphered)
328 FO MSS 65/977, 5 June, Ricketts to Derby
329 FO MSS 65/977, 8 May 1877, Ricketts to Derby
330 FO 65 MSS, 26 May 1877, Ricketts to Derby
331 FO Mss 65/977, 5 June, Ricketts to Derby
332 FO MSS 65/1092, 3 December 1877, Ricketts to Derby no.141; Allen and Muratoff 1953, 148
333 Allen and Muratoff 1953, 140
334 Allen and Muratoff 1953, 141-150
335 Allen and Muratoff 1953, 166-167
336 Allen and Muratoff 1953, 158, 169
337 Allen and Muratoff 1953, 186-187
338 Allen and Muratoff 1953, 195-196
339 Allen and Muratoff 1953, 199
340 Allen and Muratoff 1953, 148
341 FO 881/4012 Report by Acting Consul Lyall on the Russo-Turkish Campaign in Armenia 1877 (printed for the FO 1879). See also Notes on the Caucasus 1883 by Wanderer (most likely Consul Lyall)
342 FO MSS 65/1092, August 1877, Confidential, Ricketts to Derby; FO MSS 65/1092, 21 September, translation from Karajal to War Office
343 FO MSS 65/977, 15 April 1877, Ricketts to Derby; FO MSS 65/977 May 14, 1877, Ricketts to Derby
344 FO MSS 21 October 1877, no.121 Ricketts to Derby
345 FO MSS 65/1092, August 1877, Memorandum, Ricketts to Derby
346 FO MSS 65/977 28 May 1877, Ricketts to Derby
347 FO MSS 65/978, 7 October, extracts from Westnik (24 Sptember-6 October 1877), Ricketts to Derby
348 FO MSS 65/977, 28 May 1877, Ricketts to Derby
349 FO MSS 65/978, 7 December 1877, Confidential on the fall of Kars 145, Ricketts to Derby
350 FO MSS 65/1015, 7 September 1878, Gardner to Salisbury
351 Medlicott 1963, with references for the full text of the Treaty
352 FO MSS 65/1018, 30 April 1879, Gardner to Salisbury
353 McCarthy 2011, 443
354 Tsiutsev 2014, Map 14
355 Mouradian 1995, 50-56
356 Laycock 2009, 103ff.
357 Forsyth 2015, 307
358 FO MSS 65/1056, 30 April 1879, Gardner to Salisbury
359 FO MSS 65/1056, 30 April 1879, Gardner to Salisbury
360 MSS 65/1124, 14 September 1881, Lyall to Granville
361 FO MSS 65/1092, July 1880, Private and Personal, Lyall to Granville
362 FO MSS 65/1093, 30 July 1880, Lyall to Granville
363 FO MSS 65/1092 14 November 1880, Confidential 30, Lyall to Granville
364 FO MSS 65/1092 September 27, 1880, Confidential 28, Lyall to Granville
365 FO MSS 65/1092, 14 November 1880, Confidential 30, Lyall to Granville
366 Tanriverdi 2011, 454-455
367 FO MSS 65/1124, 14 September 1881, Confidential 14, Lyall to Granville

368 FO MSS 65/1093, 30 July 1880, Gardner to Granville
369 FO List 1882
370 FO MSS 65/1124, 27 April 1881, Confidential 10, Lyall to Granville
371 Marvin 1891, 98-110
372 FO MSS 65/1369 Commercial Report for 1888; 65/1427 12 February 1892
373 FO MSS 65/1369, 13-25 Jan, Peacock to Sandworth (consul at Odessa)
374 Dennis 2011, 273
375 FO MSS 65/1427, 18 March 1892. Murray to Salisbury
376 Tanriverdi 2011, 463-473
377 Tanriverdi 2011, 472
378 FO MSS 65/114, 24 January 1881, Confidential 4, Lyall to Granville
379 FO MSS 65/1054 8 February 1879, Lyall to Salisbury
380 FO MSS 65/1124, 21 July 1881 Confidential 13, Lyall to Granville
381 FO MSS 65/1054 10 May 1879, Lyall to Salisbury
382 FO MSS 65/1124, 31 March 1881, Confidential 9, Lyall to Granville
383 FO MSS 31 65/1124 March 1881, Confidential 9, Lyall to Granville; FO MSS 65/1124 27 April, 1881, Confidential 10; Lyall to Granville
384 FO MSS 65/1124 27 April 1881, Confidential 10, Lyall to Granville
385 FO MSS 65/1124, 1 February 1881, Confidential 5, Lyall to Granville
386 FO MSS 65/1124 24 May 1881, Confidential 11, Lyall to Granville
387 FO MSS 56/1124 20 January, Confidential 2, Lyall to Granville
388 FO MSS 56/1124 1 February 1881, Confidential 5, Lyall to Granville
389 FO MSS 65/1124, 31 March 1881, Confidential 9, Lyall to Granville
390 Morrison 2021, 20-28, 533, and passim
391 Morrison 2021, 10-13, 159-160
392 Barthop 2002, 157
393 FO MSS 65/1124 24 January, 1881 Confidential 4; 1 February, Confidential 5; 5 February Confidential 6; 1 March 1881, Confidential 9: all Lyall to Granville
394 FO MSS 65/1124 9 March 1881, Confidential 8, Lyall to Granville
395 FO MSS 65/1124 2 July 1881, Confidential 13, Lyall to Granville

PART 2

Tiflis

'A most powerful and most pleasurable impression'

Tiflis (Tbilisi from 1936), at the heart of the intersection of routes from the Black Sea to the Caspian and coveted by invaders across the centuries, 'shared all the triumphs and misfortunes which have befallen Georgia'.[1] It also developed as a thriving multicultural centre.[2]

Tiflis was an old city, according to the myth founded in the sixth century by King Vakhtang Gorsalgali and his son Dachi. It was annexed by the Arabs in the eighth century and stayed as a khalifate until the Seljuks took control in the eleventh century until the early thirteenth century, when Tiflis was made the capital of Georgia by King David IV (The Builder), who unified Georgia into a kingdom, recovering land from the Seljuks and annexing lands belonging to feudal lords. This period and the subsequent reign of Queen Tamara, who expanded Georgian dominance into an empire and vassal states stretching into Armenia and present-day Azerbaijan, are known as the Golden Years of Georgia's history. From the early fourteenth century onwards, Mongol invasions were followed by forces of Turkmen and Persians who sacked the city. It remained under Persian Safavid influence until Georgia was annexed by Russia in 1801, a move that, to this day, has proved fatal. The town became the administrative and military capital of Georgia, under a succession of viceroys and military commanders of which the better known were the notorious General Aleksei Yermolov (already encountered) and one of the most constructive, Prince Michael Vorontsov (in post 1844-54).

Visitors' impressions

All travellers needed at some point to visit Tiflis to obtain travel passes, prepare for their journey, gather provisions and/or rest.

It would be fair to say, however, that Tiflis did not strike all with 'a most powerful and most pleasurable impression', as given to Wardrop in 1887, when considerable development had taken place. The Eurocentric Lyall (in 1825) agreed with Ker-Porter about Tiflis' gloomy aspect, Asiatic dirt and 'barbarism'.[3] It had very few 'European' streets, few glazed windows, filthy baths, dirty markets, no straight streets, was 'excessively nasty' in parts and surrounded by hovels on the hills. In a rare positive note, he comments on the fine architecture of the Sioni Cathedral (originally sixth-century, but with much rebuilding). The town was then small and still partially in ruins after its sacking by the Persians in 1795 yet parts of what it was to become and some of its chief landmarks were there (e.g. a main square (Erivan later Freedom Square), whence ran the principal road, later boulevard Golovinski (now Rustaveli), the Sioni Cathedral and other churches, the Kale (citadel) and city walls, the bazaars, the baths. Intersected by the River Kura (also Mtkvari today) and at the time crossed by only one bridge, the town, hemmed in by hills, fell into distinct zones: the left side of the river was to develop as the administrative European town around Yerevan Square going northwards with the Viceroy's Palace (moved from near the Arsenal in Yermolov's time) along Golovinski (Rustaveli), gardens, museum(s), theatre and main cathedrals; on the same side to the south-west was the Holy Mount (Mtatsminda), further south were the citadel, the Botanical Gardens, the baths, bazaars and caravanserais. Over the river to the north was the later railway station, the Mushtaid Park, gardens, the military depot, arsenal, barracks and bazaars to the south and in between the German settlement (see further below).

Yermolov was keen to make Tiflis a completely European town and to allow only one area, by the fortress, to remain Asiatic. As such, old houses were being pulled down.[4] By Freshfield's time (1868) the town 'was a success'. The streets 'were wonderfully European' with tall houses, shops with plate glass windows and well-dressed ladies in Parisian costumes. The Russians had spent 'a lot of money' to Europeanize it.[5] This transformation had been in part due to the work of Vorontsov, who did much to stimulate literacy, intellectual activity and Russian (European) culture in Tiflis. Under his administration there was a proliferation of schools and gymnasia, encouragement of local languages, and a multitude of clubs and societies were formed (e.g. Society for Agricultural Production and Geography, the Archaeological Commission, the Medical Society and even a Society for the Revival of Georgian Music). Local journals existed but often folded (as did newspapers, see below). Stipends were given to students to go and study in Russia.[6] In 1867, a statue of the viceroy, towering over the Kura, was unveiled in a grand ceremony attended by royalty, notables, official guests, elders from outside Tiflis and many others, attesting perhaps to his popularity. Sycophantic speeches looking back at 'enlightened' times were made, turning Vorontsov into a cult figure. However, as Jahn had rightly argued, the statue was also a provocation.[7]

Freshfield was the first (1868) followed by Telfer (1875) to mention two new significant Tiflis landmarks: the Opera House (1851), where *Crispino e la comare* was playing in 1864[8] and *La Traviata* and *Faust* in 1868,[9] and the Museum under Director Gustav Radde (still in some confusion in 1875, according to Telfer).[10] This hints at the cultural and intellectual life of Tiflis at the time, but barely scratches the surface. None of the travellers properly engages with nor shows any real interest in the culture of contemporary Tiflis, except for the future diplomat and champion of Georgia, Oliver Wardrop. Freshfield, focusing on his mountaineering goal, visited the Topographical Department to purchase the standard Five Verst map, and met the geologist and academician Hermann Abich (1806-86), who gave him advice and information on Mounts Kazbek and Elbruz.[11] Grove (there in 1874), keen to get to mountaineering, thought Tiflis was worth seeing, but not worth going to see.[12] Those who visited the Museum usually met the Director Herr Radde. However the travellers were not visiting Tiflis out of interest (except for Wardrop) and had the added disadvantage of not knowing Russian or Georgian, nor having real social connections (except for Telfer, who with his Russian wife, was received by the governor general and his wife by the Grand Duchess Olga, who lent them *The Times* for the duration of their stay).[13] This lack of curiosity (and knowledge) seems bewildering today, but commensurate with the then colonial mindset of visiting a town that was neither wholly western nor eastern, governed by an erstwhile enemy, Russia, and subject to the frustrations of Russian officialdom.[14] It was to be passed through solely for practical purposes.

Only the 'sportsman hunter' Clive Phillipps-Wolley, whose main interest in the Museum was hunting trophies, met Consul Lyall, who helped him and gave him a frank account of the 'state of the country', for Phillipps-Wolley later refers to the 'Augean stables', Lyall's unflattering words (see Part 1 and below).[15] Wardrop, who had done extensive research on the geography, travel literature, history, literature and arts of Georgia prior to his trip (demonstrated by dedicated sections in his book and extensive bibliography), was aware of Georgian history and the local and international political climate (see below).[16] Equally, prior to Bryce (1877), who gives an overview of the town's main districts, and Wardrop (1887-88), who offers a walking topographical tour of Tiflis, its quarters and its monuments, travellers generally provided only descriptions of the key landmarks of the town, with varying degrees of enthusiasm shown for the bazaars and surrounding area considered by most to be the more curious part of town because of the variety of nationalities and costumes seen there. Bryce describes the European side with its wide and open streets, tree fronted European shops, houses 'high and new looking', and the 'handsome' Grand Duke's 'palace' on Golovinski. South of this area by the river was old Tiflis, he writes, with its narrow, crooked streets, ill paved or unpaved, with houses of one or two storeys, two mosques, 'incomparably more picturesque' (than the European town).[17] Bustle was at its highest on the bridge spanning the Kura by the eastern gate: here all traffic from Armenia, Persia and the steppe came through, with camels, donkeys, bullock carts and mounted Cossacks. Kakhetian wine and fruits from the German orchards could be bought here. The bazaar in the 'old town' is succinctly described by Phillipps-Wolley (1881): besides being ankle deep in mud (depending on the season) and sometimes clogged by carts drawn by buffalo or bullocks everything was sold here by 'every race'. Each street had its own speciality: boot makers, silversmiths, armourers, carpet merchants, furriers, vendors of vegetables. Besides wearing high boots, Phillipps-Wolley felt obliged (as advised by the consul) to dress modestly so as not to attract pestering from 'avaricious Armenians'. He notes that even Armenian children had their own stalls.[18]

Tiflis was in continuous development. Wardrop mentions the several bridges now crossing the river, how Golovinski would soon become 'one of the finest streets in the world', the caravanserais (one in Erivan Square, the other off the square, by the Georgian Theatre, owned by an Armenian, Mr Artsuni), the Land Bank of the Nobles, founded in 1874 to aid farmers, and where all profit was spent on the 'furtherance of philanthropy and encouragement of national education'. Here Wardrop mentions how the Georgians were too often swindled by Armenian moneylenders: 'made Shylocks by the peculiar conditions they have lived in'. He continues his tour mentioning the Museum (with an accurate and more accurate account of its departments than the other travellers). He lists geological, zoological, ethnographical, entomological, botanical, archaeological and numismatic sections, the frescoes, a large collection of photographs (see below) and library.[19] He enumerates schools in 1886 (gymnasia, lower, municipal, private and - the greatest number - elementary), a new unfinished theatre, the trams (from a Belgian company), the publishing office of the *Kavkaz* (established 1846), the Vorontsov Bridge and Vorontsov statue (coiffed in a sheepskin hat by youths). The Mushtaid Gardens and area were considered the 'finest promenade' in town, with the best restaurants and clubs, where all sorts of people were to be met (including political exiles from Poland, Russian officers, German professors and representatives of many other nationalities). Music, 'fancy fairs' and dancing took place there, but all weapons had to be left at the entrance.[20] While Bryce dismissed the city, seeing 'no future for Tbilisi', despite its picturesqueness, as 'it had no glimmer of national life', as well as having no real sights or institutions,[21]

Wardrop shows Tiflis to be a thriving city with an intellectual life and the opportunity to exchange ideas. By the beginning of the twentieth century, it was a city with multiple institutions (banks, theatres, hospitals, cinemas etc.) as well as being a centre for the Caucasian press.[22]

Architecture

No traveller engaged with the wide-ranging and eclectic architectural styles of the town shown in public buildings, caravanserais and private stone and brick houses. The range of styles was as wide as the range of architects, many with an international formation, especially in the later part of the century. Thus the Viceroy's Palace, which was reconstructed many times (first in a neoclassical style) was redesigned in 1865 by the Swedish architect Jacob Simonson according to neo-Renaissance trends with a Persian style ballroom; the Museum (of Radde's day) by Albert Zaltzman in neoclassical style; the City Hall (1882-86) by Paul Stern and Alexander Ozerov in neo-Moorish form with the second theatre (by Victor Schroter as mentioned below) with an outer neo-Moorish appearance but European interior; the Baroque Catholic Peter and Paul Cathedral (Zalstmann 1870-77); the Alexander Nevsky Church (1871-89), originally conceived to commemorate Russia's victory over the North Caucasus mountain people, by David Grimm and Robert Gedike) in a Russo-Byzantine style. Caravanserais also had many lives moving from Islamicizing (Persianate or Moorish) interiors in the first part of the century to exteriors in the latter part. An example of such evolving styles in one building is the Armenian merchant Gevork Artruni's caravanserai of the 1850s (now the Ethnographic and History Museum), one side neoclassical, the other, later Art Deco, with an interior Islamicizing structure and ornamentation. There were two mosques, a Shia one (the Blue Mosque, allegedly built by Shah Ismail in the sixteenth century) by the Metekhi Bridge (later destroyed) and another, Sunni, below the fortress (destroyed in the eighteenth century) rebuilt by Scudieri in the mid-nineteenth century and renovated in 1895 with neo-Gothic elements.[23]

Tiflis

'Tiflis'

A feature of many private house in Tiflis were carved or plain wooden balconies attached to brick or wooden houses, which acted as a projection of living space. These were mostly to be found in the crowded old parts of the town (Wardrop mentions balconies, with no details, on the Asiatic side[24] around the baths). But elaborate Islamicizing balconies facing an inner courtyard (sometimes also the street) were also attached to private mansions in hybrid styles built by architects such as Paul Stern, Alexander Szymkiewicz, Ghazar Sarkisian and K Tatischev. The interiors of official and private mansions were also eclectic, with the use of coloured, faceted glass in the Persianate style (made by Persian craftsmen such as Abdullah, Mirza Riza-khan or Mirza Mohammed Kazwini) and Islamicizing stucco decoration, merging with European decoration.[25] The absence of Georgian architects for much of the century is being debated today.[26] In the *fin-de-siècle* period and early twentieth century, Art Nouveau styles, often with balconies attached, became popular for private houses of the wealthy. Architects included Simon Kliadishvili and Grigol Kurdiani.[27]

Prints of old Tiflis, more than anything, convey the contrast between od and new and the urban bustle. The favourite view of Tiflis was from high above (as from Mtatsminda) where 'churches, cupolas, public buildings and red tiled houses, so handsome in the distance' seemed magnificent, as opposed to the view from the plain to the west where Tiflis appeared 'squalid and dirty'.[28]

'Strange confusion of tongues and dresses'

All travellers mention the mixed population of Tiflis: in 1825 it was estimated to number 20-30,000 (including the military), in 1834, c.25,000 and in 1886, 735,000 in total (from official papers, not to be 'too implicitly believed', according to Wardrop).[29] It had become a migrant city, with less than half its population born or brought up there.[30] Tiflis was three (small) towns and six nations, wrote Bryce.[31]

Contrary to expectation, the majority of the population was Armenian: wealthy middle-class merchants, entrepreneurs (owners of tobacco firms, leather plants, a paper factory), administrators, *literati*, shop-keepers and money-lenders, living on both sides of the river; they were powerful and controlled Tiflis' industries and trade.[32] Except for a few writing in the second half of the century such as Telfer[33] and Bryce, travellers' opinions were quiet on the Armenians or were governed by the money-lending trope and/or the assertion that they were the 'Jews of Europe', detested by their neighbours for their selfishness, thriftiness and astuteness.[34] They were also seen as trusted by the Russians and enjoying privileges.[35]

Armenians had their own cultural life in Tiflis with numerous writers and playwrights (such as Khachatur Abovian (d.1845), Grigori Artsuni (d.1852), Horhannes Tumanyan (active 1886), Gabriel Sundukyan (d.1912), Arfiar Arfivian (d.1908), mostly spanning the second half of the century and promoting their language and own nationalistic ideals. Armenian newspapers such as *Mshkak* (Worker, 1872-1920) and *Nordar* linked Armenians to the diaspora.[36]

Georgians, who were traditionally rural, numbered only about 22 per cent of the population at the beginning of the nineteenth century, but increased after the 1860s as peasants came into the town after the abolition of serfdom, employed as servants or factory workers (later, with education, becoming militant, see below). Georgians from noble families, many co-opted by the Russians, worked in the civil service and the military but from the 1860s became more politically active in movements to revive Georgian culture and identity. Bryce's opinion of Georgians as lazy and having little future has already been mentioned. This shows how ill-informed he was, and he was later to be openly contradicted by Wardrop. Tropes of female beauty or the reverse, impassivity and exotic national dress are also *de rigueur* as regards Georgian and other indigenous women when depicted by most travellers (see Part 3, Ethnography).[37]

Persians (c.10,000 in 1876-77)[38], who lived in an area called Seidabadi, or city of Seids (by the baths), worked in construction, crafts and decoration, in the carpet trade, as street vendors and in the bath-houses. They were not considered to be strict Muslims.

Russians, mostly administrators and military, usually lived in the centre by the Viceroy's Palace and in Mtatsminda. There were also various religious sects deported from Russia (Molokans, Dukhobors and Baptists) of which the Molokans were the most numerous. They had their own district in Akhali Kukia. Jews (few according to Bryce),[39] Poles, French (purchasing silkworms and wood)[40] and others such as Ossetians, mountain Lezgins, Georgians from other areas, even Abkhazians lived or stayed in areas depending on their trade.[41] Settled Tatars (Azerbaijanis) contributed to the intellectual life of the city but also came and went as did migrants from the Caspian and Persia.

Germans, known as 'The Colony' (c.5-6000 in 1886), originally migrants from Wüttenberg and Baden, had established themselves on the right bank of the river, with their own schools and churches, 'cherishing their Protestant faith'. Here you were no longer in Russia or Asia, but 'on the Swabian Neckar' with 'exiles from a higher civilization planted in the midst of a lower one,' concluded Bryce, not hiding his contempt for Georgians.[42] According to Murray's *Handbook for Travellers* (1888), the German colony 'was a model of neatness and prosperity'.[43] But they were not popular as they were too insular,[44] spoke little Russian and despised Orthodoxy. They nevertheless opened successful breweries (the first in 1850 advertised in town as 'Deiches Bir')[45] and lucrative market gardens.[46]

High culture

The first Opera House was 'scintillating in gold and azure'. But the English observers do not do justice to this extraordinary building on the main thoroughfare of Tiflis, built to commemorate fifty years of the official annexation of Georgia and, as suggested by the Viceroy Michael Vorontsov, to inculcate the Russian way of life into the capital. The Italian Giovanni Scudieri was hired as architect, with interior design and stage curtain by Grigory Gagarin. An engraving and full description of the theatre appeared in the French *L'Illustration*, 25 October 1851, by Edmond de Bares. It showed a beautifully proportioned, highly decorated, delicate interior in the Moorish style: the amphitheatre had two superimposed rows of boxes, with a top row of arcaded slender columns and the lower with square topped staggered columns, all decorated with geometric and arabesque motifs. Large chandeliers decorated in geometric motifs hung from a domed ceiling. A parterre led to a large, arcaded stage and a grand curtain which on one side (the right) depicted Russia (St Petersburg, the Neva, Moscow and the Kremlin), with at the base the symbols and produce of the Empire - the cross of St Vladimir, the fish of the Volga, the grain of Ukraine, the fruits of Crimea and on the left Georgia (Tiflis with its fortress and bazaars, the Kura) - and fabulous textiles, musical instruments, arms and wine. Alexandre Dumas *père* saw its political message: Russia as sovereign and conqueror, Georgia as happy, exotic slave.[47] The Emperor's Lodge, in the form of an oriental pavilion with a cupola, was directly in front of the staggered, square topped entrance. The whole 'was a fairy palace' and resembled 'the most delicious motifs of the Alhambra scintillating in gold and azure,' Dumas wrote. Of all the opera houses he had seen it was 'the most charming'. The English called it 'pretty' and 'fitted in great taste in white and gold'.[48] The theatre, which became a competition ground between Georgian and Russian (or rather European) culture, burned down in 1874 amidst swirling conspiracy theories (insurance, political motives). It took until 1890 for a new theatre design, with a neo-Moorish façade but European interior, to be approved (by Victor Schroter), and the new Opera and Ballet Theatre opened in 1896.[49]

The Caucasus Museum

The Museum under the directorship of the ethnographer and ornithologist Gustav Radde was established in 1867 with the support of the Grand Duke. Both in its décor and displays it was an unequivocal symbol of Imperial power and the appropriation of the valuable asset that was the Caucasus. But it was also a source of knowledge as well as propaganda; there was a library and books and journals on display tables for those interested in the Caucasus and the intelligentsia working on the area. It became one of the major institutions of Tiflis.

Although associated with Radde, the collections of the Museum had had a pre-history, in which the Russian Geographical Society, set up in 1845, played an important part. In 1851, a local branch of the Society had opened in Tiflis, with the support of Prince Vorontsov and the collaboration of leading scientists and intellectuals (such as the archaeologist A.P. Berge, the orientalist U.V. Khanikov, the numismatist I.A. Bartolomei, the writers V.A. Sollogub, R.D. Eristavi, the editor of *Kavkaz*). One of their aims was to establish a museum based on donations from already existing private ethnographic and other collections, (such as A.V. Ivanivski's collection of minerals and Sollogub's ethnographic material) and for future material. By 1852 rooms in a private house had been located and by 1854 the founders had over three hundred items (mostly costumes, household wares, weapons, musical instruments, geological specimens, miscellaneous articles from Dagestan, Persia and Turkey, some antiquities and coins). A sample catalogue was made in 1856. After Sollogub, the management of the Museum passed to the naturalist Frederick Beyer, helped by academician

Hermann Abich, who both travelled collecting samples. The Museum moved premises, but Beyer's collection was vast and much of it remained at his house. Internal disputes about the management of the Museum ensued and things slowly ground to halt. The Museum lost its premises and by 1864 it had closed, with the material stored in the military district and elsewhere.

Renamed the Caucasus Museum under Radde, the collection became an institution, not only as testament to the Russian Empire but to science, with contacts with leading scientists both in Russia and abroad. Unfortunately, this was a fairly closed circle and seems to have been bypassed by most travellers, some of whom only met Radde. The hugely prolific Radde travelled extensively to gather material, publishing works on natural science and ethnography (see Part 3). Where the Museum itself is concerned, among his most valuable contributions (for those visiting and later scholarship) are the printed *Kratkii Putevoditel' po Kavkazkomy Muzej* (Guide to the Caucasus Museum), first edition c.1878,[50] which then ran into several editions (including a French one of 1885). The publication gives a detailed layout of the Museum and summary of its collections, as well as the history and catalogue of the Museum, *Sammlungen des Kaukasisches Museums*, in several volumes from 1899-1912 (1 Zoology, 2 Botany, 3 Geology, 4 Ethnography, planned but not published, 5 Archaeology, and 6 Radde's Autobiography and Biography) with invaluable photographs of the displays. Photographs show a handsome two storied neoclassical building set in a lush garden in its late stages, with a plinth to commemorate the educator, linguist and orientalist Adolf Berge or Berzhe.[51] The second floor was added with funds raised from the Grand Duke and collaborators. The first suggested design of the Museum, however, was far more fanciful: a one-storey building with two semi-circular wings and pointed arches around a central pavilion in an Islamicizing style. Yet there was more than a nod to 'orientalism' inside the neoclassical building; the octagonal entrance, domed ceiling and hanging lamp were in a Persianate style and Persianate decorative elements flowed throughout, including pointed arches, multicoloured windowpanes and decorated ceilings.[52] In the Ethnography section, the crowding of peoples (as mannequins and in photographs) and materials was suggestive of the bazaar.

The material was based on historical collections, with added contributions from ongoing expeditions, scientists, royalty and amateurs, many from abroad. The arrangement was systematic: the lower floors displayed Geology (Room 1), Zoology (Room 2), Mammals (Room 3, including a small 'anthropology' section (see below), continuation of Zoology (Room 4); then up the stairs to Ethnography (Rooms 1-2), Botany (Room 3), Entomology (Room 4) and two rooms for Antiquities. Displays from all over the Caucasus, and also beyond, were either in cases, or in the case of Zoology and mammals, in dramatic taxidermic installations on stands. These seem to have captured the travellers' imagination and appreciation the most, and were consequently included in Murray's 1888 *Handbook for Travellers*.[53] All rooms had either maps (added gradually), a large amount of photographs on walls or columns, relevant paintings, tables with catalogues and information leaflets. Some rooms had armchairs and tables with decorative bouquets. Donors were listed with their relevant collections or gifts. The preface to the fourth edition of the Museum's Guide (1885) shows how donations fluctuated, decoration progressed and extra space was needed. For example, a large recent collection (donated by V.I. Moller) of rocks and fossils was waiting to be exhibited, the addition of plants to the herbarium made the Botanical collection one the richest, it boasted, after St Petersburg. As Radde's book on Ornithology could be purchased, more attention had been paid to the Mammal section. Major publications were underway.[54]

The publication provides an invaluable source of who was active in the scientific community or as private donors at the time. Donations and acquisitions were so numerous that consecutive numbers could not be attributed to the items, and recent acquisitions (after the catalogue had been printed) were shown with explanatory notes. In the Antiquities section acquisitions by the Museum were shown in black numbers on a yellow background, those by amateurs in matt yellow, those sent by the Provisional

Committee of the Vth Archaeological Congress with black on a pale yellow.

The Museum was open three times a week, for 20 kopecks, children under seven were not admitted, school children and cadets had to be accompanied by their masters having agreed the time in advance with the Director, all outer garments had to be left in a cloakroom, smoking was not allowed, nor dogs. All complaints had to be addressed to the Director, and most importantly, there was no touching as all objects had been sprayed with poison.[55]

The entrance made a formidable case for Empire and its myth of unity, its rulers and its scientists. It was faced by a veritable shrine to the Imperial family. Beneath an inscription *Viribus Unitis* (with united forces) on an arcaded arch, were at the very top a portrait of Alexander III (1845-94), followed by His Royal Highness Grand Duke Michael and the Grand Duchess Olga Fedorovna, and below Prince Vorontsov. Beneath him were views of Tiflis and of the Military Highway (the fought over highway from Vladikavkaz to Tiflis, symbolic of Russia's military control of the Caucasus). The portrait of a female saint was on a carpeted altar beneath them.[56] Specimens of the signatures of the Imperial family and of the Shah of Persia (the Qajar shah Nāṣer al-Dīn Shāh, 1848-96) were framed in niches and to the left were photographs of members of the 1881 Archaeological Congress held at Tiflis. The message was to continue, but evoking the classical mythology of the Caucasus, also appropriated by the Imperial family. There was a circular staircase running to the upper floor (subsidized by the Grand Duke to the tune of 5,000 roubles) along which were a series of frescoes painted by an artist named Sim from Vienna and his wife. Frescoes in Baroque style depict mythological themes and one a Biblical one. The first depicts Prometheus chained to the Caucasian mountain range and shaking his fist at a threatening vulture, with four Ocaeanid (nymphs) heads rising from the Euxine (Black Sea) looking compassionately at him; the next shows the arrival of the Argonauts in Colchis (west Georgian coast in classical antiquity, known for its riches), with the Grand Duke Michael standing as a heroic, conquering Jason on the prow, holding a spear and a shield, indicating with his arm the land they have left behind, and being greeted by Aethe and her daughters in a chariot. The third, at the entrance of the Ethnography section, represents Jason and Medea in the temple of Hecate. The fourth shows Noah planting the first vine (a nod to Christianity and Georgia's wine production) with in the background the Araxes valley and Mount Ararat, and the fifth, between two windows two mounted Amazons charging into battle. Two others show heroes of (distant) Georgian history: King David the Builder and Queen Tamara.[57]

Interested visitors walking through the lower rooms of the Museum and those upstairs showing earth sciences and natural history would have noticed the geographical classifications and settings. Maps, paintings, photos of locations adjacent to exhibits, together with vivid topographical installations, plants and taxidermy, conveyed the variety of the natural world of the Caucasus. These rooms displayed the lands, their very geology, fauna, flora and peoples, acquired and ruled by Russia on the path to greater industry and 'civilization' while asserting and promoting Russian (and European) 'science'. The message of scientific knowledge through its natural history rooms (Geology, Zoology, Botany, Entomology) was easier to convey than through the rooms devoted to Ethnography and the jumble of Antiquities on the upper floor. The former were classified according to systems devised by local experts (such as Academician Abich in the Geology section or Arzrouni)[58] and precedents and current practices in Europe (e.g. geological epochs according to the geologist and palaeontologist Karl Alfred Zittel).[59] Ornithology was classified and arranged by Herr Radde himself. A reference to Darwin and the evolving science of physical anthropology was evident in the Mammals room, where beneath photographs of gorillas, two cupboards displayed a Russian woman's skeleton, the skulls of a Turk, two Lezgins, an Imeretian, a Laz, a Russian from Archangel, a Frenchman, one Tekin (Tonkin, Vietnam?), a Turcoman, four Armenians and two Mongolians. A depiction of models of the human race, according to Johann Friedrich Blumenbach,[60] hung on the walls.

In Russia, physical anthropology (craniology and skeletons) as a field in its own right had been championed by Anatoli Bogdanov, the Director of the Zoological Museum in Moscow, in the 1860s. Inspired by Karl Ernst von Baer (1792-1876), the 'father of Anthropology' as he was known in Russia was an ardent anti-Darwinist.[61] Others in the field were Nicolai Mikhukho-Maklay and Dimitri Anuchin. Human specimens were actively sought and collected from *kurgans* (burial mounds), thus allying two disciplines. By the mid-to-late 1870s physical anthropology was included in the Moscow University curriculum, and in 1876 a Chair was established, but soon discontinued as it became incorporated into Geography and Ethnology.[62] The reception of Darwin and evolution of Darwinist thought in Russia was a long and tangled affair with both supporters and critics, the latter the older generation of scientists or those entrenched in their own systems (e.g. von Baer, who also objected on moral grounds), the Orthodox Church and Slavophiles. In the mid-1860s there was a positive trend towards evolutionary science. Both critics and recognition (under Anuchin and I. Borzeknok) grew during the 1870s and 1880s. Moscow University became 'a bastion' of Russian Darwinism and the seeds were sown for a home-grown Russian tradition of evolutionary thought both pro-and-anti Darwinist. By the 1890s experimental biology and genetics emerged as fields in Europe (e.g. neo-Darwinism, neo-Lamarkism) in which Russia at first lagged behind but participated in from the early twentieth century onwards.[63]

The Caucasus Museum was visited by over 2,000 people in the first two months of opening.[64] But it never achieved the cachet of the International Exhibitions, which since the Crystal Palace exhibition of 1851, had been one way of displaying European superiority to the world.[65] It was too small, too remote and perhaps too rural and not industrial enough, despite photographs of roads, bridges, railways, new buildings, mines and telegraph posts. Sections did, however, include materials used in industry, such as mining and minerals used in technology (copper and cobalt), and there was a whole section devoted to Baku and petroleum production and stone for construction.[66] The sections on Ethnography and Antiquities are discussed separately in Part 3.

Society and Dissent

Beneath the state institutions mentioned above and the 'glitter of (Russian induced) society',[67] trumpeted in the almanac *Kavkaskii Kalendar* (the Caucasus Calendar, 1846-1917), much disquiet was felt with the colonial government, its cultural impositions and social divisions, wrote Consul Lyall.

From the 1850s to the 1860s, especially under the Europeanizing Vorontsov, literacy (in Russian and Georgian), learning and culture had been promoted in Tiflis' schools and societies. Some of the aristocratic Georgian elite, participating in the colonial bureaucracy and elaborate state functions, were assimilated, but others saw dangers to Georgian identity. Three groups promoting national unity and progress (known as the *tergdaleulni* or 'those who cross/drink from the Terek', the traditional boundary between Russia and Georgia), emerged with different degrees of emphases in the 1860s and 1870s.[68] The first was spearheaded by the writer, poet and founder of the newspapers *sakartvelos moambe* (the Georgian Messenger 1863-64) and *Iveria* (1877-85, 1886-1906), Ilia Chavchavadze, born in 1837 and assassinated in 1907. He championed the use of vernacular in written Georgian, Georgian national identity, national struggles abroad and, at home, a socially conscious nobility. While radical at first, by the 1880s Chavchavadze had acknowledged loyalty to Empire. The second group (*moere dasi*), which included Niko Nikoladze (1843-1928), Giorgi Tsereteli and Sergo Meskhi, was different and more pragmatic. It promoted urbanism, economic growth and trade, the establishment of commercial banks for working people, and self-government rather than independence. Nicoladze considered co-operation with the Russian 'intelligentsia' acceptable. He later became a nationalist. The newspapers *krebuli* (The Collection, 1871-73), *Droeba* (Times, 1866-85), and *kvali* (1893-1904) were associated with this movement.⁶⁹ Other eminent figures promoting Georgian culture and challenging Russification were Ivan Machabeli (1854-98) and Dimitri Qipiani (1814-87), who was exiled and murdered. Wardrop is the only traveller to mention contemporary Georgian writers and he was well aware of their nationalistic feelings. He refers to Chavchavadze ('in many respects as an awakener the most remarkable man that Georgia possesses'), Orbeliani (who celebrated Georgia's glorious past and encouraged Georgia on the road to progress) and Ivan Machabeli, who with Chavchavadze was the most influential among his contemporaries. Able to read English literature in the original and a translator of Shakespeare, Machabeli was a radical educated abroad, whose journal *Droeba* was supressed 'because of an impudent article'. Wardrop also mentions the 'young and energetic' Prince Kazkek (writer of historical pieces) and Alexander Tsagareli, and encourages readers to delve into Georgian folk tales, fables, ballads and riddles.⁷⁰

Intellectual life was not only confined to Georgians: the educational opportunities of Tiflis had been seized by many. There was a strong Azerbaijani cultural scene. As early as the 1840s, Azerbaijani translators and teachers (of Persian) also worked as poets (such as Mirza Vazeh (d.1852), the playwright Mirza Fatali Akhundov (d.1878), and Abbas-Kuli-Aga Bakhinov. The latter two became friends with the Georgian and Armenian *literati* mentioned above. There was also an Ossetian theatrical group, while a Kabardian (Shora Nogmov) published the first history of Kabardia in Tiflis (1861).⁷¹

Georgian and other writers did not need reminding that they lived in a police state, which had become even more vigilant after the assassination of Alexander II and the adoption of Alexander III' s repressive Russification and centralization programmes. The Russian language and Cyrillic alphabet were imposed in Georgia, and Georgian ousted from the curriculum, although local Mingrelian, Svan and Abkhazian were encouraged at primary level. This was felt to be a deliberate undermining of the Georgian language.⁷²

A consul's voice: back to revolution

Consul Lyall gave a frank assessment of the situation while at Tiflis. The country was generally in a miserable state after the war, he wrote.[73] There was a huge deficit (due to the continuing war in Central Asia and the building of railways), there were shortages, and law and order seemed to have broken down; the rural police themselves were part of gangs of 'brigands', magistrates were open to bribes, and murders committed 'under revolting conditions' constantly went unpunished in Tiflis, while outside the city assassinations, cattle-lifting, arson, affrays, burglaries and robberies were daily occurrences.[74]

Consul Lyall also appears to have been a victim of the chaos. In July 1880 accusations had been made against him by a Mr Murtagh and a Mr Rodkes. The former (of 'petti fogging turn') was monopolizing the sale of cheap Birmingham goods in Tiflis by bribing Russian officials and the latter had already been in prison for forging receipts and took umbrage when Lyall refused to support him in his claim of innocence. They ganged together with other British subjects to sign a document indicting Lyall. The main charges, however, were that that he had been too involved in the lives of his housekeeper at Tiflis (who had become a drunk) and in consequent dramas involving her daughter who wanted to be repatriated but without her mother.[75] The Russians may well have encouraged this petition, as they did not want Lyall (or anyone else perhaps) as consul there. His reporting had not dissimulated his contempt for what was happening at Tiflis. The Russians' attitude is revealed in a letter to the Treasury where the abolition of the Tiflis consulate is discussed (December 1880), together with how to save money (£650) by appointing an unpaid vice-consul at Batum instead.[76] As Wardrop later pointed out, the abolition of the consulate at Tiflis was a mistake.

Nearly all British travellers, either unaware, dismissive or possibly not wishing to offend, fail to refer to any social unrest; the exception is Phillipps-Wolley (1881), who repeats the 'Augean stable' analogy (used by Lyall) when writing about his discussion he had with his servant regarding the corruption of the civil service at Tiflis and the emperor's efforts to have it cleaned up by sending agents.[77]

It was not only the intelligentsia who were dissatisfied. Peasants had already revolted in Samegrelo in 1856-57 against their landlords' unreasonable rents.[78] These problems were only exacerbated after serfdom was abolished, creating an influx into towns of peasants in search of wages. Peasants had to start paying taxes and landlords had kept certain rights, including charging for wood collected in forests and water from waterways, as well as retaining police functions.[79] The rise of workers' associations and education in towns all promoted social discontent and by 1887 Karl Marx had been published in Georgian.[80]

By the late 1890s the first organized strikes took place in Tiflis.[81] In 1894 a third, more radical group emerged in Guria (*mesame dasi*), where in a speech by Silbistro Jibladze at the funeral of one of the founders of the group (Egnate Ninoshivili) a clear distinction was made between 'parasitic capitalists' and the representatives of physical and mental work, whose duty it was to spread literacy and follow world trends. It has been called the first Marxist demonstration in Georgia.[82] Such events, with roots in the ideas of the *tergdaleulni*, the *moere dasi* and the *mesame dasi* groups were to lead directly to the social democratic and Marxist movements of the early twentieth century in Georgia.[83]

An idealistic diplomat

Oliver Wardrop seems to have written *The Kingdom of Georgia* (1888) partially in response to Bryce's focus on the Armenian cause and negativity about Georgia (the book was dedicated to Bryce) and partly in response to the changing world after the Russo-Ottoman War and the 1878 Berlin Treaty. He also uses the book not only as a travelogue in Georgia, but to give the first (in English) proper account of the history, language and politics of Georgia, as well as a 'compendious bibliography' and statistics on population, trade and agriculture, including a specimen of Georgian music, in appendices. The impact of his reading of the Georgian nationalist *literati* discussed above can be seen in his arguments on the future of Georgia.

In light of the bad feeling in Russia towards Britain which had ensued after the Berlin Treaty another war was feared. What action would Georgia take? Wardrop asked. Where the Caucasus was concerned, out of the three native groups deserving consideration (the Lezgin tribes, Armenians (740,000) and Georgians (1,000,000) made up of various highlanders, Svans, Mingrelians, Kartlians etc.) the Georgians, in the majority, were now politically homogeneous and not inferior in historical importance or intellectual development to the 'regnant race'. The country was no longer fragmented into disparate tribes but was now unified. There had been a growth of national feeling, borrowed from western countries, and intellectual and social development in Georgia. Politically, the population was now Georgian, partly due to 'irritating' Russian policy such as enforced military service, excessive policing, taxation and the arrogance of functionaries. Resentment had grown against the limited benefits of Russian rule overall, where roads were being built for military purposes rather than trade, adding to neglect of the Caucasus' industrial and commercial interests.

Wardrop speculated over which direction this nationalistic movement would take. He suggests that there would be a time when Georgia would 'be ripe for action'. Its hopes were turned to Britain once more (how true this was is debatable) for the establishment of a strong independent state, which would be of 'enormous advantage' to British interests in the Black Sea and the Caspian. He did not foresee Armenia, Georgia and the Lezgins (Dagestan, Azerbaijan) uniting into one state, but they could be allied in common interests. The mountain tribes would help defend Georgia's borders. He concludes by writing that if the Russians attempted to crush the national spirit, then the descendants of Irakli (1762-98, unifier of eastern Georgia but ultimately placing Georgia under Russian protection) would 'show despots how men can die'.[84]

Wardrop's ideas were later to be tested and proved sincere. Georgia declared independence in 1918, calling itself The Georgian Social-Democratic Workers Republic, recognized only by Germany. At the end of the Great War the British occupied

Transcaucasia, but there was widespread disagreement about the future independence of the Caucasus. The British had on the whole supported the Russian White Army and were unsure of who would prevail. In 1919, Wardrop now appointed as High Commissioner in Transcaucasia, fought to persuade the British to support the cause of Georgian and Azerbaijani independence. As the Bolsheviks advanced in May 1919 Lord Curzon, the ex-Viceroy of India (then in the war cabinet), officially requested the recognition of Georgia and Azerbaijan. Yet the British dithered, still opposing the idea, until the Bolsheviks occupied both Georgia and Azerbaijan in early 1921.[85]

TIFLIS

1. Wardrop 1888, 9
2. Chikovani 2018, 233-234, from Gachechiladze 2010
3. Lyall 1925, 513
4. Lyall 1925, 521-522
5. Freshfield 1869, 176
6. Jones 2005, 33-34; Chikovani 2018, 235-236, 247
7. Jahn 2014, 163-180
8. Ussher 1865, 91
9. Freshfield 1869, 106
10. Telfer 1876, 145
11. Freshfield 1869, 102
12. Grove 1875, 24
13. Telfer 1976, 1, 158
14. For the latter e.g. Phillipps-Wolley 1881, 188-189
15. Phillipps-Wolley 1881, 197, 231, 245
16. Wardrop 1888, 173-196
17. Bryce 1877, 135-138
18. Phillipps-Wolley 1881, 182-186
19. Wardrop 1888, 15-16, 407
20. Wardrop 1888, 9-32
21. Bryce 1877, 148
22. Chikovani 2018, 241
23. Chikovani 2018, 238-239; Kutishvili and Cachola Schmal eds. 2018, passim
24. Wardrop 1888, 25
25. Shkolna 2022, 138; Mania 2014, no page numbers
26. Mania 2014
27. Tatarashvli 2008
28. Ussher 1865, 96-97; Wardrop 1988, 24
29. Wardrop 1888, 197
30. Chikovani 2018, 236
31. Bryce 1877, 134
32. Rayfield 2012, 298-297
33. Telfer 1876, 76
34. E.g. Spencer 1838, 28-33; Telfer 1876, 255; Phillipps-Woolley 1881, 211
35. Spencer 1838, 33. He was hosted by an Armenian family at Kutaisi.
36. Chikovani 2018, 245-247;
37. E.g. Telfer 1876 158, 164
38. Bryce 1877, 145-146
39. Bryce 1877, 147
40. Murray's Handbook for Travellers 1888 ed., 413
41. Bryce 1877, 145-146
42. Bryce 1877, 138
43. Murray's Handbook for Travellers, 1888 ed. , 413
44. Phillipps-Wolley 1881, 166
45. Wardrop 1888, 25
46. Chanishvili 2008, 2-7
47. Dumas 1859, 143
48. Ussher 1865, 91; Freshfield 1869, 106
49. *Museum Studies Abroad, A Brief History of the Opera and Ballet Theatre of*

Tbilisi, 2/8/2023, no author, but references given; Chikovani 2028, 240
50   Radde 1878 *Das Kaukasische Museums in Tiflis*, Dresden 1878
51   Radde 1912, Pls. 4-7
52   Radde 1912, Pls. 8, 18, 19, 20, 25-28
53   Murray's Handbook 1888, 413
54   1885, Russian edition, 1-3
55   1885, French edition, 2
56   Radde 1912, Pl.8
57   Radde 1912, Pls. 10-13; 1885 French ed.26,27
58   Radde 1855, 7,8,13
59   Radde 1885, 9; Zittel 1839-1904
60   German naturalist and physical anthropologist (1752-1840) known for establishing the concept of human varieties or race (from a single species) by comparing skulls and to a lesser extent skin colour. Five groups emerged from his studies: Oriental, American Indian, Caucasian, Malay and Ethiopian. The Caucasian was the most primeaval. Georg-August-Universität, Johann-Friederich- Blumenbach Research Institute of Zoology and Anthopology.
61   Vuchinich 1988, 90, passim. Von Baer was a pioneer in many fields: embryology, physical anthropology, ethnology.
62   Krivosheina 2014, 275-305; Vuchinich 1988, 68.
63   Vuchinich 1988, 9ff.,33-34, 45-46, 156ff., 197, 377ff.
64   Jahn 2014, 165
65   Knight 2001, 3
66   Radde 1885, 9,11
67   Jones 2005, 22
68   Jones 2005, 34
69   Jones 2005, 37-39
70   Wardrop 1888, 148-154
71   Chikovani 2019, 243-244
72   Rayfield 2012, 305
73   FO MSS 65/1124, 31 March 1881, Confidential 9, Lyall to Granville
74   FO MSS 65/1054, 10 May 1879, Lyall to Salisbury
75   FO MSS 65/1092 13 July 1880, Lyall to Granville
76   FO MSS 65/109, 3 December 1880, Granville to the Treasury
77   Phillipps-Wolley 1881, 203
78   Jones 2005, 22
79   Jones 2005, 25-26
80   Rayfield 2012, 309
81   Jones 2005, 28
82   Jones 2005, 49-50
83   Jones 2005, 40ff.
84   Wardrop 1888, 15-168
85   Aleksidze 2028, 125-137

PART 3

Ethnography

The conquest of the Caucasus and the imposition of Russian administration brought with it a plethora of mapmakers, geographers, statisticians, ethnographers and scholarly societies, some already mentioned in Part 2. Most had Empire-serving agendas wrapped in the hyperbole of a 'civilizing mission'. Romantic notions of travel in the Caucasus from Russian literature by Pushkin and Lermontov had also fostered curiosity and a type of voyeurism among Russian writers and the press but less so among British travellers.[1]

The tradition of gathering information on peoples of the vast Empire by the Russian Academy of Sciences was longstanding and had been systematic since the eighteenth century, but once the conquest of the Caucasus had begun, information on what was mostly *terra incognita* presented its own discursive forms which developed according to region, changing administrative practices and scholarship. The study of mountain peoples thus came about by a melding of different disciplines and practices, such as military cartography, geography and language studies over time.

Early Imperial cartography was at first not concerned with peoples but with geography and territory acquired and to be acquired, and once peoples, from the early nineteenth century were inserted, it was according to the military's experience or what informants told them.[2] It was consequently random[3] and accuracy was always a problem (as with information given to travellers). Ethnic identity, including tribal identity shown on maps from the early 1840s onwards, was not an expression of ethnographic interest but a means of understanding borders.[4] The names were not those used by the mountain peoples (as mentioned by Abercromby, see below), who employed different designations for each other depending on their ethnicity; it was more practical to name ethnic groups after villages or geographical boundaries as knowledge of local social structures and how best to adapt them was needed for administrative purposes.[5] Thus from the very beginning there were distortions in how the mountain peoples were perceived and in the transmission of this knowledge.

The study of languages was equally pragmatic, despite some genuine interest. Again this had roots in the eighteenth century.[6] The aim of scholars in the Caucasus was essentially to civilize, Russianize and Christianize through the use of the mountain peoples' own languages.[7] Adolf Berge (1828-86) was a pioneer in this field: he produced dictionaries for various north and south Caucasian languages (Abkhaz, Avar, Lak, Khiurkil, Kiurin, Tabarasan).[8] Peter Karlovich Uslar devised seven alphabets to represent Caucasian languages, whose particular sounds were accommodated to the Cyrillic script.[9] This was achieved with the help of native writers and teachers who reasoned that some literacy for their own people was better than none. Abdullah Omarov, for example, taught in Kumukh at Uslar's schools. Ossetian folk tales and proverbs were published by Ossetians.[10] But here too there were compromises; Omarov believed the way of life of one 'tribe' (the Lak) could be representative of all Dagestan.[11] Other native scholars were Khan Girei (Adygei) and Nogmov Shora (Adygei). The Society for the Restoration of Orthodoxy adopted Uslar's system to transcribe Abkhaz and Svan.[12] The alternative to the Russian language and Cyrillic script would have been Arabic, the other *lingua franca* symbolic of Islam, unacceptable to Russia's 'civilizing' mission as well as a potential threat.[13]

The imposition of colonial rule and administration needed both a knowledge of indigenous legal practices and the means of adapting them. For example, in areas like Dagestan or Chechnya, where Sharia law was in use mixed with native practices but actively promoted (as under Shamil), the Russians opted for favouring *adat* or 'customary law' in order to override the effects of conservative Islam and powerful imams. 'Unacceptable practices' like the blood feud were, however, made illegal,[14] even if this was ignored. Customary law thus served both the Russian pragmatic agenda and also the ideological one, as such customary laws predated, they argued, the advent of Islam.¹⁵ Special military (*voenno-narodnoe*) courts were instigated from 1865 to 1870,¹⁶ and survived for many years despite efforts in the latter half of the nineteenth century to introduce the centralized, uniform Russian code.¹⁷

In a discussion of the development of ethnography as a discipline in Russia under German influence (mainly geographic, with the idea of classifying, stratifying and categorizing people) Elfimov stresses the importance of the concept of *narodnost* and *inorodcy* (nationality, national spirit) in the evaluation of the peoples of the Empire where indigenous people (*inorodcheskii*) were subsumed politically and ideologically to nationalistic Russianness, where Orthodox values were paramount. The Slavophile element intensified as the century progressed.¹⁸

The Museum and the '*Civilizing Mission*'

The Caucasus Museum's ethnographic rooms (Upper floor Rooms I and II) may not have been of much interest to the travellers but were an extremely important component of the institution for the narratives they presented. What they did not show was also significant. The Director Gustav Radde had himself researched both Svaneti and Khevsureti with genuine application, collecting ethnographic material, but always in the context of the 'civilizing mission'.¹⁹ The descriptions below are taken from the 1885 French edition of the catalogue combined with the photographs in Radde's *Sammlungen*.

The entrance to Room I made an immediate statement: it was flanked by two cannons with trophies once having belonged to Shamil. Three groupings of mannequins, with an emphasis on Christianity, greeted the visitor: Georgians - Imeretians, Mingrelians and Gurians; Christian mountain peoples of Georgian origin - Khevsurs, Pchavs, Tush, Svans and Ossetians, even though many of them were not; and Abadzes/Abhaze and Kabardians (see Appendix). A table displayed further small models of Caucasian 'types' (by Mr Chorodovich), with five other tables with publications on the Caucasus for the public to read. There followed cabinets which put on show the vast array of material collected and donated. For example, Cabinet I contained a melange of arms from the Caucasus (Khevsureti, Kurdistan, Dagestan, Gouria, Svaneti, Lenkoran) and Persia. Objects of significance were pointed out, such as item no. 52, an axe used in capital executions given to Shamil by *naib* Bouk-Mahommed and taken in 1852 by General Suzloff on an assault on the village of Khelegui (in Kataichi), or no. 178, a walking stick having belonged to Prince Vorontsov, or no. 179 a walking stick having belonged to a Persian minister, Hadji Mirza-Agacy. Cabinet II contained musical instruments, drinking vessels and smoking apparatus. These included Turkish and Tatar (Azerbaijani) material as well as Georgian, Ossetian, Kurdish, Dagestani and Mazanderani objects. The third cabinet contained various headdresses, shoes and feminine luxury items. Among the Ossetian, Svan and Abkhaz material were headdresses (various pieces of wool nos. 46, 50) worn by Svans of old, Don Cossack and Persian hats. Among the shoes and slippers were those currently worn by Svans (and commented on by Freshfield and others, see below). Luxury feminine material included items of clothing (Lezgin, Tush, Svan, Chechen, 'Asian' embroidered slippers, stockings, items of silver, gold caskets, hairpins and necklaces). Further Khevsurian arms were displayed by the window and under a display case with a Khevsurian banner (*drocha*) used to rally 'fanatic' mountain people and on the ground Khevsurian and Ossetian furniture. Cabinet IV contained agricultural implements, models of the same, whips from Baku and the Caspian. Cabinet V contained domestic utensils (from Adjaria, Akhaltsik, Gilan, Persia, Kurdish areas, one Circassian box (see further below) and models of the same.[20]

At the entrance to Room II were mannequins of Jews and Armenians (removed from the mainstream) and in a nearby cabinet (IX) vases of copper, silver, bronze and clay from Persia and Akhaltsik, Shemakha and Shusha. Beside this a Russian-style niche with the bust of Alexander II and models of 'all Russian types' to one side was an immediate reminder of Empire. The rest of the area was taken up with drawings of vegetation and forests from Colchis, the Black Sea, tree limits by Lapuri in Svaneti (7,200 metres) and various views (Elbruz, the source of the Ingur) and paintings of the last Transcaucasian war offered by General Kaufmann and 'types' from the bazaar in Tiflis (Georgians, from Ratcha, mountain peoples: Svanetians, Abkhases, Ossetians). On the wall hung various embroideries (from Persia and Nukha). In the second part of the room were six cases with examples of industrial products and in cases and on tables various artefacts from Nukha, Akhaltsik, Shemakha and Persia (vases, smokers' paraphernalia, combs, silk ribbons, various ornaments, slippers). Dominant in this part of the room were photographs of Christian Caucasians, grouped by language (with sample scripts attached); another column showed Mohammedan and Jewish 'types' grouped by language and diverse German colonists. Scenes of war were included. Yet another column displayed more ethnographic groups and their principal industries and domestic animals, and images of Levantine baths. Another column had views of Tiflis and places already mentioned and representations of the Trans-Caspian desert (by August Schaffer). Strewn around were vases and utensils, including vases from Turkestan (offered by General Kaufmann). To one side stood a mannequin group of Turkomans and Abkhazes, with textiles and embroideries associated with these peoples and Turkoman tent decorations. The last part of the room was even more of a mixed bag: fine vases from Persia and Georgia, views and paintings of landscapes and rivers (the source of the Rion, Mounts Kazbek and Ararat), of carpets (by August Helvig), and of Kurds, Tatars, Jews of Erivan, Akhaltsik and Tiflis, Georgians, Adjars, Imeretians, Guriels and 'beautiful' Mingrelians.[21]

This deliberately detailed description confirms that contributions were not lacking, that space was restricted and that classification and order were not easy to follow. The cramming may have served a purpose as it conveyed not only the richness of the acquired lands but also their bazaar-like messiness and crude orientalism when compared to ordered Imperial sophistication and the 'civilizing' mission of the colonial presence. Overt signs of this Imperial presence have already been noted: the shrine to the royal family and ruling bodies at the main entrance, the frescoes with the Grand Duke as Jason, the niche with the bust of Alexander the Great in Room II, trophies from Shamil's day and the war in Turkestan. Other signs can be seen in the progression and manner of the layout and in what was missing. When it came to mannequins, models and photographs the layout was careful to separate ethnic groups according to race, geography and religion. Where mannequins were concerned pride of place in Room I was given to Christian groups. However, here the Georgians seem to have been defined by and reduced to the folk 'Lesginka' dance. Armenians and Jews[22] were classed as minorities with Molochans in Room II, even though Armenians were successful and not in a minority in Tiflis and had far greater presence than Jews and Molochans (see Appendix). Photographs of the Museum interior (all from Radde's *Sammlungen*) show mannequin groups of Chevsurs and Tush,[23] Dagestanis,[24] Duchobors and Kurds,[25] Abkhazians,[26] Tatars and Persians[27] and finally, the most removed, Turkmen.[28]

Where were the Circassians? a visitor might have asked. The groups are all shown in their best male, female and children's national costume with either vistas of their natural environment and samples of craft and industry (e.g. looms, a primitive forge, manufactures such as pottery, textiles, animal skins, domestic utensils) and animals. The preface to the 1885 edition of the Museum guide states that full exact scale models of dwellings were to be made by a certain Vyrubov. Despite attention being given to the mannequins' physiognomy and height, their immobility and stiffness and their 'Sunday best' clothes (clearly not worn by everyday working people) share the artificiality and immobility of the same peoples in photographs dotted around the Museum (see Part 6 for types of photographs) and not only objectify the indigenous but convey an idea of capture and a sense of a static, tribal, past primitiveness isolated from the march of civilization.

The display of mannequins was first used on a grand scale at the first major Moscow ethnographic exhibition of 1867, where three hundred mannequins were on show. The layout followed some of Bogdanov's suggestions at the time, a geographical system, in the sense of regions, their flora and fauna, in which 'representatives of tribes should be arranged as much as possible in their natural setting with attributes of domestic life' and productions. It touches on the admittedly difficult, second recommendation, which was 'to express some sort of character trait of their way of life'[29] only by conveying, again, a mode of life stuck in time. Any sense of geographic determinism to explain the simplicity of the 'tribes' in the conquered territory was subsumed under the general category of primitiveness.

Photographs not only of the indigenous peoples but of industry as well as maps, showed the Empire's march of progress in the midst of backwardness. The displayed artefacts on mounts and tables were sometimes piled together to make a mound, such as the looms and cots in Room I.[30] This probably occurred because there was not enough space, but it also signalled not only abundance but also evoked a pile of ancient stuff ready for a bonfire. The display cases attempted to show a range of artefacts arranged by function and geography, but as the later cases reveal, this aim was defeated by the sheer volume of material. This failing does not detract from the value of the actual material and the magnificent textiles and ceramics on display, yet certain omissions were glaring. The Circassians (except for one box) were obliterated from the record nor were the Ingush represented. There is no reference to the literature or oral folk traditions of the mountain peoples, nor of the highly literate Armenians, the Georgians and Jews, nor any allusion to their religious beliefs, unless this information was contained in the books on display.

Did the Director of the Museum think this presentation was a fair or actual representation, to use the phrase of Cvetkovski?[31] It is possible. It was undeniable that the indigenous people represented were for the most part not civilized in the European, western context of the times, but they had social structures, mixed belief systems, oral and some written literature. They were also authentic to the area unlike the Russians. It was difficult to convey the complex reality of the life of the mountain peoples in a museum (while also ignoring the effects of Russian rule, diseases, deportations, displacements, isolation): it was easier to show the mountain peoples as stuck in remote time.

Nevertheless, the displays were partly authentic because they did show genuine articles (while ignoring others). There is a significant absence of indigenous religious iconography such as local shrines, local mosques, mountain churches. The emphasis was on a Christian and a Christianizing country where Islam was the enemy. The understanding by specialists such as Radde, Berghe or Uslar was, of course, far more sophisticated, and the nuances of indigenous culture would presumably have been available to read in the publications, themselves promoting the 'civilizing' message, strewn around the Museum.

The Caucasus Museum's messages would have been absorbed without question by the westernized public, but also surely laughed at or looked at with contempt or bewilderment by anyone from the varied mountain peoples. The gap between the statement of Empire and the depiction of these peoples is so huge at the Museum, that to speak of orientalism in this context is not appropriate; there was nothing very exotic or romantic here in terms of material culture or history (as for example in Crimea), and now that the Circassians and others had been done away with, it was the scenery that inspired. The remaining mountain peoples were portrayed as primitives and curiosities whose future and identity in the Empire was ambivalent, leading to extinction or in time and with effort partial civilization. It could be argued that the Museum, reliant as it was on royal and official patronage, was in its own time capsule.

Observing customs

None of the travellers discussed here would have claimed to be ethnologists, except Abercromby, whose chief interest was language (and antiquarianism), nor were many even interested in the subject. The field as such had emerged comparatively late in Britain, pioneered by Edward Burnett Tylor (1832-1917) in 1871. He defined culture in its wide ethnographic sense as 'a complex whole, which includes knowledge, belief, art, morals, law, custom and any other capabilities and habits acquired by man as a member of society'. As Freshfield wrote, dodging the subject, in the Preface to his 1869 *Travels in the Central Caucasus and Bashan*, ethnographic details had not been included in his account because information filtered through an interpreter would not be trustworthy, and besides the subject had been tackled by German travellers, whose works were translated into English.[32] He was right: access to the large literature in Russian on the subject would have been available but it had to sought out or discovered (as for example with Abercromby). Ethnographic details, then known as 'custom/s', were, however, expected in travelogues and some travellers obliged more than others. Bell and Longworth spent enough time in the places they visited to report on what was going on. Other information was derived from previously known and out of date sources, such as Chardin, Pallas, de Marigny and Klaproth, but also anecdotally, telling both in terms of context and attitudes.[33]

A feature that was common to many was the inclusion of vocabularies and even phrases in appendices and the transcription of ballads and war songs in the text (see below). This was essentially geared towards other travellers but also highlights the languages the British visitors considered important.

Circassia and the West

Bell and Longworth, and to a lesser extent Spencer, stand out from the rest for having stayed for prolonged times in Circassia. Bell, essentially a merchant, had a vested interest in promoting the cause of Circassian independence and its possible significance for trade, while Longworth was on missions to gauge the political situation. Spencer, whose publications preceded those of Bell and Longworth (1837-38), wrote as a champion of Urquhart and as a travel writer at pains to sell the Circassians to the British public. He relied on his servant and miscellaneous sources as informants while deriding Pallas, Klaproth and Clarke[34] and not referencing others, for depicting the Circassians as plunderers and robbers. He praises the beauty and simplicity of the land, its fertility, the 'semi-barbarous' Circassians and their skills, honour, virtues and values such as respect towards elders.[35] He mentions the neglect of agriculture (except for millet and barley), the slash and burn techniques, bee-keeping, the water mills attached to every village, the use of oxen and mules (never horses) and primitive cloaks and felt tents used by shepherds.[36] The picture evokes a romantic, bucolic, pastoral life.

Travelling in the manner of Bell and Longworth, Spencer spent time with chieftains up and down the coast, dramatizing his encounters. He mentions the heightened power of military chiefs in wartime, chosen if no hereditary prince or elder was a suitable candidate, and recounts how Lezgin tactics were adopted for the open warfare with divisions into platoons, each carrying lances and flags or flags of different colours.[37] He met ferocious mountain people, 'hardy, abstinent, armed only with bows and arrows or a light gun and black shields'.[38] In Abkhazia warriors were attached to special trees (like the Circassians) in groves, where every tree appropriated by a warrior was hung with trophies and offerings. Before battle an elder would strike an oak exhorting the young to be brave and slay the enemy, addressing the oak as a witness to past times and victories. It was a sacrilege to cut down such trees, punishable by death.[39] The Russians cut down such groves as punishment and used this as a weapon to drive locals out of areas.

Religion

In his section on religion Spencer makes the link between the distant Christian past of the area (under Byzantium), 'a relic of Christianity', and some of the figures of the Circassian pantheon, whom he calls 'saints' and some religious festivals (such as the New Year spring festival which he considers close to Christian Easter).[40] His listing of the major and minor deity protectors, some of their Christian associations, such as the worship of Elijah or the melding of Miriam (the goddess of bees) with Mary is corroborated by modern scholarship.[41] Spencer was more systematic in his presentation of the material than Bell or Longworth, even if similar observations on major deities or customs such as local divination and fortune telling, festivals (notably that of Sozeresh in the first days of spring, with people dancing around an effigy), the importance of sacred groves and trees for warriors and the adoption of the Muslim Bayram festival (commemorating by animal sacrifice Abraham's willingness to sacrifice Isaac) are found in passing in Bell and Longworth.[42] Some of this information would have been already known from previous travellers' reports. Much information was piecemeal and accidental, for example certain celebrations, such as weddings or the feast of Miriam or Merem in October were witnessed.[43] Longworth describes 'a heathen' harvest festival beside a grave and never supposedly attended by strict 'Mahometans' but nevertheless with a 'hadji' present. 'Lads and lasses' danced round an effigy, a post with a stick placed cross wise at the top, perhaps a deity. Then an old 'patriarch' came forward and delivered thanksgiving and offerings (bread, honey, cakes and 'boza', a fermented grain drink) and a bull was led to the post and sacrificed. The carcass was roasted and distributed to 'the multitude'. It was unlikely that these old pagan rites would be abandoned until Islamism could provide similar 'joyous occasions', commented Longworth.[44] Other family affairs, such as the 'celebration of the hearth', were not accessible.[45]

It should be noted that modern ethnographers, such as Jaimoukha 2009, derive much information from Bell and Longworth's accounts.

Law and brotherhoods

Law was referred to as *adat* (or customary) but the specific, local Circassian (*xabze*) code of conduct law which prevailed at councils was not named as such or referred to specifically. The law of brotherhood discussed below may have been incorporated into it, but this is not clear.[46]

Bell and Longworth's valuable and new contribution to western knowledge about the Circassians took the form of their observations on the councils and the Circassian system of voluntary brotherhoods or associations united by oaths. Councils (*medjilis*) favoured their own societies (and laws) over Islamic law, although its representatives were allowed to sit on councils. Mehmet, a judge, carried a Turkish law book with him, with an index of penalties.[47] These brotherhood associations were formed for judicial and social purposes: punishments and fines were meted out, revenue and subscriptions raised. Their primary purpose was mutual social responsibility; they could be rich or poor and allied for the sake of influence. Members ranged from fifteen or twenty to two or three thousand.[48]

Longworth's discussion of Circassian institutions was meant to gauge to what extent they might be viable for a unified government. Manning has argued (rather forcedly) that Longworth saw liberalism 'writ large' in his description of Circassian institutions.[49] Longworth does use terminology associated with liberal vocabulary in Britain (such as 'joint stock company' or 'liberal ideas of property') in order to make parallels intelligible to the British public (and the Foreign Office), yet also categorically compares their system of 'voluntary organisations' to the self- protecting burghs of the medieval system in Europe.[50] Longworth stresses the supreme importance of oaths in this system (or the Circassians' assertions of such) which bound the societies to a sense of social responsibility as regards crime, security, property and hospitality.[51] The practice of oath taking, which was also an Islamic practice,[52] was increasingly used and enforced as influence from Dagestan arrived and the war gained ground. But as mentioned above, Islam was never to gain whole sway in Circassia. The societies were not free from personal jealousy and competition. Thus, for example, the Chipaquo society was united with the Tocav or Natquo one to give them ascendancy over the Natkuvich.[53] Autonomy was central to their institutions, and any idea of 'supreme authority' was totally incompatible with their mutually understood sense of identity.[54] This explained the interminable debates at council, where elders, religious authorities and the nobility were given voice. Consensus, Longworth argued,[55] was eventually reached by a system of 'virtual' representation by several voices derived from the notion of common interest, not from one representative of party.[56] In military matters local influences were of greater importance, where nobles of feudal and military merit were given greater voice.[57] Longworth transcribes a lament to the hero Pshukei Bey, fallen in a Russian campaign, sung at a council gathering, possibly the same as the war song referred to by Bell.[58]

Longworth concluded that despite some parallels with a system of government as the West understood it, and any potential use and development of the system (such as the machinery for collecting revenue), a centralized government was not a viable outcome for Circassia and would clash with the societies.[59] The travellers also emphasized the use of fines over blood feuds.[60]

Women and slaves

Women were considered the property of fathers, husbands, or the tribe. They were considered a threat to 'martial spirit' and were basically slaves. This was contrary to Islamic law, where according to the Koran, women have rights, wrote Longworth.[61] Slaves, the majority of whom were prisoners of war (with more menial duties given to Russian prisoners), were nevertheless entitled to keep 'half the fruits of their (agricultural) industry'.[62] Many slaves and women of lower rank were sold into slavery, often of their own volition to find a decent harem in Turkey or marry and be free.[63]

Language

In vol. I of his *Travels in Circassia* (1837) Spencer gives vocabulary and phrases (including modes of pronunciation) in Tatar and Circassian.[64] In an 'Advertisement' to the 1838 edition, Spencer strongly refutes (among other things) the accusation made by a 'quarterly oracle' of not having provided sources and of plagiarism made regarding the vocabulary.[65] The question of plagiarism in travel writing in general was easy to make given how often previous sources were used and not acknowledged, but may have been accurate in Spencer's case as he was so keen to publish quickly. The phrases in Spencer are very much of the tourist kind ('what will it cost'?) and giving orders ('open the window', 'make a fire'). Predictably, Bell gives specimens of simple vocabulary from the three languages of the Abkhazian coast (Azra, Abaza, Adige) in an Appendix.[66] The Circassian ballad and/or war song transcribed by Bell and Longworth has been mentioned above.

The North

Travellers who took pains to go to the northern range of the Caucasus, some travelling from Tiflis across the whole range westwards (Freshfield, Grove) were going for the specific purpose of mountaineering or investigating the mountains as the area opened up from the later 1860s. They were not particularly interested in the indigenous peoples and their customs per se. They focused on the landscape and mountains (see Mountaineers below) and viewed the mountain peoples essentially as porters, guides and providers of shelter and sustenance, while not stinting on often derogatory comments.

However, as they traversed parts of Ossetia, Ingushetia and Svaneti, they came across indigenous villages, including Muslim ones, where Russian influence was either evident or still totally absent, and had multiple experiences attesting to the far from uniform status of the villages and villagers. It was inevitable in these regions to come across the presence, influence, resentment and grievances of the Russian Empire's impositions as the century wore on.

Adventurers used the Russian Five Verst map and the general printed map in Freshfield's book (by Sampson and Low and Co. Ltd.). The latter shows a simplified geography: Ossetia, encompassing Svaneti, was placed immediately adjacent to Chechnya. The travellers depended heavily on local information, sometimes hostile to neighbouring peoples, to establish where they were and for nomenclature, and it is not always clear which region they were in except when they name a village that still exists. (The plethora of regional names and details on mountain passes, glaciers etc. and summary maps is confusing to the uninitiated and was intended for professional mountaineers.)

Ethnography

While choosing porters for Freshfield's party's first foray towards Mount Kazbek they found four aged men (for 2 ½ roubles, 7 shillings per day) who carried out their part of the bargain with 'an honesty and good humour which led us to form an unlucky premature estimate of the general character of the people we should afterwards deal with'.[67] In the Upper Terek region they 'were delighted to get rid of the Res (village/area ?) men' who had been 'most provokingly insolent during the descent'.[68] This set the tone for Freshfield's trip, which more than those of the other travellers, demonstrate the English imperial mind set. The area was still remote for foreigners, and local reception (friendly, adequate or rough) and porters recruited along the way were essential to their survival in the region. The locals would also have been curious and bewildered by these dependent foreigners, and were determined to extract as much pay as possible from them.

North-East: Ossetia, Ingushetia, Khevsureti, Chechnya

Most of the observations on the indigenous people are either incidental and/or the result of overnight stays in different localities. On the first trip to Kazbek, near the village of Goslet, Freshfield's party came across a pile of stones resembling an altar covered with the horns of chamois and ibex. The 'tribe' that worshipped there were Kists (a scattered Ingush-Chechen sub-ethnic group) according to Freshfield's informant, who gathered there once a year to sing strange songs and make offerings to the 'genius loci'.[69] On their second trip (from Kazbek to Elbruz) they passed an 'Osset' village in the vicinity of Kobi (east of the Jvari pass, south Ossetia), distinguished by the 'great number of stone towers', many ruined, and houses which were 'gloomy masses of rough masonry' with small holes for windows. The men were 'handsome', dressed in long frock coats, high fur hats, carrying swords, daggers, guns and pistols.[70] While on their first trip they witnessed a fully armoured Khevsur (people on the border between Ingushetia and Chechnya) sword dance but not in Khevsureti (see below). Khevsur fights in full gear, like the Circassian horsemanship displays of the past, had seemingly already entered the entertainment business[71] and their depiction in chainmail became their 'calling card' image.[72]

Reception in the north was not always cordial. At the village of Zacca, for example, crowds jostled, pushed, were 'not content' with staring, wrangled over money and behaved insultingly. This escalated into a fight and a sheepskin coat was stolen.[73] The incident gave the travellers a particularly bad feeling about the Ossets, later 'modified' by better treatment.[74] The travellers' goods and dress provoked great curiosity among villagers, especially their heavily nailed boots,[75] which Freshfield compared to the natives' 'peculiar' footwear (shown in the Museum), which consisted of a tangle of leather bands stuffed with dry grass and bound, which surprisingly were highly protective against both rocks and cold, including steep snow slopes.

Possibly at the prompting of his publisher (Longmans, Green and Co.), Freshfield includes known generalities on the Ossets (originally Christian, worship partly pagan, custom of vengeance and feuds, men handsomely dressed and few poor) without giving his source. The latter detail can hardly have been true to what Freshfield and the others experienced. In summary the Ossets made both a bad (robbery) and a good impression (physique).

The pro-Russian Telfer touring almost ten years later was keen to incite curiosity about the area, now much more open, and includes details on ethnography, antiquarianism, botany and mountaineering. He is telling about the Russification and primitiveness of these areas. He makes value judgements about the 'tribes', informed from others (Professor Brosset of St Petersburg, Ph. Bruun of Odessa, the University Library at Odessa, and DuBois de Montperreux)[76] and which probably coincided with what he thought.

Telfer was particularly keen to show the 'civilizing' influence of Russia on and their attempts at conversion of the Ossets, as well as their ancient history (the ancient Alans). Out of a population of 65,000, 50,000 Ossetians were said to be Christian, Telfer writes.[77] He visited schools supported by the Society for the Restoration of Christianity in the Caucasus in Zalutch, a village of relocated

Ossetians near Vladikavkaz, and in Vladikavkaz (see below) where the pupils were taught to read and write in Russian, the elements of arithmetic and to sing to the Tsar. Books in Ossetian were nevertheless available since a vocabulary had been made by a Dr Sjogren in 1844, *Ossetische Sprachlehre*.[78] Zalutch (Zaluch) itself was clean and tidy: the modern houses no longer had towers (trapezoid towers particular to the Ossets had rooms on either side of a 'court' and raised beds).[79] The entertainment here consisted of the *lezghynka* dance, a sword dance, wrestling and a pantomime of a stag hunt.[80] It was as if all traditions of the west and north Caucasus had been boiled down to these sketches and the village well on the way to civilization. This did not hide the fact that the Ossetians were poor; they were used to clear mountain roads in winter, a menial task they accepted as it exempted them from taxes.[81]

Telfer demonstrates the complexity of these village identities by listing the sub-groups of Ossetian 'tribes' (Digor, Tagaour, Kurtalins, Alaghyrs) living in different parts (north and south) and themselves forming sub-groups.[82] He remarks on the appearance of the Ossets (highlanders and lowlanders), not 'fine' looking but with fair hair, light coloured eyes - suggestive, with the cleanliness, of superiority to dark skinned indigenous peoples. The women were plain.[83] Telfer then, from various sources including Russian literary ones presumably advanced by his Russian wife, such as Pushkin's observation of an Ossetian funeral (*Journey to Arzum*, 1835) and Lermontov, 'who knew the country well' and romanticised it in *Byelia* from *Hero of Our Time*,[84] informs the reader of the customs of the Ossets (from the history of their partial conversion to Christianity in the eighteenth century, their mixed Christian, pagan and Mohammedan practices, their reverence for Christ, the Virgin Mary, their great divinity Elias (Elijah) to whom they pray for rain and good harvest). They wore both crosses and amulets. They avoided Christian churches, preferring their own idols and their supreme being (H'tsaov) and views of paradise according to the Koran.[85] Each wood was supposedly under the influence of its 'own genius', as were mountains. When Telfer reached the station of Gudaur near the Mountain of the Cross (a rendezvous for caravans over the narrowest pass of the Aragvi and the station of Pasanur) he quoted from the Ossetian legend of the mountain spirit god (from a St Petersburg publication of 1871).[86] Telfer continues with marriage customs and the abandonment of bride stealing, and burials ('pagan' rites involving offerings, holding a horse's bridle, shearing a widow's hair, throwing in a horse's ear, burial under a cairn). The Christian funeral rite was amended to include self-whipping and loud beating of breasts (reminiscent of Shia rituals), following the corpse to its resting place, crying over the cross. The feast of remembrance (*Baden-ty*) was comparable to the day of Russian remembrance, he writes, yet finished in drunken orgies.[87]

Mixed 'pagan', Christian and Muslim religious practices and 'mysterious ways' were also characteristic of the Ingush village of Bazorkyn (near Zaluch) where according to Telfer's informant they avoided intercourse with all Christians, dispersed when a party approached, and left all the doors open to let out the spirits of the departed. They adored a deity called Galgar and their supreme being was Deammeh. They swore by certain stones and a sacred tree that had been struck by lightning. Confessions for murder were made at a dead man's grave, with an oath sworn by the Archangel Michael. Telfer quotes the oath and gives the Ingush vocabulary for the days of the week.[88] His source for the Ingush was a publication of 1847, *Roukavodstvo k' paznany you Kavkaza* (Guide to (knowledge of) the Caucasus).[89]

To what extent which or any of these customs were still practised in the mid-1870s is unclear, but Telfer manages to give the impression that the 'civilizing mission' still had a lot of work to do or perhaps that such people were a lost cause while being a source of curiosity.

Distinguishing between 'tribes' or peoples was not necessarily simple in these areas, as Georgians and others were mixed with Ossets, Pshavs and even Chechens. Pshavs mixed with Tush and Khevsurs, partly for ethnic relations such as between the Ingush with Chechens, Bats and Kists, and partly as villages were displaced for administrative reasons. Names given locally were also confusing: the Ingush, for instance, knew themselves as Ghalghaj. Telfer describes the Khevsurs (to the north-east of the Aragve river) as a 'rude tribe, proud, supercilious, known for hand to hand combat, dirty, inimical to Russia, who call the Russians *bahale* or frogs, because of their uniform'.[90] From conversations with Radde Telfer would probably have been aware of his seminal and forthcoming book on the Khevsurs, *Die Chews'uren und Ihr Land* (Kassel, 1878), the result of an expedition taken in 1876, but he makes no mention of it. Radde's book is exceptionally detailed, with chapters on geography, ethnography, population (Chevsur, Tush, Pshav), a botanical section with a list of plants, and sketches and plates of furniture, clothing, weaponry, the mountain scenery and clusters of towers). Radde was far from impartial himself, as his comments on the Svans, quoted by Freshfield below, show. On the Khevsurs Telfer repeats the myth that (apparently claimed by the Khevsurs themselves) they were descended from the Crusaders on the basis of the cross motif on their festive garments. Radde does not dispute Christian elements in Khevsur religion but does not mention this myth.[91] The Crusader myth was to be expanded by the serviceman Arnold Zisserman's 1879 book *Dvadtsat pyat let na Kavkaze 1842-1867* (Twenty-Five Years in the Caucasus 1842-1867),[92] where he claimed to be the first one to make the connection. The book was otherwise much dependent on Radde. According to Telfer, the Khevsurs rejected priests and the use of churches but St George was their god of war. The Ph'tchavy or Pschavs were another 'rude tribe' of the area with puzzling religious tendencies and very superstitious according to Brosset's *Histoire de la Georgie* (1858).[93]

Language

Telfer, keen to promote the special status of Ossetians compared to other 'tribes', stresses how remarkable the Ossetians were for their link with groups of Indo-European languages. This had long fascinated linguists and others (Klaproth, DuBois de Montperreux, Potocki). For Ingush Telfer gives the vocabulary for the days of the week.[94]

Vladikavkaz and the Dariel pass:
'more savage than beautiful'

The iconic and obligatory sight for travellers in this part of the north (currently in Georgia and north Ossetia) was the Dariel Gorge leading to and from the fortress of Vladikavkaz, on the Terek river. Founded by Potemkin in 1784 and named 'Command of the Caucasus', the fortress and the gorge or pass leading to the only military road south were essential to any war effort in the region and hugely symbolic of the Russian presence in the Caucasus. The area was on permanent alert for most of the century.

Lyall with Ker-Porter before him (in the nineteenth century), Cameron, Ussher, Cunynghame, Telfer, Bryce and Wardrop all used the pass and visited Vladikavkaz, and informed readers on the development of Vladikavkaz across the century (even though it was a hard sell). The pass, however, was one of the more illustrated subjects of the travellers' books (see Part 6).

'Dariel Fort and Ruins of Tamara's Castle'

When Lyall arrived at Vladikavkaz (still mainly a fort) from Georgievsk and Mozdok on his way to Kazbek (1824) he stressed the importance of its location: it commanded one of the passages between the chain of mountains that formed the barrier between Asia and Europe, in use since antiquity (*Pylae Sarmatica* or *Porta Causica*). It had been founded on the relocated village of Zaluch. The fort served as the headquarters of the Russian forces on the north side of the mountains, but was also 'an emporium' of military stores for nearby troops.[95] The number of troops at the time varied according to circumstance, ranging from one battalion to a regiment, they but was always defended by a number of canon. Within the fortress (he gives no dimensions) were numerous magazines, barracks, rows of stores (well stocked with many kinds of wine) and whitewashed houses for the governor and officers. Lyall does not mention any other inhabitants except for the military. With regards to the Dariel 'defile', over whose description travellers were at first to compete, Lyall criticizes Ker-Porter's Plate illustration of Dariel,[96] saying that it does not correspond to his (hyperbolic) prose of 'a rugged world' and a 'sight to make the senses pause' but rather with a more sober passage 'a chasm' rising 'upwards of a thousand feet'.[97] A small fortress, which had been built with much engineering effort, commanded the 'gloomy' defile, but was in ruins. The elevation of the mountains behind the fort was estimated at 3,786 feet.

Cameron, coming from the south, waxes lyrical about the approach to the gorge looking 'with awe and admiration' at the 'sublime', 'gorgeous', 'magnificent' spectacle before him,[98] but focuses on the strength of the flowing river alongside, skipping descriptions of the defile, and only mentioning the small fort in passing. Reality hit him when he reached Vladikavkaz: war was raging in the west (1844) and he was advised by the local commandant not to continue unless with a properly escorted group. These were always needed in this region but could vary in size depending on circumstance and who was travelling: from a group of Cossacks to, with ladies, a battalion of infantry, a body of cavalry and four gun. He took the advice of his servant who said they would be far less conspicuous without such a train (which would be extremely slow) and he proceeded, with the chance to flaunt the courage of an Englishman, without an official escort towards Kabarda.[99]

For Ussher (in 1864) again coming from the south, the defile 'was unsurpassed for gloomy magnificence', showing features of utter desolation and chaos'. He mentions the 'enormous sums' spent on the road, which 'was the only means of conveyance by land of heavy materials' from Russia to Persia, Turkey and Europe, but it seemed to be in a permanently bad condition, being either snowbound or subject to avalanches and heavy rain and disruption from mountain peoples.[100] Telfer writes that the military road had cost £4,000,000.[101] Ussher notes the military importance of Vladikavkaz, which, however, seemed 'a poor looking town' defined by lakes of mud with an almost impassible road through it, wide streets and one-storey houses. His party found the 'large stone' inn or post-house with a drunken landlord and minimal comfort: a large table, closets (with no beds) and a bench for sleeping on. After a flea-bitten night they hurried to Grozny.[102]

Cunynghame, coming from Grozny, was received by Governor General Loris Melikoff (an Armenian), 'a most intelligent officer' ready to assist them. The town was preparing for an Imperial visit, the planning of which seemed to be in the hands of a Mr Upton, employed by the Emperor as architect. The cost of the visit to the citizens was to be 12,000 roubles, defrayed by house-tax. The citizens had resolved to charge 15-20 roubles per night when the Emperor was there.[103] Accommodation had not improved; the travellers had to share with a Swiss officer and his family. Cunynghame does not dwell on the pass but illustrates it. Leaving for the south they had to pay a toll at the military road (barred with a huge length of wood painted in the Russian Imperial colours).[104] The local fort had been rebuilt, but it must have been dull for the officers on duty, he notes.[105]

When Telfer visited four years later, things had changed a little, but he still paints a forlorn picture. There was a conspicuous residence for the governor, a large, untidy public garden, a few stone houses, while numerous uniforms (civil and military) testified to the 'predominating influence of absolute power'.[106] There was a new military hospital (for 360 people, partially filled with soldiers suffering from miasmic fever from work on the mountain roads), but much was left to be desired in its surgical department and in its 'foul atmosphere'. The bazaar was 'poorly furnished' and Russian heretics ('wanderers', *strannyky* or *begounny*, 'runaways') hung around the railway line.[107]

From a military outpost Vladikavkaz had evolved into a Russian provincial town (having become an *oblastny gorod* in 1861) with a population of some 15,000. For the traveller lodgings were still dire. Telfer attributes, with rare criticism, the lack of decent hotels to the Russians' sluggishness and laziness, preferring to put up with discomfort rather than 'suffer his indolent spirit to be disturbed.'[108]

Bryce (1876), travelling from Piatogorsk, comments on the military road's importance during Shamil's time and currently to the Russians as troops were being sent through it to Armenia. Svaneti was also in uproar at the time.[109] A railway had been installed from Moscow to Vladikavkaz and because the whole area was on alert, Bryce's party took the six-hour train journey from Piatogorsk, running along the open steppe to Vladikavkaz. To Bryce Vladikavkaz was 'a large straggling sort of place', lately improved by rows of trees planted by some wide streets and enlivened by the 'picturesque' Caucasian dresses of the mixed population.[110] The inn was still highly primitive, and they left for Kazbek the next day. The famous Dariel pass, he writes, 'was striking in its grandeur', the scenery around 'more savage than beautiful'.[111]

Wardrop, as is to be expected, goes into detail about Dariel's 'awful cliffs' and its history, including a legendary castle (not the fort) associated with Queen Tamara (written about by Lermontov) and the general scenery vaunted by Pushkin and Lermontov. The fort itself was 'a romantic looking place with old-fashioned battlemented towers', clearly not in much danger and garrisoned by a few Kazakhs. Vladikavkaz was developing and now had several quarters: the best being on the right bank of the river, where there were shady gardens. The town had a respectable boulevard, fairly well-paved streets, several decent hotels (he recommends the upgraded Pochtovaya and the Frantsiya), a market (although hardly any trading), a cathedral under construction, a little theatre (often closed) and the 'old fort', which seemed to be the only tourist attraction. The population now had risen to 30,000 and was mixed (Russians, Circassians, Georgians, Armenians, Persians), and if it were not for the 'Asiatic' costumes and 'Asiatic' tongues you could be in any Russian provincial town. There was nothing to see or do: it was not a town 'anybody would care to settle in'; it was better to take the train to the fashionable inland watering place of Piatigorsk. (He illustrates all these places.)[112]

Chechnya: a scholar's journey

Abercromby, travelling in the late 1880s, approached this region (east of Vladikavkaz) from Dagestan (Gumuk, Gunib towards Veden). The area was still not considered safe: all through 'Chechents' country, every six to ten miles, there was a police post.[113] Police were taken from the local yeomanry, who did their turn of duty for six days in each month, for ten roubles a month. The post road to the west was considered particularly unsafe: those using it were not allowed to carry arms.[114]

The area was of interest to him, not only 'anthropologically' and ethnographically (even though his observations were brief) but mainly for linguistic reasons. This aspect would mainly be of interest to specialists. Abercromby did not indulge in political commentary.

Approaching Chechnya Abercromby details the different names given to the 'Chechents' in the area: they were known as the Michikhisch (or Mizdsheg) among the Tatars, the Avars called them Chachan or Burtichi, and the Chechens called themselves Nakhchuo, or Nakhchuoi (a derivative of the Nakh people).[115]

At Karachai, the first village in 'Chechents' country where they dismounted (causing a sensation), Abercromby observed the local physique: tall, fine-looking men, with both aquiline and straight

Ethnography

noses, blond hair and light eyes. They were finer looking than the Avars and other Lezgins, he thought, and better dressed, wearing white *beshmets* and black *cherkaskas* of very good cloth,[116] although nearly all were barefoot. The women were conspicuous from their red dresses (see Appendix).

The remoteness of the place was evident (locals did not look one in the face, but they were more stared at and observed than in Dagestan) and conversation was almost impossible: no-one spoke Avar and Tatar was useless. People knew only a smattering of Russian. He noted the importance of dress and hairstyle there: no-one believed Abercromby's guide to be a Tatar because he did not shave his head and his dress was different. They all thought he was a Georgian.[117]

Abercromby contrasts the local houses with those of Dagestan; here the houses were directly on the ground (not over a stable or cow-house), with 'singular', enormous, dice-shaped chimney pots.[118] Near Shali the houses were not piled beehive-like on slopes (as in Lezgin villages) but lay on the level, surrounded by gardens, orchards and outhouses. Here they stayed at a yeoman's house: a whitewashed building of one storey and a veranda. Their room was clean, covered in native carpets with a wooden divan and a shelf for crockery. He was struck by the archaic shape of local milk-jars but noted that the rest of the crockery and utensils were of Russian patterns and manufacture.[119] The hostess was tall and nice looking, dressed in white. They were entertained in the company of both men and women by dancing, of a man alone with a woman accordion player, and a 'light footed child'.[120] In contrast with the Lezgins Abercromby seems to have been impressed by the Chechens.

Svaneti

Svaneti (south of Elbruz) was an area visited by most from Freshfield to Abercromby (see Map 4): it developed its own curiosity factor because of its remote landscape and characteristic high stone towers.

Freshfield's party was the only one to have traversed the whole east to west range from Kazbek to Svaneti-Elbruz, and his book opened up the area: it promised good sport for mountaineers (Grove) and hunters (Phillipps-Wolley); it was interesting territory for ethnographers (Abercromby) and for those who, while touring, observed the 'progress' or not of Russia there (Telfer, Cunynghame). Most travellers do not make overt political comments but give more than tacit endorsement to the status quo (which after all facilitated their travels) while railing against inefficiency and bad roads.[121] On the road Freshfield and his party became used to 'queer company'.[122]

Readers of Freshfield's book would be reinforced in negativity towards the Svanetians by his quotation of Radde, who had travelled there collecting information and bad experiences. Radde assessed rather viciously that 'in their countenances insolence and rudeness are prominent, and hoary-headed obstinacy is often united to the stupidity of savage animal life… individuals are often met who have committed ten or more murders, which their standard of morality not only permits, but in many cases commands… their manner when endeavouring to impose upon strangers is most disagreeable.'[123] This is perhaps more revealing of the colonial outlook than of Svanetians. Freshfield added Malte Brun's equally negative opinion of the Svanetians, whose 'dirt, rapacity, and skill in weapon making' made them the 'eaters of vermin' mentioned by Strabo. Freshfield added that now the vermin had 'taken over' (presumably referring to bedbugs). The Svan porters seemed to be 'universally lazy and stupid' but 'more fools than knaves', 'free from more active vices'.[124] Porters were usually anxious not to stray too far from their territory,[125] a hint of past and ongoing rivalries and feuds.

The people at Gebi, where they stopped en route to Elbruz to make excursions into the Rion mountains, for example, had 'faces…of lazy stupidity', not fine looking like the Ossetians. They found that as the 'natives' were brought into contact with their rulers, they improved in manners and civilization, and that the districts which the Russians had left to take care of themselves were those in which the old customs of petty warfare, robbery and murder still prevailed.[126]

'A Native of Jibiani'

Svan villages in the community of Ushguli (Jibiani, Murkmur, Tchubiani) were in 'strange and picturesque' clusters, with stone-built towers. Three villages had sixty towers between them.[127] At Jibiani the villagers looked wholly savage, especially the children, where girls looked more like brute animals than human beings.[128] The men were well armed but shabbily clothed, some wore an inside out sheepskin hat to shield their eyes. The women were shapeless bundles of rags.

Freshfield's party had a bad experience at Jibiani, which no doubt contributed to his bile against its inhabitants. They were incessantly stared at in the village and when they retreated into the barn where they were lodging jeering men kicked the door open while items of clothing put out to dry outside were stolen. Exasperated, Moore 'fired five rounds of his revolver' which 'had the intended effect of no further annoyance'.[129] Next day, when preparing to leave, they 'were assailed' by clamours for money and the men refused to load the horses until they had been paid what they asked for. The party gave them what they thought was fair and they left pursued by the men. They were later told that if they had not had their pistols they would have been robbed.[130] Travelling to Elbruz and Uruspieh they had no further trouble with porters. An idea of the remoteness of the region and isolation of the people is given by the porters' ignorance of England and the English, only knowing of Russians, Turks and Franghi (or foreigners).[131] This must have piqued the patriotic Freshfield.

Heading north, they passed the 'castellated' village of Becho and arrived at the 'mean-looking' village of Pari. One rebellious prince's property at Pari had been replaced by a Cossack military post, and Freshfield found it natural that as Russia succeeded in converting her 'suzerainty over the Caucasus into real dominion', native princes should be seen as landed proprietors only. Eventually, however, the Cossack post was removed and with only ten Cossacks left in the district, the area (Upper and West Svaneti) was left independent and its people at full liberty to follow their 'own wicked ways of theft and murder, to their hearts' content.[132] Here Freshfield cites Radde on the deliberately slow Russian policy of 'taming' the free Svanetians, who were felt to be beyond the pale. Freshfield thought the Russian government's hope was that these people would self-exterminate.[133]

The low flat-roofed village of Uruspieh (Upper Baksan valley, Kabardino-Balkaria) was entirely different from the Svan 'fortresses' and provided a completely different experience. It was already known to European travellers (and photographers), and they were looked after by friendly Cossacks delivering them from 'barbarous natives'. They slept in beds in a clean looking cottage.[134] Here too, in the conventional comment on physicality, the men were judged a 'fine race' while the women were prematurely old.

The local princes of Uruspieh (after whom the well-stocked village was called) were their hosts. The princes were 'men of taste', well informed and tolerant in their views (Freshfield does see the irony of this assessment). One of their first conversations evoked Kars and 'Williams Pasha', which must have pleased the English. The princes had been in Russian service but were exempt from conscription, and so at Uruspieh, Freshfield wrote, 'the imperial sway of Russia did not press hardly'.[135] Freshfield preferred the term patriarchal to feudal when describing the princes' standing; they were the heads of the community and the richest, and the duty of hospitality fell on them. Their word was not law, however. They were nominally Mohammedan and spoke Tartar.[136]

Having climbed Elbruz the party travelled north to Piatigorsk and Naltschik in the Upper Terek to investigate the northern part of the central range. At Naltschick the Russian commandant was not to be relied on to negotiate a fair price for porters and they had protracted negotiations over pay, but stayed in a clean room, which nevertheless lacked creature comforts.[137] They proceeded to villages in the region of Balkar, annexed by Russia in the early nineteenth century (now the Karbardino-Balkarian republic), inhabited by Turkic peoples. Freshfield asserts that they were the first western Europeans to be seen in Balkar.[138] At Muchol (Uruch valley), for example, Freshfield's party was received in a friendly way by the Mullah dressed in a turban and loose robe of a Turk. Knowing that Britain was a friend of Turkey made him very civil. The locals had a fear of Russian proselytising and 'being compelled to worship the relics and pictures of a hundred saints, instead of the one God and Mohammed his prophet'.[139] They clung to their faith, writes Freshfield, and the call to prayer resounded night and morning in all the villages. Some wanted to leave for a more Islamic district.[140] Freshfield praises their corn cultivation and contrasts the industrious and well-to-do Muslims with their lazy and neglectful Christians neighbours. In another village (Novo-Christianski in the Upper Uruch), however, the party came across what could happen: they were met by a native, Mohammedan chief of military rank (with several wives), whose whole village had recently and simultaneously converted to Christianity (presumably nominally) in response to the remission of taxes.[141] Here the carpets and cushions associated with Muslim households had disappeared 'under Russian influence' and they were forced to sleep on bare boards.[142] On the way to Vladivostok they met Digors (a sub-group of Ossetians) who had been traditionally Muslim, many of whom had emigrated, but the remaining seemed to have been thoroughly Christianized.[143]

Svaneti continued: new mountaineering routes

Of the next two travellers to visit these regions, Grove and his party from the Alpine Club were mountaineers (trav. 1874-75) while Telfer was touring (trav. 1875).

Inspired by Freshfield's expedition, Grove's party (F. Gardiner, A.W. Moore, H. Walker) were also keen to make their mark and explore new routes.[144] Grove acknowledged Moore (one of Freshfield's party) for his information on the topography of the Caucasus.[145] His tone is far more conciliatory, warm and observant than Freshfield's, for example naming porters, and their cook Paul (who had accompanied the previous party) or describing more of the life of the villages.

The men set off from Kutaisi, noting the Jewish presence - for Grove positive - at Utsova ('the limits of civilisation') but seen as a great 'infliction' by the people of Kutaisi.[146] He does not elaborate. They explored many of the same places as Freshfield's party (Gebi, Uruspieh, the Elbruz region) but also Bezingi, east of Elbruz, and other new villages such as Tchegem, Kunim and Uchkulan.

Grove, in a veiled criticism of Freshfield's negative opinion of Gebi's 'hovels and strong towers', gives a more considered opinion; the towers were built against marauders by the people there, having command of the two main passes of the region. They were the merchants of the area, but where travellers were concerned 'cheating scamps'.[147] Grove generalizes on the northern Caucasians: they were generally good people, but sharp in sales, ready to take advantage, like some at home, but with little inclination to murder and theft (and less so with the advance of civilization).[148] At Gebi Grove observed what he thought was a village parliament discussing municipal matters, but in fact was a daily congregation.[149] The village was governed by six elders, one of whom was the headman (appointed by the Russian government),

'The Men of Gebi'

who had fought against Shamil. There was a local school, built with no help from the government, teaching in Georgian.[150] The villagers were poor, eating once a day.

At Kunim, over the great chain, he remarked on the construction of houses, like cowsheds and dog-kennels, but inhabited by handsome, well-to-do people. They were coldly but adequately received, because the chief had not been forewarned of their arrival.[151] At Bezingi (due north, western Terek), received by the local chief and his two wives in national costume (most probably forewarned) they encountered the usual crowd, examining their clothes and boots.[152] He later wonders what would happen if a Caucasian chief in full national costume were to enter a Surrey village and ask for lodging: he would probably be kicked half to death.[153]

At Tchegem on the approach to Vladikavkaz, they were welcomed by three handsome chiefs (one marked by smallpox, current in the region), who having been prepared by the Governor of Vladikavkaz in advance, treated their guests to luxuries such as white sugar, tea and a whole sheep. Nothing was stolen. They had a conversation with a passing 'Caucasian', who answering the question of whether the Russians had treated them well, said 'No'. The Russian government was not just, for everything depended on one man, he argued, and he was likely to make mistakes, whereas a council of many men was far less likely to make mistakes. He seemed to know about the 'great British council' (Parliament) but was clearly referring to local and traditional decision-making bodies, wrote Grove. The Russian government did not respect the rights of men: it was about to confiscate the Prince of Uruspieh's forest (this was mentioned by Freshfield, and one of the princes was then in Vladikavkaz pleading his cause). Furthermore, the princes now, after emancipation, had to pay men to work for them. Grove did not engage with him, but wrote that he did not see oppression around him, that taxation was light, there was no religious coercion, that each village had its priest, but no-one forced them to attend church. He did agree that confiscating property was unjust (unlike Freshfield) but there may have been mitigating circumstances, and he conceded that if universal military service were to be applied it would cause great discontent.[154] He was willing to disregard the decades of Russian war and interference in the region and the grudges people still held.

Uruspieh was as friendly as before, and despite being close to Piatigorsk the people were still curious about strangers and crowded around when Grove wrote in his notebook.[155]

Having tackled Elbruz, they continued west of the mountain (where Freshfield did not get to) to Uchkulan, in the valley of the Kuban. Here they found the usual 'hovels', except one of 'Russian construction' belonging to an unhappy clerk employed to interpret for the chief of Uchkulan. The chief (Tokmak Akaiev), despite working for the government, was 'ignorant of the language' (Russian). He acted as a government banker for the people around (at the time possessing 50,000 roubles or £6,875) and showed the travellers his account book and a treasured watch, given to him by the Grand Duke Michael. The chief proved to be kind, but the travellers' nemesis, the porters, were troublesome. They asked for more than what was agreed despite the chief's entreaties. Other porters were found.[156]

On the way to Abkhazia, Grove noted the religious observances of the porters: they prayed three times a day but were 'rogues' and complained about the food they were given and demanded extra payment.[157] The chief porter stopped arguing when he was told his name would be given to the Russian authorities. On the approach to the military post of Lata and Sukhum-Kale the party noticed than the men became more and more cowed, finally parting company with great relief.

Grove's conclusions regarding the 'Caucasians' were positive: they led primitive lives yet far removed from barbarism, they were simple, pastoral, kindly, hospitable, there was an absence of theft among the northerly mountain peoples, nor were they violent. However, they were indolent, procrastinators, unreliable and took advantage of travellers. In terms of physique, the men were graceful, spare, did not indulge, except for the priest 'in many countries a fat class' and were capable of walking a long time without food, almost on a par with Scottish Highlanders or the Swiss.[158] Yet when food was available and 'indolent' natives galvanized into action, the traveller with money could fare well (in a rich village): sour milk, coarse white cheese, brown bread, mutton, fowls, sometimes eggs, tea and cakes, were better than any traveller had any right to expect among a 'primitive people'. But this proved difficult when travelling in areas when there were no villages.[159]

Both Freshfield and Grove contrast the decency of the northern tribes with the more southern ones, but by generalizing for the benefit of future visitors, show the extent of their objectification. The indigenous peoples' particular identities and protective and defensive attachment to their land were considered almost as a curiosity and connected to ancient history, to be subsumed under the blanket term 'Caucasian' for the public. Yet the realities on the ground showed that identities and territoriality were not to be lost so easily. Grove himself assumed that these peoples' 'destiny would soon yield to the monotony of civilization' and what was so singular about them would be lost for ever.[160]

A tour of inspection

Telfer, travelling at the same time as Grove, met him and his party at Kutaisi, but as Grove stated, their objectives were different and they parted ways.[161] What is especially informative about Telfer's account, in contrast to the piecemeal information gleaned from the previous travellers, is that he gives insights into the realities of the Russian administration of the region and its political divisions: Dadian Svaneti, Independent Svaneti (valley of the Ingur to the commune of Latali) and Dadeshkeliani (Ingur valley from Betcho to Zugdidi).[162] The first and last areas were named after princely families. Telfer also interrupts the narrative with copious notes on the history of Svaneti and its ethnography (costume, arms, religious practices, names etc) taken from various sources.

Telfer travelled with a cavalcade of officials comprising Russian law officers, an interpreter, four Cossacks and Prince Tenghiz Dadeshkeliani, whose family had been sent to serve in distant provinces after a sedition, and who now served as an assistant police-officer of his area. At the head of the party was the chief of Kutaisi, Colonel Theodore Hrinewsky, on tour of inspection of the Ingur valley.[163]

Leaving Kuatisi they went from Lentekhi over the Laptary pass, to the Ingur, Ipari, Mestia, Betcho (near Mount Ushba), the Upper Ingur and towards Mingrelia. The clustered villages of Svaneti belonging to one commune were home to about 450 'souls'. A table from a census of 1874 gives the total population of Svaneti (from 84 clusters of habitations) as 11,591.[164]

One of the objectives of the chief's tour was to superintend fresh elections, held every third year, in the areas where there were *mamasaklysy* (elders) and their *pamoshtnyky* (assistants). These were elected posts, and the men of Kala and Ushguli were to be gathered for the purpose. When they were chosen (not all were willing), they would cross themselves, kiss the Bible and be invested with a brass badge and thumb ring. In Ushguli, however, where the people were the 'most irreclaimable', the native practice of swearing, ('there before Christianity') consisted of making an oath by throwing a bullet at an image.[165] In Appendix XIII[166] Grove writes that the Svanetians had not forgotten past injustices, including the fairly recent 1869 invasion and show of military force after another show of disaffection. In 1875 there had been serious opposition in Independent Svaneti over the survey of the valley ordered to equalize land tax (to change capitation tax to land tax) and they had refused to accept the chief's authority. At the centre of the insurrection were men from Mulachi and Lataly who argued that the survey was intended to deprive the landowners of excess land, that cattle and domestic animals would be numbered and taxed and that younger members of the family would be conscripted. (They after all had plenty of experience of the different aspects of Russian interference.) As there was precedence for the falsity of Russian claims, continues Grove, the men swore to unite and resist Russian oppression. Reminiscent of the war, a Russian force was assembled (four companies, two mountain howitzers, one hundred cavalry and militia men). Meanwhile the Laptary pass had been blocked by the mountain people. The chief got through and eventually managed to speak to the insurgents who said they would not back down unless the troops refrained from entering their country. The reply was that unless they backed down, went home and sent leaders to the government the troops would attack. The men replied that they would be willing to go home on condition that the leaders would not be made to surrender and a legitimate 'peace treaty' be made. One leader nevertheless, in a show of defiance, shut himself in his tower, which was then set alight. He was captured and eighteen prisoners were taken.

The party proceeded to Mestia and Kala, where things had calmed down. One leader was condemned to death, the others detained at Kuataisi under various charges, including murder, and were condemned to death, but died in prison. The one survivor was banished to Kharkoff for five years. This disorder resulted in changes in the administration.

Grievances were ongoing: the Russian army was felling trees

indiscriminately in the Betcho region.[167] The 'Svanny' disliked the intrusion of strangers and especially those 'wearing the uniform of the monarch who claims them as his subjects,' Telfer commented.[168]

Local elections did not always go smoothly, not only because of local 'uproar' over the merits of favourites, but through serious local feuds which were aired, negotiated or simply deferred for fear of reprisals, or the chief's lack of authority.[169] Here the party needed the help of Tenghyz, as one of their own. Feuds was still very much alive, contrary to previous travellers' reports: there were over twenty cases of murder which had never been settled, the chief heard.[170] Women were being sold off, one girl was sold as a serf to an old man against her will, people exchanging gunfire from the towers.[171]

In the commune of Dadeshkeliani, Telfer visited the house of Tenghyz, which was newly built, near the ruined stronghold of his ancestors. He was shown two heirlooms: a silver drinking bowl of the seventeenth century and a silver casket with a twelfth-century Kufic inscription containing a massive silver belt (Such items were already in the Tiflis Museum). After the elections, which were orderly here, there was dancing and singing.[172]

'Villages of Mulach and Mugal'

A fraternizing traveller

The hunter Phillipps-Wolley (1882) was keen to track, hunt, sensationalize and amuse by his adventures with bears and other creatures, rather than address ethnography except anecdotally. These accidental ethnographical comments, however, can be informative because of details not mentioned by others. This was because he fraternised with the natives, such as Simon his guide, staying with local hunters,[173] seeing them as individuals and witnessing some of their customs. For example, he saw at close hand a feast (of the Death of the Virgin) outside Gebi where meat (the remains of nine bullocks) was cooked in giant cauldrons and afterwards distributed among the heads of houses.[174] Such cauldrons are still to be found in villages in Svaneti. He noted the trophies hanging inside towers (bear paws, ibex and chamois heads and horns), the selling of ibex horns, encounters with other hunters - 'wild looking creatures like satyrs' in goat skin garments,[175] the unease between the men of Racha and those of Svaneti, the poverty, the instance of goitre.[176]

He describes the life of Simon, the richest man in Ushguli, and his favourite hunter. Simon had been baptized and brought up in Racha, returned to Svaneti, and in early summer he went to Racha to find work, and when the time came, threshed his barley out (about 450lb in one year), which he sold for profit. He owned nine small cows, six bullocks and three horses. His staple diet of oat cakes or rye bread and fresh cheeses was supplemented by chamois or ibex, which he shared with the village. His only luxuries were his red linen shirt, his wife's silver earrings and a little coarse tobacco.[177]

The priest's house, where Phillipps-Wolley stayed, was a different matter. He was a man of Racha who had spent eleven years in Svaneti and would stay until his sons ceased to be an expense. One of the sons was an officer in the artillery, the other studying for some profession at one of the 'great' Russian universities. Phillipps-Wolley notes here that such a life of contrasts and hardship when plunged into new lives would spur Nihilists or other violent revolutionaries.[178] The priest lived in a low house of rough stones, with a timber edifice and balcony approached by an external ladder.[179] There was no privacy here, the priest having no authority in the village. The key to the church was kept by six villagers and they had to let the priest in and keep guard until the service was over. Women were not admitted under penalty of stoning.[180] The priest stressed that the isolation of 'the wonderfully uncivilised Svanetia' was responsible for its lack of development: the passes were only available for six months of the year, they had no traders, and the villages were isolated from each other.[181] There was a priest in every hamlet, but no schools at the time although Phillipps-Wolley's interpreter informed him that a 'set of young men', educated natives, had formed a society and raised funds for educating a few peasant children.[182]

Customs were of old: betrothals occurred early, from babyhood sometimes, bigamy was common, marriages were sometimes probationary, blood feuds were still 'very alive' and most of the men Phillipps-Wolley encountered had some sort of problem with their neighbours, and fights with *kinjals* (daggers) and rifles were common. One of the hunter's brothers, George, had a hand missing from a blow by a *kinjal*, but had never received compensation for it. Contrary to travellers before him he stresses the lack of theft in Svaneti.

'An "Independent Svanny"'

As yet no forester (to safeguard the forests) had been established in Svaneti, despite trying. In Racha family tax was eight roubles annually and there the government did something, such as keeping the roads in repair, whereas in Svaneti it was six kopecks (rich and poor alike), and the government did nothing.[183]

At Becho Phillipps-Wolley was no longer among hunters. There he met the local prince and Russian officials. The prince, a tall handsome man, seemed alone to command the respect of his people. His house, better than the rest (one storey, wooden with a balcony) was his headquarters where he lived with a deputy governor. His entourage was a 'judge', another man 'more Russian than Caucasian' and half a dozen minor officials. All were scruffy except for the prince. He was followed everywhere by two courtiers, one holding a bottle of red wine and tumbler, the other the means for lighting a cigarette.[184] The place thronged with people, wrote Phillipps-Wolley; the prince fed at least one hundred and fifty retainers daily, with no signs of any enforcement of emancipation. He was dependent on a tithe of flocks and herds, collected in a 'rough and ready' way by his agents. He dealt with local (presumably minor) offences by cuffing the offender. One evening they dined at the judge's house, where they met members of a government expedition sent from Tiflis to make a report on the agricultural potential of the region (local crops were mainly oats, barley, some wheat, millet, peas and beans, some flax. It was difficult to grow tobacco. Dwarf apples and pears were grown but mostly fed to the bears).[185] Phillipps-Wolley spoke to Mr Schemanovsky, 'agronome to the government of the Caucasus', about Svaneti and the trouble its people gave the Russians. Even in Tiflis they seemingly knew little about it, and the region was not taken much notice of despite the occasional trouble. The people were undisciplined, useless for military purposes, and if brought down to the lowlands to military stations or the Black Sea coast, they died in droves.[186] This was the cost of semi-independence.

Parting with his companion Frank, who headed to Kutaisi, Phillipps-Wolley left Becho (heading for Lachamul) and stayed at yet another, very different Svanetian village. This was Etseri (south-east of Zugdidi), a rich village which prided itself in being a 'royal' village or principality, 'since antiquity', and the traditional burial seat of the regional princes. This refers to the Dadeshkiliani family, known since at least the eleventh century, and who controlled much of western Svaneti in two clans. In the nineteenth century a blood feud broke them up, resulting in exile for the perpetrators of the crime. The princes had resisted the Russians in different ways, one prince being executed for stabbing the military Governor of Kutaisi. By the 1860s this area was under Russian control.[187] Phillipps-Wolley was received by the priest's wife.

The village was more populous than others (c.3,000) and its wealth derived from its open and southern aspect, making it 'a marvel of fertility', and its industry of good cloth, excellent soap, 'abominable' bees'wax candles and worse vodka.[188]

A last look at Svaneti (1895)

In his last major publication on mountaineering in the region, 27 years later, Freshfield was more expansive and informative towards the places he visited (while also recycling his more dramatic experiences). At Mestia, for example, there was a schoolhouse and a *starshina* or government representative, but Freshfield does not develop the subject. At Becho, the new capital of Svaneti, he mentions the courthouse and headquarters of the police (a shed). Prince Dadeshkeliani was his host in Svaneti based in Ezeri (in a large Swiss cottage style house filled with Persian divans). While educated in government business and speaking French, the prince lived like a feudal chief in the Middle Ages, surrounded by retainers, receiving rents in services and kind. Freshfield does not seem to grasp that any major change to the status quo of local princes would have upset the whole balance of order and sown even more disquiet. At Ezeri Freshfield notes that a Georgian priest had lately arrived and heard for the first time here the sound of church bells.[189] In general, there was far less mobbing, provisions were easily found and horsemen were less intractable. At Ushguli that 'wild, hunted look' in the land of vendetta was far less universal.[190] But changes had been gradual and feuds ongoing.[191] Overall Freshfield's tone is still disparaging, and his focus is still on mountaineering, glaciers and the beauty of the landscape, while being wistful about places he had not visited.[192]

Dagestan

If the travellers' information on the north and the west was anecdotal but could be complemented by other sources (from previous travellers to Russian reports), ordinary western knowledge of Dagestan was even more incidental and rare. For the travellers (except for Abercromby who was particularly interested in the languages associated with the indigenous people and produces a map and an Appendix on linguistic groups), people are described as they came across them (notably who hosted them) depending on the routes they took and the locals (whether indigenous guides, hosts or Russian officers) who gave them information. Here they were more dependent on the goodwill of local officialdom, thus giving greater insight into the life of co-opted indigenous officials and Russian officers in these remote places than that of the indigenous populations.

In 1865 it was still risky to travel in parts of Dagestan such as Gunib, which were mostly *terra incognita* to westerners. Cossack escorts were needed as well as local guides. Other areas were still recovering from the recent Shamil wars and experiencing Russian rule. By the 1880s the provinces established in Dagestan and parts of the Caspian from north to south were: Temir-Khan Shura, Khunsakh, Gunib, Levashi, Kumukh, Majalis, Kasumkent, Akhty, Baku Province, Kuba and Shemakha.[193]

The main indigenous groups referred to by the travellers, irrespective of accuracy, were the Avars and Lezgins (the latter widely used to designate Dagestanis in general), often intermingled with others, which must have been confusing. The Avars were one of the largest Caucasian ethnic groups found traditionally from the west central area of Dagestan to the north-east. Mixed with these were the Lak or Qazikumuk, the Dargins and mountain Jews in the north. Tatars were local coastal Turkic people from present-day Azerbaijan. The Lezgins were predominantly a strongly clan-based southern group, but could be mixed or subdivided depending on location. Only Ussher and Abercromby differentiate more carefully between groups, mentioning the Lak, Qazikumuk, Udi, Tats and others. Most travellers would not have been aware of ethnic histories of the ex-khanates, now districts (*okrug*), they were passing through and of the past administrative and population changes imposed on them nor of their boundaries. Thus areas and indigenous distinctions were sometimes blurred: for example, Ussher put Gunib in Chechnya and called Lezgins Circassians.[194] Most used the general term 'Lesghian' or 'Lesgees' for the inhabitants.

Avars

Ussher writes that the Avars were an offshoot of the Huns in their westward migration. Modern scientific research has shown the Avars to be descended from east central Asians migrating to the Carpathians.[195] The linguist Abercromby devotes time to the Avars and places them in the historical context of other linguistic groups and dialects (see below) and does show a marked interest in local physiognomy. He was influenced by Roderich von Erckert's *Der Kaukasus und seine Völker* (1888), which he recommends. At Gumuk, near Gunib, Abercromby observed that the Avars were no different from other 'Lesghians': they had pallid complexions and children's hair was dyed bright red with henna, men had shaved heads, low receding foreheads, were sometimes unbearded or only moustached or whiskered. The faces were not uniform, yet they were dressed the same with the same sheepskin hats or *papaks*.[196] This attest to the mixed population of this region, inhabited by Lak and others, as noted above.

One of Abercromby's informants regarding the 'customs' of the Avars was a Cossack Avar, who had married an Avar woman for a very low price, bringing him property (as Avar women were allowed to inherit property and money).[197] Homicides, with feuds and blood money (the latter paid to the government) appeared to be frequent here: thus demonstrating a mixture of supposedly forbidden *adat* (customary law) and Russian sanction. The Avars still practised trepanning at Botlikh as a 'remedy for pains in the head' and in 'folk tradition' to allow the 'evil Being in the head' to egress with permission from the authorities.[198]

Ussher first mentions the Avars as he entered from the north via Grozny, Gunib, Kutaici, Shura and Baku en route to Persia. He enters their 'territory' at Gengutai, within site of the Caspian in the distance.[199] Here he mentions the comfortable 'fortified' house of Reshid Khan, decorated with horse trappings, arms, Persian 'embroidered' carpets, a German silver teapot and willow pattern dishes. The Khan was the brother of the Khan of the Avars and a lieutenant of the guards. He was Russified but not wholly trusted: he had a guard of one hundred Russian soldiers to both guard and keep check on him.[200] People were slowly returning to the village, which had suffered during the Shamil wars and which used to have a thousand houses, the Khan said.

Similarly Abercromby, on his way to Botlikh, stopped at Khunsakh at the 'comfortable' house of the local governor, whose lodgings were hung with Turcoman carpets from Merv and who told him of the 'customs' of the Avars.[201] At the village Kharaki he met the St Petersburg-educated local naib, Abd el Mejid, living in a house furnished in the European style on a pension of six hundred roubles per annum (£60).[202] Such educated local officers could be in charge of a sub-district, but the governors or *nachalniks* were always Russian. Native houses were quite different, and not all was comfort. In the Avari district, commanded by General Prince Chavchavadze, Cunynghame came across one of the 'most curious' villages - Inkulluk on the River Oor - he had ever seen, inhabited by 'strange people'. It was partially built in caverns in the rock with underground streets and houses.[203]

Forts were a new feature of the landscape here, and the well escorted military man Cunynghame describes a new fort being built at Kunsakh. The fort was being especially adapted to the mountains; it had good flank defences and could be easily defended by a comparatively small force. It could accommodate forty pieces of canon, it had comfortable headquarters for officers and men,

Ethnography

'On River Oor, Inkulluk'

a church was in preparation, yet it had not enough ditches, he concluded. The greatest drawback in the region was the lack of timber.[204]

Most who travelled here post-Shamil (an Avar) were fascinated by his character and exploits. Western newspapers at the time had already been full of the story, but these travellers put Shamil and his 'final stand' at Gunib on the western tourist map. It would also be a publishers' selling point. For the locals Shamil was a legend even before his death, and people treasured laments, stories and mementoes from those times (see Antiquities).

Ussher went to Gunib despite being advised not to. No native was to be allowed to live at Gunib and a fort was to be built, a Russian captain informed Ussher.[205] Gunib induced hyperbolic language: 'it was the scene of the last struggle against the detested invader with dauntless courage'.[206] Ussher gives details of Shamil's defences and observation walls, of the small house where he surrendered to Baryatinsky and where a commemorative pillar was erected. Shamil's house was now lived in by a Russian captain.[207] A Polish guide recounted the details of Shamil's story. This gave Ussher the opportunity to indulge in further sensationalism and tell the story of Hadji Murat, an Avar rebel commander (1818-c.1852), who had a career of defection and counter defection between his own people and the Russians.[208] He was ambushed by the Russians and his head cut off by an Avar. The head was sent first to Tiflis then to the *kunstkamera* in St Petersburg. His story was made famous by the Tolstoy novella *Hadji Murat* (1912). It was also an opportunity for Ussher to retell the story of the captured princesses (see Part 1).[209] At Khunsakh, north of Gunib, rebuilding itself after being ravaged by the war, Ussher heard further tales of Shamil, and describes the stone house of the 'handsome' Russified Khan. He notes the curious combination of eastern and western architecture in the Khan's new house 'among the devastation' of war: there was mahogany furniture, prints and photographs, multiple Shamil trophies, a 'gaudily coloured' carpet, while niches and shelves were well stocked with quilted cotton coverlets (local bedding custom). This gives an insight into the hybrid lives and aspirations of this new co-opted class.[210]

Cunynghame, touring in 1871, by which time Shamil had already died, also wrote in strong terms about the 'situation' of Gunib and the 'excessively fanatic' but 'energetic and decisive' Shamil.[211] Cunynghame reminds his readers of a fine picture of the assault on Gunib by Growsinski exhibited in London.[212] He had met Shamil's son Ghazi Mahomet effendi in Constantinople, where he received a pension from the Russian government, while his second son served in the Imperial army.[213]

'Tartar House, Chok'

Abercromby also visited Gunib but only devotes a few sentences to the capture of Shamil,[214] preferring to observe the geomorphology of the area and its antiquities. He notes that in the area some villages did not understand each other's languages. For example, at Atsi complaints had to be translated into Avar, then into Lak or Tatar and finally Arabic or Russian. Arabic was widely spoken in Dagestan and judicial decrees were recorded in it.[215]

Lezgins

The hunter Phillipps-Wolley (1880), as in Svaneti, went off the beaten track for the sake of his 'sport' and indulged in storytelling. Beyond Gerdaoul, reaching the mountainous 'lords of Daghestan', they passed a Tatar village famous for its silk, with fine orchards, magnificent walnut trees and endless rows of mulberry trees. Here the houses were like chalets, the lower half made of mud and stone, and the top of beam and wattle covered by a wooden or thatched roof. The women 'drew up their white wrappings' as they drove through the main street and 'scuttled away'.[216] Another village (Lezgin) came into sight but they were immediately cursed at when they asked for food. Here they found an uninviting *duchan* (inn), where, driven by hunger, they stopped. When seated a host of 'the worst looking scoundrels', with the owner 'of shifty eyes and high cheek-bones', 'looking like an illustration of Chinese hell', surged around them, breaking down the wooden walls of the house, spitting and gesticulating. Things escalated but then a messenger arrived from the village elder telling them that on no account should they spend the night there: the people were beyond his control and might well slit their throats. They left into the night, careful to keep their guns close at hand. A tiny hamlet 'in the deepest recesses' of 'a shadowy ravine' then appeared, where they were greeted by clamorous dogs and a swarthy faced man who ushered them into a one-room cottage. This belonged to a Lezgin Tartar shepherd. Cushions and carpets were brought out and the 'hospitable fellows' served them chicken and rice amidst few other signs of civilization. The men were rough and tanned, their clothes ragged, and all were armed to the teeth: *kinjals* were never laid down. But their eyes were broad and friendly, looking the stranger steadily in the face. The children who came in to look at them were sturdy and handsome. The women, including two very pretty faces, retired to an outhouse and stayed there during the whole of their stay. As a final seal of approval there were 'no insect gymnastics', in other words their hosts were clean.[217]

The episode, and his use of Lezgin guides to look for game in the mountains, allowed Phillipps-Wolley to romanticize for the sake of his readers: Lezgins 'lead a happy life… a simple one' amid magnificent mountain scenery. The mountains 'give them all they want: water, wood, game, fuel'. The Lezgins of today (those that remain, he stresses) were an honest race of sturdy mountain folk, who have little love for Russia, and 'concern themselves in no way with the outside world'. Their following of Shamil had been due to superstition and isolation, he reasoned.[218]

Arriving from Tiflis and the south-east with his guide Mejid, en route to Nukha, Abercromby had his first 'sighting' of people he ascertained to be Lezgins at the posting station of Bielokani near Zakatali. He notes that their faces were rounder and paler than those of Georgians, and they wore *papaks* (woollen hats, see Appendix).[219] He describes the village houses, made of stone, two storeys high with wooden verandas, with domestic animals below and the family above (having to pass through the filth below, but only entering the living quarters in bare or 'stockinged' feet). He encounters shepherds by the village of Shin, whose only protection was their *burkas*, *kinjals* (daggers) and a few native flint guns and long thin sticks.[220]

Other groups: Tatars, Kurds, Jews, Armenians

Tatar was the common language of some Dagestanis. Tatars were to be found miscellaneously and living mixed with other communities (see Derbend below) but also at Richa on the way from Akhti to Gumuk and Nukha in the Elizavetpol district.[221] They also allegedly operated as highwaymen in remote areas, where the Lezgins never left home unarmed.[222]

Kurds are mentioned by Cunynghame as 'a rude people', nomadic shepherds moving close to the mountains on the Turkish frontier (from Alexandropol) in summer to pasture their sheep, while in winter migrating to the foot of Mount Ararat.[223]

The mountain Jews of Dagestan were widely distributed, although there was a concentration of them in Derbent. They were also to be found at Tarki, Majalis, Aksay and other places in Tabarasan.[224]

Arriving at the Armenian mountain village of Gerdaoul in Dagestan (from the west), Phillipps-Wolley, finding himself surrounded by haystacks 'like white sugar cones' perched on wooden scaffolds to save them from marauding buffaloes, saw that it was well-off and thriving. The Armenians were good colonists and very hospitable, 'almost as good as the Germans', but detested by others and speaking only Tatar. The village was known for making carpets, sold as second-hand Persian ones in Tiflis or as Armenian in Shusha or Shemakha. A large wool-work frame was before every door, and beside the door frames he noted a covered bird trap painted in brilliant daubs of colour that was used as a shield by hunters so that 'the bird never sees the hunter'. Large 'ant-hills' stood around the village; they were wine cellars for huge jars of native wine.[225]

The Caspian

Four travellers came to this region (Ussher and Phillipps-Wolley from inland, Cunynghame and Abercromby from Astrachan). The areas such as Quba, Tarki and Baku were historic khanates which had been incorporated and transformed into Russian provinces, with parts of Baku province subdivided into smaller administrative districts and the Tarki *shamkalate* abolished in 1867.[226]

Again, the travellers' experiences were in the hands of the governor, General Prince Melikoff, and his staff,[227] unless they were willing to go off-piste like Phillipps-Wolley and Abercromby.

While visiting Shura, Derbent, Baku and places in between and back to Schamachi Ussher showed no interest in ethnography. There seems to have been a distinct desire from Ussher and Cunynghame to stress the difference between the comfortable lodgings and education of the local governors and Europeans living there and those of the Asiatic others.

Ussher describes Shura, or Temir-Khan-Shura, considered the entrance to Dagestan from the west, as a large town (c.6,000 inhabitants), built in the style of a frontier fortification (square with a deep ditch topped with thorny brushwood). The houses were stone, with well laid out streets but ankle deep in mud. An entire regiment was based here, with well-built barracks, a handsome governor's house, pleasure grounds tastefully laid out with trees, shrubs and flowers. Here they saw ladies in European costume. Ussher says nothing of the mixed population, except that most of the town had gone to a celebration in Gunib and that it was difficult to tell the Tatar Mohammedans in the regiment who were dressed in the Russian uniform from the Christians.[228] In fact a multitude of different nationalities lived in Shura.[229]

Cunynghame mentions Shura, but did not visit it, rather staying at Petrovslk Fort on the coast. This was an 'improving' town, with prosperous bazaars and a good bathing establishment.[230] Keen to get to Gunib, Cunynghame had no time to visit Derbent or Baku.

Derbend (now Derbent), writes Ussher, was rarely visited by strangers, although he mentions Dumas' account.[231] He briefly describes the town and citadel in the form of a parallelogram of three miles by one mile, and the citadel half a mile and its famous wall, which around the town was in good repair, their antiquity, the unprotected harbour, a small and shallow port and a large but uncomfortable post-house. In the centre was a church or cathedral and a mosque. Streets were narrow and dirty, some also being built. The flat roofs gave an 'oriental' aspect to the whole, a unique and almost 'Middle Age' appearance. The bazaar was by the waterside where 'natives' came from surrounding districts to sell their cattle, horse and sheep. This the only mention of the indigenous people. The citadel, Ussher believed, was in much the same state as it was when taken from the Persians (with the same guns in some instances).[232] Other objects of curiosity around the town were sites where Peter the Great had quartered. He also mentions a certain Michelevsky, in exile from St Petersburg for having written anti-government pamphlets and having corresponded with Herzen, the editor of *Kolokol*, a newspaper 'professing more advanced principles than are tasteful to the Russian cabinet'.[233]

Ussher concentrates on his time with General Melikoff (later killed by mountain people) the brother of Prince Melikoff, the Governor of Dagestan, Armenian by birth, who had fought at Kars and wanted to talk about General Williams and Colonel Lake.[234] He had a handsomely furnished drawing room and a grand rosewood piano sent from St Petersburg via the Volga and the Caspian. The general also talked much of the 'numerous languages' spoken among the mountain communities and of the European words found amongst them.[235] Either informed through his Armenian host or from his own opinion, Ussher writes that the 'natives' were unwilling to accept any Christian ancestry.[236]

At Baku Ussher mentions a 'manufactory' lately established by Germans for naphtha extraction with machinery from Manchester. He also visits the local attraction, the 'renovated' but very poor Indian fire temple, with only two old Indian men in attendance.[237] There was 'nothing to attract the visitor' here, Ussher writes.[238] But Baku was not yet the boom town it was to become. By 1883, when visited by Charles Marvin (see Part 1, Batum), the Nobel brothers were revolutionizing the oil industry on the ground (installing pipelines, refineries, oil-well 'fountains') and developing the town itself. British involvement in the oil industry was to come from the later 1880s-1890s at first with Russian concessionaries and the likes of the entrepreneur and mining engineer Leslie Urquhart from the early 1900s.[239] At Quba, Ussher meets a Mr Kotzbue, an entrepreneur (surrounded by comforts) specializing in rose madder pigment.[240]

Discussing the variety of settlers in the region, Phillipps-Wolley mentions exiled Molochans (heretic, 'vegetarians' or 'milk-drinkers') and the eunuch sect (Skoptsi) at Tchaillee (all spelling on maps being different, 'crack-jaw' and unpronounceable) in the vicinity of Lenkoran. There were also 'half-naked' Tatars celebrating Bairam in 'a wilder scene than the witches' meeting' in *Macbeth*.[241] Having found basic comfort at Lenkoran (the one roomed 'club', a fair bazaar, few Europeans) and a Mr Muller's offer of a hunting hut ('shabby-shanty') he set to hunting wild boar.

Abercromby took Derbent, its people and antiquities seriously.[242] He mentions the mixed population (Russian, Turks i.e. local Tatars, Armenians and Jews), with the former limited to the garrison. The current language was Tatar. The Tatars, he writes, looked more like Tats or Persians, they all shaved their heads except for a patch above each ear. They were Shiites - but not according to his guide Mejid, who said they were Sunni - who celebrated the feast of Hosein. They were now very poor as the market for madder manufacturing had dropped, and the richest community were the Jews and some Armenians.

Leaving the 'wide streeted' European part of the city (attesting to the development of the place since Ussher's day), he passed through the 'squalid' Jewish quarter, with an unimposing synagogue. They dressed much like 'natives' except for having no *kinjal* and a twisted lock of hair. He proceeded to the Tatar quarter (rough, narrow, irregular streets) to his guide's drapery shop. This was an elderly Bey, educated, who informed him on the ancient walls of the town. Hawking was a regular practice here.[243]

Mixed communities

Other specific groups noted by Abercromby were the Tats, defined by him as Persians, around Derbent. The Tats of the Caucasus were of Iranian origin, speaking their own Iranian dialect and were concentrated in Tabarasan (the Azerbaijani coastal area), originating from Fars according to the nineteenth-century Abbas Qoli Aqa Bakikhanov's *Golestan-e-Eram*.[244] On walking around the wall Abercromby came across a Tat village (Metegi, with a Tatar Beg who had served in the Russia army), where Tats were called locally 'unfree people' because they were under the authority of Begs, whereas the 'Lesghians' in Tabarasan considered themselves 'free' people.[245] Tats to the east of Derbent all spoke Tatar (Azerbaijani Turkish) as well. Areas where Tat was still spoken in parts of Azerbaijan were in the process of becoming wholly Tatarized.[246]

On the way inland to Kubaichi (Kubachi) Abercromby came to the village of Majalis, inhabited in its lower part by a one hundred Jewish families, the rest being Tatars. At Kubachi, where he arrived to witness the *kurban bayram* festival, the white haired local elder-headman (*juzbashi*), confirmed that the people of Kubachi spoke their own dialect and were descended from the Franks.[247] This did not convince Abercromby, who noted that the people had nothing European about them, except that they seemed mild mannered and were less 'wild looking' than other Lezgins, and the women had uncovered faces.[248] The same Kubachi dialect was spoken in neighbouring villages.[249] Kubachi was of particular interest to Abercromby because of its ancient metal-work (see Part 4). Its modern metal manufacture was in decline. Other industries he mentioned were a strong textured cloth (?) and felt made by women. He questions the Kubachi custom, known from Arab writers, of putting the bones of the deceased in a sack and allowing the flesh to be eaten by birds. He rightly thought it was a Zoroastrian custom brought over when families from Khorasan settled in Kaitakh and Kubachi.[250]

The scholar-linguist goes into detail

Abercromby's essential interest, apart from antiquarianism, was comparative linguistics. He demonstrated this by his research, correspondence and reading from the 1840s onwards[251] as well as in his travel book on the eastern Caucasus. The book is not only peppered with linguistics comments on vocabulary and possible origins, pronunciation, differences between one region and another, native terms for villages[252] but he also devotes a whole chapter (X) to the grammatical structure and affinities of the Caucasian languages. He isolates them into the 'seven best known tongues' (Ud, Kurin, Hurkan, Kasikumuk, Avar, Chechents/Chechen and Tush). He also lists some of his scholarly sources, such as several volumes from the *Mémoires de l'Académie Imperiale des Sciences de St. Petersburg* (Series VI-VII) and studies by Anton Schiefner on Tush (1851), Ud (1863), Chechen (1864); Peter von Uslar on Kasikumuk (1866), Hurkan (1871), Avar (1872) and Kurin (1873). He provides a map showing the main groupings and distribution, and places the languages starting from Ud in the south-east to Tush in the north-west. The Ud language, then spoken in two small southern villages on the south side of the great Caucasus range, was nearly extinct, as the people 'were almost entirely Tatarized or Georgianized'. He also lists the dialectic subdivisions of the Hurkan or Dargo group (north and south of Kubaichi, such as Aqusha, Kaitakh, Urqun?) and notes the influence of Tush vocabulary on Georgian.[253] He then proceeds to compare in detail the vowels, consonants, grammatical cases, adjectives, numerals, pronouns, verbs, moods and tenses of the various groups, pointing out similarities and differences in tables and charts. He then analyses syntax, indigenous expressions and comparative vocabulary, giving parallels with Tatar, Persian, Armenian, Finnish, Georgian and Mongol. The section on comparative expressions would have been, and still is, particularly interesting to folk ethnographers. He points out what still needs to be done (such as laws regarding the sounds between language groups) and speculates on historical development.[254] He ends the chapter with his deductions. First, he looks at languages that he considers were originally unintelligible to each other yet also show similarities in systems (e.g. between Chechen and Tush and Hurkan as a separate group), languages were not the result of foreign influences but descended from a common stock. Even Ud could not be ejected from the east Caucasian family, he argues. The central question, therefore, for Abercromby (and others involved in this field at this time) was whether these 'peoples' entered from the north or the south. He concludes, on the basis of correspondences with Armenian (an Ud language) and Median (Lezgin, Tush and Tatar groups) that 'the primitive inhabitants of the eastern half of the Caucasus came from the south-east' and spread over the Kur and Araxes. The Turkic languages of the area (Kumyk, Azerbaijani Tatar, Nogay, Balkar, Karachay) were no of interest to Abercromby as they were introduced in historical periods.[255]

Debates about Caucasian linguistics, which are thought to be divided into three main groups, are ongoing today. The three groups are the North-Western group (Abhaz-Adyghian) with speculations about its Indo-European origin; the North-Eastern group (Nakho and Dagestani); and the South Caucasian group (Kartvlian or Iberian, Georgian Mingrelian, and Laz), possibly of a single language. The consensus seems to be that they did descend from a single proto-language because of their correspondences. Svan, with four dialects, remains a separate language, differing from the others in its more archaic vocabulary and possibly separated early on. Of all these only Georgian (and Armenian) had an ancient literary tradition whereas the others stayed oral.[256]

The scholar goes public

On his return to Edinburgh Abercromby gave a public lecture, possibly to promote his book, which simplified much of his research and presented the Caucasian peoples as much more of a unit than they were and had been thought of, while indulging in known tropes regarding men, women and Circassians.[257]

He briefly mentions the number of dialects spoken in the area (30-40 from five or six stocks, not naming them) and concentrated on four of the greater groups: the Georgians, the Circassians, the Avars and the Ossets. He was also perhaps the first in Scotland to show his audience the mass produced, cardboard ethnographic 'calling cards' which he had bought in Tbilisi showing Caucasian 'types' (see Part 6 and Appendix), which were printed in his book (and this one).

He starts with physical appearance, stressing the difference in physical type between the first three groups (Georgians, Circassians and Avars) who were tall, slight, sometimes fair, usually dark, whose women had regular features, beauties if wealthy, but lacking animation, while poor women were like hags) and the Ossets, who were short, thick-set and dark-haired. They spoke a language different to any in Europe or the world, but one allied to Persian and thus having attracted notice in Europe. He continues with dress: the Circassians were 'the swells of the Caucasus', but with some 'cut-throat' looks; the Georgians and Avars were fine and gallant, but in the mountains were maimed through blood-feud fights with spiked iron rings. He continues to follow 'the various stages of life' of the 'Caucasians' from infancy through marriage to the grave. For example, the Circassian infant was bathed in cold water as soon as it was born, and the Georgians had the habit of binding babies' heads and keeping them tight in their cradles. For men, he stresses their martial education, for working women their subjugation and 'humiliating' position. In the mountains, he asserted, they give birth in a hut away from the family home. He mentions widespread hospitality but notably among Circassians, where it was almost a duty. He asserts that despite being nominally Christian or Muslim, traces of 'old paganism' remain (sacred groves etc.) as did old superstitions. Regarding funeral customs he tells of the long defunct practice of setting up the corpse outside on a scaffold for seven days, surrounded by relatives, while gifts were presented to it, before it was placed in hollowed tree trunk and buried under a mound. For Georgians the dead person (in the case of a male) was dressed and washed, accoutred with his best weapons, with professional and other mourners wailing and lamenting over the body for four days, then transporting it to the family cemetery, where it was buried with modest gifts, followed by horse racing.

No doubt discussions followed this talk, which was clearly meant to entertain, but which lacked facts and nuances.

It is also clear from the above section that the majority of travellers followed basic norms of the day, based on precedents and the requirements of the publishing trade, when discussing the 'customs' of the regions they travelled in (such as comments on law, religion, marriage etc). They had neither the language, the means nor the interest (except for Abercromby) to enquire further into customs they generally thought primitive, antiquated and on the way to extinction.

1 Jersild 2002, 72; Gutmeyer 2017, 137
2 Jersild 2002, 75
3 Jersild 2002, 75
4 Jersil 2002, 84
5 Jersild 2002, 79
6 Herder (1744-1803) was a German philosopher who fostered the notion that language and education were linked to family and tribal identity.
7 Jersild 2002, 80
8 Dettmering 2014, 356
9 Jersild 2002, 82
10 Jersild 2002, 84
11 Jersild 2002, 82
12 Jersild 2002, 83
13 Dettmering 2014, 357
14 Kemper 2005 147-174; Jersild 2002, 90-99; Dettmering 2014, 342
15 Jersild 2002, 97
16 Tsiutsev 2014, 28, 32 , Map 11
17 Jersild 2002, 106-107
18 Elfimov 2014, 70; idem 2017, 149ff.
19 Radde 1878 *Die Chevsuren und Ihr Land*…Cassel
20 Radde 1885, 27-35
21 Radde 1885, 36-43
22 Radde 1912, Pl.25
23 Radde 1912, Pl.24
24 Radde 1912, Pl.26
25 Radde 1912, Pl.27
26 Radde 1912, Pl. 28
27 Radde 1912, Pl.29
28 Radde 1912, Pl. 30
29 Jersild 2006, 9-11
30 Radde 1902, Pl.18
31 Cvetkovski 2014, 216
32 Freshfield 1869, vi
33 Chardin, *The Travels of Sir John Chardin into Persia*, 1686, London; P.S. Pallas *Reise durch verschiedene Provinzen des Russischen Reichs*, St. Petersburg 1771-1776 (translated into French 1788-1789) and *Travels through the Southern Provinces of the Russian Empire, in the years 1793-94*, London 1812; J.H. Klaproth *Tableau Historique, geographique, ethnographique et politique du Caucase*, Paris 1827 and Dr J. A. Guldenstadts *Bescheribung der Kaukasischen Lander*, Berlin 1834; Chevalier de Marigny *Three Voyages in the Black Sea to the Coast of Circassia*, London 1837
34 Spencer 1837,351-354; E.D. Clarke, *Travels in Russia, Tartary, and Turkey*, Aberdeen 1810, 1848
35 Spencer 1837, 2, 8, 351, 421
36 Spencer 1837, 99-102, 220-226
37 Spencer 1837, 1, 136-139
38 Spencer 1837, 1, 95-98, 128-129
39 Spencer 1837, 1, 261-263
40 Spencer 1837, 1, 396-398
41 Jaimouka 2009, list of deities 6

Ethnography

42 Bell 1840, 1, 189-192, 2,271ff.; Longworth 1840,2, 79-80
43 Bell 1840, 1, 284
44 Longworth 1840, 2, 206-207
45 Jaimouka 2009, 47
46 Jaimoukha 2009, 5
47 Bell 1840, 2, 246
48 Bell 1840, 1, 193, 202-203,220; Longworth 1840, 233, 229-240
49 Manning 2009, online, Just like England: On the Liberal Institutions of the Circassians. *Comparative Studies in Society and History*, 51(3), 590-618. doi:10.1017/S0010417509000243
50 Longworth 1840, 1, 229
51 Manning 2009, 30-31
52 Jaimoukha 2009, 20
53 Longworth 1840, 1, 233-234
54 Longworth 1840, 1, 231, 239; Manning 2009, 32-33
55 Manning 2009, 32, quoting Longworth
56 Manning 2009, 41-43
57 Longworth 1840, 1, 238
58 Longworth 1840, 2, 49-52; Bell 1840 1, 304-5
59 Longworth 1840, 1, 236
60 Longworth 1840, 1, 242; Bell 1840, 1, 178, 193
61 Longworth 1, 234-235, 278-279, 282-285; Bell 1840, 2, 27-28, for closeted women.
62 Longworth 1840, 1, 279-80
63 Longworth 1840, 1, 279
64 Spencer 1837, 1, xxii, 347-355
65 Spencer 1838, Advertisement, i-viii;
66 Bell 1840, 2, Appendix XIV
67 Freshfield 1869, 195
68 Freshfield 1869, 217
69 Freshfield 1869, 205
70 Freshfield 1869, 213
71 The depiction of Khevsurs in traditional chainmail fighting gear became one standard images of ethnographic 'calling cards' (see Part 6): cf. Mamatsaschvili 2001, 14-14 (by the photographer Roinashvili)
72 Mamatishvili 2001, 14-15 (a series of photographs by Roinashvili, see Part 6).
73 Freshfield 1869, 217-218
74 Freshfield 1869, 226
75 Freshfield 1869, 215-216
76 Telfer 1876, 1, ix; 2 23, note 1
77 Telfer 1876, 1, 292-297
78 Telfer 1876, 2, 23
79 Telfer 1876,1, 275; 2, 2, 7
80 Telfer 1876,2, 4-7
81 Telfer 1876, 1, 279
82 Telfer 1876, 1, 276-278
83 Telfer 1876, 2, 20
84 Telfer 1876 ,1, 276-278; Pushkin Sotchynenya Poushkina 5, 63; Lermontov, Hero of our Time , first Russian ed. 1840

85 Telfer 1876, 2, 20-23
86 Telfer 1876, 2, 276
87 Telfer 1876, 2, 20-22
88 Telfer 1876, 2, 7
89 Telfer 1876, 2, 9 note 1
90 Telfer 1876, 1, 274
91 Radde 1878, 96-98
92 Zisserman 1879, ed. 2017, 162-163
93 Telfer 1876, 1, 274
94 Telfer 1876, 2, 9
95 Lyall 1825, 1, 463
96 Kerr-Porter 1821, Pl.3
97 Lyall 1825, 1, 469
98 Poulett-Cameron 1845, 141-144
99 Poulett-Cameron 1845, 153-154
100 Ussher 1865, 110
101 Telfer 1876, 1, note 1
102 Ussher 1865, 111
103 Cunynghame 1872, 238-239
104 Cunynghame 1872, 244
105 Cunynghame 1872, 247
106 Telfer 1876, 1, 290-291
107 Telfer 1876, 2, 12-14
108 Telfer 1876, 1, 291-298
109 Bryce 1877, 83
110 Bryce 1877, 68-69
111 Bryce 1877, 73-74
112 Wardrop 1888, 68
113 Abercromby 1889, 77, 122
114 Abercromby 1889, 127
115 Abercromby 1889, 124
116 From Abercromby 1889 ix: *beshmet*: a close fitting garment with an upright collar, terminating in a long skirt reaching the knee or further down; *cherkaska*: collarless garment of stronger stuff than *beshmets*, fastened at the waist and with diagonal pouches across each breast for cartridges
117 Abercromby 1889, 123-129
118 Abercromby 1889, 123
119 Abercromby 1889, 150
120 Abercromby 1889, 132-134
121 Freshfield 1869, 224
122 Freshfield 1869, 215
123 Freshfield 1869, 295
124 Freshfield 1869, 299
125 Freshfield 1869, 350
126 Freshfield 1869, 271
127 Freshfield 1869, 298
128 Freshfield 1869, 301
129 Freshfield 1869, 304-306
130 Freshfield 1869, 308
131 Freshfield 1869, 347

Ethnography

132 Freshfield 1869, 292-293
133 Freshfield 1869, 333
134 Freshfield 1869, 335
135 Freshfield 1869, 355
136 Freshfield 1869, 355-357
137 Freshfield 1869, 397
138 Freshfield 1869, 407
139 Freshfield 1869, 407
140 Freshfield 1869, 407
141 Freshfield 1869, 432
142 Freshfield 1869, 423
143 Freshfield 1869, 424
144 Grove 1875, 30
145 Grove 1875, 44
146 Grove 1875, 60-61
147 Grove 1875, 66-67
148 Grove 1875, 88, 119
149 Grove 1875, 70-72
150 Grove 1875, 84-75
151 Grove 1875, 107
152 Grove 1875, 125-141
153 Grove 1875, 148
154 Grove 1875, 156-161
155 Grove 1875, 199
156 Grove 1875, 289-293
157 Grove 1875, 301,304,306,313
158 Grove 1875, 256
159 Grove 1875, 194-196
160 Grove 1875, 251
161 Telfer 1876, 2, 38-39
162 Telfer 1876, 2,112
163 Telfer 1876, 2, 48-49
164 Telfer 1876, 119
165 Telfer 1976, 2, 66
166 Telfer 1876,2, 262-267
167 Telfer 1786, 2, 85-86
168 Telfer 1876, 2, 121
169 Telfer 1876,2, 74-75, 83-84
170 Telfer 1876,2, 83, 86, 94
171 Telfer 1876,2, 100
172 Telfer 1876,2, 90-92, 96
173 Phillipps-Wolley 1883, 2, 9-11
174 Phillipps-Wolley 1883, 1, 162-163
175 Phillipps-Wolley 1883, 1, 259
176 Phillipps-Wolley 1883, 2, 90, 117
177 Phillipps-Wolley 1883, 2, 15-16
178 Phillipps-Wolley 1883, 2, 79
179 Phillipps-Wolley 1883, 2, 73
180 Phillipps-Wolley 1883, 2, 80
181 Phillipps-Wolley 1883, 2, 24

182 Phillipps-Wolley 1883, 2, 97
183 Phillipps-Wolley 1883, 2, 93
184 Phillipps-Wolley 1883, 2, 136
185 Phillipps-Wolley 1883, 2, 140-142
186 Phillipps-Wolley 1883, 2, 139
187 Rayfield 2019, 282, 297-298
188 Phillipps-Wolley 1883, 2, 171-173
189 Freshfield 1896,1, 251-253
190 Freshfield 1896, 1, 236
191 Freshfield 1896,1, 235, 244
192 Freshfield 1896,1, 258
193 Tsiutsev 2014, Map 14
194 Ussher 1865, 131, 134
195 Online Max Planck Gesellschaft, April 1/2022
196 Abercromby 1889, 75, 85
197 Abercromby 1889, 97
198 Abercromby 1889, 114
199 Ussher 1865, 181
200 Ussher 1865, 149
201 Abercromby 1889, 95
202 Abercromby 1889,101
203 Cunynghame 1872, 210-212
204 Cunynghame 1872,202, 206; other forts mentioned by Cunynghame were Klaradat, 203, Wedden 227; by Abercromby 1889, 113
205 Ussher 1865, 139-146
206 Ussher 1865,146
207 Ussher 1865, 175-176
208 Ussher 1865, 164; Such defections were not uncommon in the Caucasus wars; see Michael Khodarkovsky, *Bitter Choices*, Cornell University Press, 2011.
209 Ussher 1865, 169
210 Ussher 1865, 144-145, 150
211 Cunynghame 1872, 191-195
212 Cunynghame 1872, 194
213 Cunynghame 1872, 196
214 Abercromby 1889, 83ff.
215 Abercromby 1889,76-77
216 Phillipps-Wolley 1881, 214-215
217 Phillipps-Wolley 1881, 217-218, 223-224
218 Phillipps-Wolley 1881,219, 223, 224,228ff.
219 Abercromby 1889, 10,11
220 Abercromby 1889, 34
221 Abercromby 1889, 14, 64, 145, 180, 210
222 Phillipps-Wolley 1981, 236
223 Cunynghame 1872, 297
224 Information based on a Russian distribution source dating to 1870 *Sbornik Svededniy o kavkazskykh gortsakh*, Volume 3, from Tsiutsev 2014
225 Phillipps-Wolley 1981, 208, 212, 239
226 For the progression and changes in size of districts from the 1860s to the 1880s see Tsutsiev 2014 Maps 11-14 with references.

Ethnography

227 Ussher 1865, 186; Cunynghame 1872, 176
228 Ussher 1865, 185-187
229 1870 Sbornik Svededniy o kavkazskykh gortsakh, Volume 3, from Tsiutsev 2014
230 Cunynghame 1872,177
231 Ussher 1865, 195; Alexandre Dumas, Le Caucase Voyage d'Alexandre Dumas, Paris, 1959
232 Ussher 1865, 197
233 Ussher 1865, 195
234 Ussher 1865, 197
235 Ussher 1865,193-200
236 Ussher 1865, 198
237 Teissier 2011, for Dagestan and the Caspian during the 18th century
238 Ussher 1865, 213
239 Marvin ed. 1891 (describing a visit in 1883): 194-ff.; 246ff; on Ludwig Nobel 275ff. Marvin was an ardent champion of British involvement in the oil trade and the author of several pamphlets such as *Baku the Petrolia of Europe, the Coming Deluge of Petroleum and its bearing on British trade*) and alarmist about Russia's threat to British India (e.g. *The Russians at the Gates of Herat* 1885). For British involvement with concessionaries, see e.g. National Archives, Kew: TR FOW/COS/47 (Museum of Rural Life) re John Fowler of Leeds.
240 Ussher 1865, 203-204
241 Phillipps-Wolley 1981, 242-243, 252
242 Abercromby 1889,209-210
243 Abercromby 1889, 211
244 Ft. W. Floor, *The Heavenly Rose Garden: A History of Shirvan and Daghestan* 2008.
245 Abercromby 1889,232
246 Abercromby 1889, 210
247 Abercromby 1889, 258
248 Abercromby 1889, 262
249 Abercromby 1889, 263
250 Abercromby 1889, 292-293
251 Edinburgh University Archives, Abercromby Papers, Gen. 1841/7; 1841/21
252 Abercromby 1889, e.g. 263-264: the native word for Kubachi was Ughbugan/Ugbugh, whereas Hürkans used the word 'warwaku' for the village.
253 Abercromby 1889, 297-299
254 Abercromby 1889, 302, 336
255 Abercromby 1889, 371-372
256 Online Britannica.com, Caucasian languages
257 Edinburgh University Archives, Abercromby papers 1841/7/3

PART 4

Antiquarianism: 'A Wonderful Harvest'

The British travellers ranged over lands imbued with antiquity and peppered with visible cultures that went back to the Bronze Age, if not earlier. Some merely observed what they came across (another requirement of the travel genre), others engaged more fully, whether in attempting their own excavations (Bell, Longworth, Telfer), by collecting significant artefacts (Abercromby) or through actual field investigation (Abercromby and the Derbent wall). Bryce recognized that 'a wonderful harvest' was awaiting 'the archaeologist' in Transcaucasia.[1] The antiquities referred to by the travellers and discussed below are mainly physical archaeological ones, such as kurgans or burial mounds and dolmens, the Derbent wall and some exceptional medieval finds from Kubachi (Dagestan). The classical period is referred to, but archaeology is dealt with mostly by travellers who passed through Crimea. The medieval churches of Georgia mentioned by the travellers are not included here as they were touristic sites, and they are dealt with fully in Wardrop and in passing by others. They were (and still are) very much part of the Christian narrative intrinsic to Georgia's identity and were promoted in the Antiquarian section of the Tiflis Museum (see below).

The 'scientific' study of antiquities for this part of the Empire was another initiative taken from the 1860s onwards (together with geography, statistics etc.) for the charting and appropriation of the Caucasus. The Archaeological Commission, under the chairmanship of Adolf Berge, was set up in 1862 and published its findings in *Akty Kavakazkoi Arkheografischecskoi Kommissieu* and other journals. The emphasis was on (private) excavations, surveys and analyses of folk material. Jersild makes the point that having destroyed all the folk life of the Adygei this Russian 'scientific' experiment was already flawed, as well as making the present suspect.[2] Fitting the past into the destruction of the present had to be calibrated.

Civilized and Primitive

The Caucasus Museum's antiquarian collections and their arrangement give an idea not only of the fairly random state of antiquarianism in the region at the time but of its positioning within the idea of the development of civilization. One problem was lack of systematic knowledge: excavations were mostly conducted privately, with private funds, and often done in a spirit of *kudos* and competition, acquisitiveness and the desire to be noted and published. Chance finds without context were also made, for example, when digging roads. There was often ignorance of what was being discovered.

The Antiquities section in the Museum was in Rooms I-IV of the top floor. Immediately to the right of Room I was the numismatic section (2,593 pieces, classified by Academician Brosset of St Petersburg). Those acquired by the Museum were classified by Mr Iversen. Twelve other donors are listed, including the Persian Consul Makhmour-Khan. The full collection was only accessible with the Director's permission.

The next room concentrated on architecture, inscriptions, and ancient and modern decorations (Armenian tomb stones, mouldings of Georgian church decorations, a cuneiform inscription from near Lake Gokchai, an ancient Svanetian door). There were photographs of churches and monasteries, of their decoration, of ruins and of 'Mohammedan constructions' (not mentioned as mosques), with explanations arranged on two columns.

The material from excavations and artefacts found randomly were arranged geographically according to the watersheds of the four great waterways of the region: the Kur and the Araxes, the Rion and the Black Sea, the Kuban (including Anapa,

Panticapeum, some Terek), and the Terek up to Manitch in the north, including Trans-Caspia. Radde acknowledged that a lack of study of the finds meant that the finds could not be classified chronologically.[3]

Material from single collections were gathered in single cabinets such as no. 41 (by Mr. Bayern, Comte de Longeuil, M. Belensky). More is learnt about the donors than about the material, mostly qualified as 'objects'. Those that are described range, for example, from a Georgian jug with an inscription, to a stone hammer used by Shamil to make gunpowder, skulls, an enamelled vase with an Arabic inscription and Stone Age material donated from Germany. Notable are a silex tool (Neolithic flint) collection and bronzes from various parts of the Caucasus including Ossetia, and the jewel of this part of the collection: a Tauro-Scythian (i.e Scythian from Crimea first millennium BC) necklace of the third-fourth century given by the Grand Duke Michael. There may have been photographs of kurgans, but these are not referred to specifically. Objects on the ground range from a stone from Mtshkheta (an early capital of Iberia, containing some of the more important and venerated Christian monuments of Georgia) with a Jewish inscription, to a stone with a Roman inscription (Vespasian), also from Mtshkheta to various reliefs and capitals from churches. Photographs show Ani (the ex-capital of the Armenian Bagratid kingdom of the latter tenth and early eleventh centuries, known for its churches), church reliefs and sepulchral stones.[4]

The whole is reminiscent of a jumble of curiosities (evoking the cabinet of curiosities of old) rather than of a gallery of antiquities. A narrative does, however, emerge from the plethora of church photographs, mouldings and actual masonry. This was a Christian and Christianizing country, with a civilized classical past of which the Russians were the natural inheritors.[5] The Georgians (and Armenians) were part of Christian culture, but now subsumed under Russian Christian Orthodox nationalism.[6] Thus Georgian and Armenian church architecture was seen as antiquity rather than as living spaces where people still worshipped. What of the non-classical, historical past (with written sources) of the area? The

Arabic or Persian past, and vast Islamic heritage of Dagestan were completely ignored. What of the non-written prehistoric and other periods? Were they, except for the Scythians and Crimean offshoots (who were considered worthy predecessors), like the mountain peoples a type of curiosity stuck in limbo between civilizations? The Museum did nothing to dispel this idea. Would it have done so had it had more information? Any scholarly information given in the *Akhty* was not reflected in the Museum's displays. The contrast, both ethnographically and archaeologically, between the high-minded classical heritage with which Russia identified and its Christian present displayed in the Museum and rest of the material in the galleries could not be starker: it was civilization versus primitiveness and mixed breeding.

Kurgans

A feature of the landscape most frequently mentioned by the travellers are kurgans or burial mounds which were seen dotting the landscape in Circassia, the Kuban, the plains of the north and Dagestan. The travellers had very little points of reference for these.

Kurgans had a long history in the Caucasus, from the Chalcolithic period (c.4800 BC) to the end of the second millennium BC, belonging to different cultures in different areas, with regional over-crosses. For example, there was the Maikop culture (c.3400-1800) named after a royal kurgan in Maikop, from Taman down to towards the River Kura; the Kura-Araxes I-III (3600-2800/500) cultures in Transcaucasia; and to the far north, on wide Pontic-Caspian steppe, the Yamnaya culture (3300-2600). Kurgans were of various sizes - at Maikop up to eleven metres high with a diameter of 200 metres - often with multiple chambers, and widely re-used. The Kura-Araxes and Yamnaya cultures had both kurgans and flat or pit graves. Grave goods varied from extremely rich (Maikop) to more modest gifts (Azerba). In addition, there was the 'Dolmen culture' (3400-1250) with some affinities with Maikop, from Abkhazia to the Taman peninsula. This culture was characterized by large constructions made from dressed stones covered by a large flat roof slab and a circular, square or triangular opening, and in places irregular paving outside thought to be for ceremonial purposes.[7] The decoration of these dolmens evolved over time.[8]

Bell and Longworth mention one kurgan in the Kuban area, locally thought to be inhabited by a 'Jin' (or returned soul), but when excavated on the spot it yielded squirrel nests, a snake, bones and pieces of terracotta.[9] This reflects the cavalier, 'free-for all' attitude prevalent among archaeological circles, local officials (see below for private collections), locals and travellers towards such antiquities, essentially excavated for their grave goods. Bell also illustrates a massive (five metres high, with a covering stone nine by six metres) stone-slab tomb with a circular aperture (Dolmen culture, but with no apparent decoration) in the Pshat valley. 'Tradition is silent as to their origin,' he writes.[10]

Telfer, who had a genuine interest in antiquities (although concentrating on the classical period) mentions reading about the excavation in 1875 of three large tumuli called 'The Sisters' in

'Ancient Tomb in the Valley of Pshat'

the region of Anapa, which had yielded gold ornaments, some Iranian. He laments that the Archaeological Commission was not excavating the tumuli on the Circassian plain around Kerch and Sennya.[11] Other travellers observed kurgans when passing. Ussher mentions groups of conical mounds some with stone figures in Kabarda after Vladivostok,[12] and other niche-shaped single or grouped mounds in lofty positions in the vicinity of Gunib[13] and 'everywhere in the Caucasus', while Bryce notes 'steppe' tumuli or kurgans with wooden idols,[14] which he presumes to be ancient and similar to Scythian ones related by Greek writers.[15] Stone anthropomorphic stelae of various sizes were memorials to the dead characteristic of the steppe in Mongolia, parts of Russia and Ukraine, as well as Crimea and Turkey. They belonged to several cultures and dated from the late fourth-early third millennium up to the early Middle Ages and possibly beyond.[16]

In and around Crimea and in Ukraine were extremely rich remains of the Graeco-Scythian culture (fifth-third/second centuries BC) not directly encountered by the travellers except in the Museum.[17]

Private collections (ranging from simple to significant) were often found either belonging to native officials or local governors. Abercromby describes the private 'curiosities' of Count Ivanoff (the Deputy Governor of Dagestan) near Khunsakh, some of which came from a kurgan in Dido country and consisted of 'small bronze figures of men and animals'. The count also had miscellaneous articles such as green-glazed chargers and samples of Avar cigarette and card cases (adorned with circles and lines of zinc thread).[18] The collection of Colonel Chilaeff (the local governor at Khotoch and Gunib) was also said to come from various kurgans north of the Terek (although some of the pieces seem incompatible with the usual grave goods) brought to him by locals as he was known to be a collector. The main artefacts included four large globular, bronze cauldrons (c.1 metre high) with figures in relief of men on horseback, wearing pointed hats (known as Phrygian hats) and carrying banners. The horsemen wore striped trousers, long pointed boots, with the ends of the pointed cap hanging down. Their hair was tied in a pigtail. Abercromby compares them to a specimen in the Historical Museum in Moscow but has no idea of the date. There is no illustration, but this may well have been an example of nomadic steppe art attested from the third century BC in areas from west Central Asia or more likely the Lower Volga, given its proximity to Dagestan, where the piece actually ended up.[19] Other artefacts were about forty objects of bronze (ewers, jugs, mugs etc.), glazed earthenware dishes decorated with flowers and monsters (not from kurgans, probably of later Iranian manufacture). The collection of Prince Maikoff (Governor of the district of Derbent) was equally mixed: two basins (again supposedly from kurgans), a Dutch metal dish and a Roman head found in the area, as well as Persian pottery, and as a reminder of Shamil, a banner taken from him as well as pieces of coats of mail.[20] It seems that it was known that material coming from kurgans was considered valuable, so it appears that often included in what excavators and purchasers tried to sell (deliberately or through ignorance) was Persian lustre ware or even more modern Russian or German plates, worth nothing.[21] Colonel Chilaeff was keen to sell his collection for 20,000 roubles.[22] The travelling museum of the photographer and collector Alexandre Roinashvili, the result of twenty years' travel in the Caucasus, shows many items that would have been seen in the Tiflis Museum (textiles, carpets both local and Persian, belts, jewellery, icons, bronzes, musical instruments etc.), but also the exceptional richness of material found in Dagestan (see below).[23]

Classical and miscellaneous

The study of coins was an established antiquarian practice, above all in regions of classical heritage. Bell lists (in Appendix XVI)[24] coins (copper, silver, gold) from Cimmerian Bosphorus, Panticapeum, Rome and Byzantium. Bell also mentions a gold and silver hoard (figurines, jewellery, coins) found by a farmer in a pit inland from Sashe. Bell requested to see it, and when brought to him it transpired that most of had been melted down. Bell illustrates the remains of a silver cup, probably showing part of a Bacchic scene with two main figures holding staves or sashes, one with an ibex on his shoulders, surrounded by horned animals and horses, an altar, quivers and cups in the field, with smaller figures in the distance beside trees, one reclining. Other remaining items were a gold bracelet and necklace with jasper fittings and some copper coins.[25] The illustrated piece appears to be part of a Roman piece with an early first millennium AD parallel in the Princeton University Museum (unsourced).[26]

Classical sources were *de rigueur* and were mentioned in passing by many travellers to the area, as Strabo, Pliny, Herodotus and Procopius were the first written sources on the western Caucasus available to westerners. Telfer and Bryce in particular indulge in classical name dropping. Both quote the classics from various periods as sources for, for example, the Ossetians[27] or for general history of the Caucasus[28] or for the Dariel pass.[29] Telfer focuses on the names of places from Odessa's and Crimea's classical pasts, but in Circassia discusses the ancient origin of Anapa, illustrating ancient 'disinterred' statues.[30]

Telfer obtained permission to excavate six graves at M'zhett (Mtskheta), The necropolis is dated from the third to the tenth millennium BC-AD. It is difficult to ascertain the date of these graves from Telfer's description. Five were formed of sandstone slabs, with bodies either seated or elongated and seem early, with simple finds: beads, obsidian tools, coarse ware, bronze pins. Some contained multiple burials (Tomb 2). Telfer presented one of the 'macrocephalous' skulls he dug up to the Anthropological Institute,[31] not specifying which one. Other graves at the site, excavated by Beiern, were of the classical period including a find of a small silver vase with the triumphs of Hercules, and the goods were sent to St Petersburg and published in the *Journal of the Anthropological Institute of Great Britain and Ireland*, Vol. IV, 1874.[32]

The cousin of the Prince of Kasbek, Prince Alexander, showed Telfer his collection of beads of coloured paste, trinkets, bronze ornaments and chains, and a bezel ring with the device of a griffin, from graves disturbed when building a road near Kasbek. Telfer illustrates the 'potin' (bezel) ring.[33] This ring can be compared to finger-rings from the Alkhagori treasure (Leningori in Ossetia), dated to the fifth-fourth century BC.[34]

A reminder of the living past was a gnostic gem of the third or fourth century worn by a woman near Kubachi on festive occasions, which Abercromby bought.[35]

Islam and Dagestan

It was inevitable that in Dagestan the cultural focus should point towards another aspect of its ancient cultures: Islam. This aspect was mostly ignored by the travellers, except in the work of Abercromby. Cunynghame nevertheless reported an important curiosity at Khunsakh north of Gunib, the mosque (no description) and the sword and shirt of a Muslim saint (Abu Muslim), which inspired bravery and had been carried by the 'most holy fanatics' attached to Shamil.[36] Roinashvili's travelling museum (not seen by the travellers, or at least not mentioned) shows the wealth of antique material that could be found in and from these parts. This included a seventh-century bronze ewer from Basra, thirteenth- and fourteenth-century bronzes (from Iran and Iraq), cauldrons of the eighth to tenth centuries from Iran (some signed), an embossed refashioned candlestick from Iran (twelfth-thirteenth century) and the base of a candlestick holder, with similar motifs to those found by Abercromby in Kubachi (see below). Included were also nineteenth-century bronzes from Iran and Dagestan. Roinashvili's ceramic collection was also impressive, from Bronze Age and Chinese Celadon ware to Dagestani embossed dishes to and Japanese ware from the nineteenth century.[37]

Abercromby was focused on the east. Arriving at Derbent from Astrakhan aboard the *Turkmen* on 11 August 1888, he observed that the town looked well when seen from the south. He saw the citadel on the mountain slope with its 'warm, russet yellow' walls and towers contrasting with the fresh green of trees, the double line of walls with towers at intervals descending steeply to the shore, with the town grouped irregularly and in-between the walls. Most conspicuous were the bright green towers and cupolas of the Russian and

Armenian churches, which dominated the low mosques and flat-roofed houses of the native inhabitants.[38] Abercromby settled there for two weeks in the house of a Russian widow.[39] It was to be one of the most significant and informative times of his stay in the Caucasus: walking and mapping most of the Derbent wall and discovering Islamic antiquities at Kubachi and recording reliefs found about that village. His intention, motivated by the ethnographer General von Erckert's own plan of the Derbent wall (*Der Kaukasus und seine Völker*, 1887), was to check the wall and presumably improve on the plan by walking the whole of it as far as possible.[40] Abercromby named and described 43 fortresses, their state of preservation and provided a map. Dilapidation was ongoing.

Abercromby quotes from the *Derbend Nāmeh*[41] for the wall's age (early sixth century, built by Khosroes 1, his father Kobad and Yezid the Governor of Derbent) and its ancient length of 25 miles from Derbent westwards to the fort of Chukna Kale, where the wall stops. He quotes further from the *Derbend Nāmeh* about who was brought in to guard it (people from Syria, Emesa, Damascus, Mosul and the governor's own forces), the new fortresses built and the reparations to it.[42]

The Derbent or defensive wall (sometimes known locally as Alexander's wall) was remarked on by Persian and Arab sources from the seventh century onwards and was one the great sites (and sights) of the region. Tradition states that it was built during the reign of the Sasanian King Khosrow (531-79 AD) but this seems to have been the completion and strengthening of earlier works,[43] and after Khosrow it at first went round the city down to the Caspian and secondly stretched south-west of the citadel to the mountains for several miles. The wall was functional from the sixth to the thirteenth century, until the Mongol invasion. Forts and towers protected the wall. The fortresses along the wall were rectangular or square with circular or semi-circular towers at the corners and were positioned 150 to 500 metres from each other. Sixth-century inscriptions in Middle Persian and eighth-twelfth-century Arabic, together with mason's marks, are to be found at various points of the wall.[44]

Abercromby's inspection started with the walls of the town, made of yellow calcareous stone, which had been damaged and repaired over time. Only a few of the step-shaped finials which once crowned the walls and gateway remained. The masonry corresponded to that of the majority of the rectangular forts extending westwards. He mentions the gates: the main one, Orta Kapi, of three arches with moulded decoration and a carved animal figure above the interior arches and stone benches at right angles; the Naria Kala Kapi, the citadel gate; the Jerchi Kapi or gate of 'public proclamations' on the northern side; the southern Baiyat Kapi gate and lower down the new gate or Yeni Kapi and the Kirklar Kapi, leading to the cemetery, with inscribed stones between the latter two. The stones of the inner wall had mason's marks on them such as lozenges, circles with dots, swastikas.[45] He recommends seeing the cemeteries outside town, which had elongated tombstones with Koranic inscriptions and names and dates of the deceased in front, but with decoration at the back: for men often of a horse and boots of the master, carved gun, a sabre, a *kinjal*, a cartouche box, slippers; and for women ornaments for head and neck, a basin, flowers, a pair of slippers, and sometimes a peacock or partridge and a vase of flowers.[46]

Abercromby's preliminary sortie to the wall from the citadel with Mejid and a guide was in a south-westerly direction. He immediately realized it was going to be arduous; among patches of scorched grass were dense evergreen shrubs. He noted the old forts to the south-west (Premeskhi Kale and Kiafer Kale). His guide knew very little. On 13 August he set off again to find an elderly Beg who knew about the wall. They headed towards Keji Kale, Kemakh and Metagi, stopping en route to look at hidden towers through dense brushwood. It was not plain sailing. The bearings Abercromby took did not coincide with those on the Five Verst map he had with him (none were quite accurate, he concluded). At Kemakh he noted masons' marks (a semicircle with two radiating strokes and two hook shaped incision).

His journey took four days, but it was disjointed, as he admits, partly as the enterprise was hampered by the Beg's (Mirza Ali) desire to divert the trip to visit family and friends along the way and spend the night[47] and partly because of the terrain: across dense scrubland, up and down wooded hills and ravines, hampering views and obliging them to make disorientating detours. Leaving the Beg, he found it was far better to use native village guides.[48] Abercromby describes fortresses with semi-circular or round towers at their angles in states of reasonable preservation (Mehmet Karim Kale, Shalkene Kale, Oghu Kale, Dervish Kale), others reduced to foundations (Duzlan Kale) or partly demolished (Noruz Ali Kale, Palangi Kale, Sezhur Kale, Kejeli Kale) or totally ruined (Mughara Kale, Ornug Kale). He notes details such as loopholed walls (Ishekli Su Kale, Kobi Kale)[49] or the fort of Yedi Gardash Kale (the Castle of the Seven Brothers), supposedly by the builder of the Great Mosque of Derbend[50] whose form (square towers on two faces, two external buttresses and loopholed walls) and masonry (small round stones) were completely different from the others.[51]

He comes across cemeteries: Pir Ganja, with the tomb of two murdered 'pious Muslims'[52] was also a pilgrimage site, and to the west of Shalkene and Kemakh a cemetery with carved tombstones, some marked by short wooden posts. The decoration of the tombstones consisted of various motifs on one stone (a *kinjal* and horse and other arms, a pair of slippers, a water jug, a basin, a dish, a pair of slippers with high heels; or two hands, a basin, boots, slippers, ornaments and a flower). Some of the ornamentation consisted of interlacing circles and semi-circles, sometimes around rods.[53] Further on, by Babanu Kale, he came across weathered and defaced stones in Kufic (the oldest form of Arabic calligraphic writing used in Korans and in architectural ornamentation), with a carved representation of a wild goat on the fort's north wall, and an undecipherable inscription.[54] It seems that the whole area was dotted with decoration and inscriptions, including villages. At the village of Tatil, for example, Abercromby noted the decorated wooden door (concentric circles interlaced with diagonals lines in relief) on the headman's house and realized that nearly all the houses in the village were decorated with

Arabic inscriptions, highlighted (as in modern times) in red and blue paint.[55] On his return to Derbent Abercromby attempted to see forts he had missed and concluded his visit by advising future travellers to explore the whole more thoroughly than he was able to do, with a 'fresh man' from village to village and to proceed via Jalgan and Metegi.[56]

Abercromby was nonetheless aware of what he had achieved. After his return he published an account and map of this survey in the *Scottish Geographical Magazine* of 1890.[57]

Whereas Abercromby had prepared for Derbent, he did not know what awaited him at the village of Kubachi. He was to stumble on a treasure trove of Iranian metalwork of the fourteenth and fifteenth centuries. Kubachi had an ancient reputation (known from early Arabic and Persian sources on Derbent) as a centre of metalworking in bronze, gold and silver of jewellery, arms and vessels, hence one of its local names, Zirigharan (or chainmail makers).[58] Some of the elite arms (helmets, chainmail, weapons) from the Shirvanshah states[59] were most probably made either at Kubachi or Shamakha.[60] Such metalwork was extremely prestigious and could be identified with a mention of place of manufacture or owner's name and date in Arabic. Others were identified stylistically, with motifs having their own names (the branch and bush motif was known as *tatta* and *markharai* respectively). Kubachi specialized in gold engraving and gold damascening on burnished steel (the latter also known elsewhere in the Caucasus).[61] Kubachi also became known for its so-called Kubachi ceramic ware (from Iran) and for its decorated stones.

Abercromby started his visit, accompanied by the *yuzbashi* or headman Omar ata Abdul Ghafar Oghli, with a description of the oldest cemetery, used according to Frahn[62] until the fifteenth century, wrote Abercromby. The still sharp ornamentation ranged from very simple to more elaborate (such as St Andrew's cross on a Greek cross, circumscribed by a circle and interlaced with Arabic letters). These stones were undated.[63] He contrasts these with the modern gravestones, which were dated and painted in bright colours to bring out the decoration and interlaced Arabic writing, which the locals could not decipher.[64] Abercromby then describes and illustrates in sketches and rubbings some of the numerous carved stones 'studded' into the walls and window heads of houses and mosques. These varied from brick size to much larger and were decorated with simple figures of rosettes or men and animals or sophisticated, intricate mythological animals and intertwined floral motifs. Some had inscriptions, with high quality pieces bearing the names of craftsmen inscribed on them [65] Two different types of style could be found in the same wall, for example; one stone showed a fox or jackal following a bear[66] and another a complicated image of a five headed dragon and an armed man to one side decapitating it with a woman on the other side, with a large eagle looming behind them. Abercromby concludes that this was an 'Asiatic' form of the Perseus and Andromeda myth.[67] As there is no illustration of the latter it is difficult assess this interpretation.

Other reliefs include wrestling men, griffins or lions entwined or facing each other, archers looking backwards, archers hunting, pecking birds, stags in movement and a Bactrian camel. Abercromby made a rubbing of a relief showing two helmeted men, one armed and holding up an animal for sacrifice, while the other holds out a cup.[68] At the women's mosque (Khunala Meshid) one stone represented two wrestling men with a Kufic inscription above them. Another stone from the same mosque shows a large bird of prey holding a smaller one with a long-tailed creature about to devour a man.[69] The reproduction (from a rubbing) is very faint in the book and the style difficult to see, but the guilloche enclosing the whole has parallels with the metalwork (see below). Abercromby admits that he did not see all the stones, mentioning that Dorn[70] had referred to seventeen mosques and eleven schools (*medrese*) with reliefs. A future tourist should come equipped with a camera and proper paper to take squeezes and rubbings, he advised. He was not particularly impressed by the stones: they evinced no skill in 'showing the human figure,' he wrote, and their best expression was in 'Saracenic' or floral motifs.[71]

Such reliefs, many still in situ, but others in museum collections, were the product of more than one workshop (local and perhaps elsewhere) and have been dated to the fourteenth and fifteenth centuries.[72] Many are defaced but show considerable carving skills. Their presence on walls of village houses suggests a secondary use. Many of the motifs (such as small plump birds, goats with great curved horns, archers on a horse looking backwards, sphinxes, floral motifs) show an affinity with Sasanian iconography[73] as well as an affinity in their decoration (e.g. the guilloche design on Abercromby's Fig. 4) with the metalwork from Iran found at Kubachi.

Abercromby was particularly impressed by the 'old brass-work' inlaid with silver, sometimes gold, which was 'quite unlike anything made in the village…[with] no-one in now in Kubaichi capable of reproducing them'.[74] He had stumbled on a valuable trove of seven pieces most of which were of medieval Iranian origin (Fars region). He speculated at the time that they may have been made in the Syrian tradition as it was known that Syrian and Mesopotamian settlers had been brought to the region in the eighth century.[75] Kubachi had an old tradition of having a mixed population, Abercromby wrote.[76]

The 'old brass-work' consisted of ewers, pots and parts of candelabra, and Abercromby provides descriptions and sketches of the parts of the distinctive decoration.[77] The technique (*champleve* incised with silver or gold, much faded or reduced to bitumen) and decoration of the pieces (hunting and drinking scenes including standing or seated figures (e.g. Figs. 9 and 100, some with animals or with inscriptions interlaced in foliate decoration) are strikingly similar in at least five of the pieces which can be dated to fourteenth- and fifteenth-century metalwork from Fars and western Iran.

The two major pieces for Abercromby, were the nine-sided brass stand (his Fig. 8). He pointed out that it was very similar to one in the South Kensington Museum (now the Victoria and Albert Museum, see below), from the St Maurice collection, either one of a pair or from the same workshop. He 'rescued' the piece and brought it back to London.[78] The other, the base of a candlestick[79] with a hunting scene and an inscription, he considered more lively and 'beautiful' than the others and 'hardly the work of a

Kubaichan artist'.[80] The 'modern art' or modern metalwork of Kubachi did not strike Abercromby as very interesting: it consisted of chased floral or 'Saracenic' designs on the sheaths of *kinjals*, gun-locks and pistol-butts, cigarette holders and silver pipe bowls, which were too uniform and not well executed.[81] The poorest craftsmanship were ivory scabbards and *kinjal* handles. Only one *kinjal* sheath was worthy of illustration, with intertwined floral decoration of damascened gold on oxidized steel.[82] Abercromby attributes the decline of this craft to lack of local demand for quality goods, changed methods of warfare (there was now peace), the introduction of Russian regulations and of cheap European 'manufactures'.[83] What was left was sold cheaply. Even so, although Abercromby did not visit the metalworkers' quarter (which he regretted), they all seemed hard at work.[84]

Abercromby was then shown the collection of ceramic wares belonging to the *yuzbashi* and others. He saw a number of lustreware plates, which he assumed to be Persian, for it reminded him of pieces in the South Kensington Museum, although the natives 'maintained otherwise'. There are no sketches of these so it is difficult to know whether any were the decorated polychrome

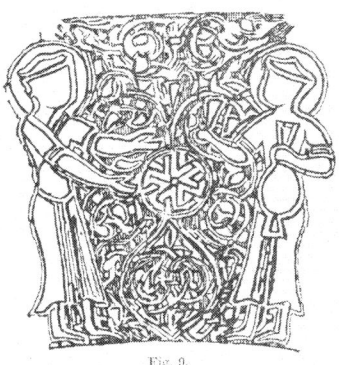

Fig. 9. Two standing men, one holding a wine cup, the other a flagon

Fig. 11. A seated cross-legged figure

slip-painted wares showing vegetal and geometric designs and portrait busts and certain derived Chinese patterns characteristic of different Iranian workshops of the mid fifteenth century to the end of the seventeenth century found at Kubachi.[85] Abercromby describes one dish with a row of lions with heads in high relief, back to back, with a row of birds above them. This iconography does not feature in the Iranian types mentioned above. Russian collectors had been 'attracted' to one type of plate (no illustration or description) and one Russian prince had carted off a total of 550 of them when he had visited. This suggests that they cannot have been antique. Cheap Russian and German plates of no value were also part of the locals' collections.[86]

Thus Abercromby displays both expertise, interest and a good eye, but also a selectivity and cavalier attitude towards what he does not like.

1   Bryce 1877, 125
2   Jersild 2002, 68
3   Radde 1895 (French edition), 51
4   Radde 1885, 52
5   See Teissier *Anatolian Studies* 67, 2017, 231-253 for the political significance of the classical remains for the Russians in Crimea
6   Jersild 2002, 70
7   Sagona 2018, 285, fig. 6.2
8   Sagona 2018, 281-297; for detailed excavations in the south see Museyibli 2008, Laneri et al 2020).
9   Bell 1840, 1, 282-283; Longworth 1840, 2, 217-219
10 Bell 1840, 154, and note
11 Telfer 1876, 1, 110, note 1
12 Ussher 1845, 113
13 Ussher 1845, 143-144
14 Bryce 1877, 67-68
15 Bruce 1877, 109-110
16 Ball 2021, 159-162, 220 for the variety of stone idols found on the steppe; Sagona 2018, 416 (menhirs)
17 For 19th-century reports of these excavations on the Taman peninsula see Meyer 2013, 64-70.
18 Abercromby 1889, 98
19 I am most grateful to Dr Warwick Ball for his comments and giving me the following reference with potential parallels for the piece: Olbrycht 2015 372 fig. 26 from Kosica near Astrachan on the Lower Volga shows a 1st millennium bronze vessel with animal handles (which the Abercromby piece does not have) with a rider in a hunting scene shown in relief. Bronze fragments with iconography reminiscent of the Abercromby piece also come from Chorasmia but with a 3-4th c. B.C. date: Olbrycht, 371 figs 25 a-c. These objects attest to the cultural interaction between the steppe nomadic groups (e.g. Massagetae, Saka in the Achaemenid period) who controlled areas such as the Trans-Caspian and the empires and elites around them. Olbrycht 2015, 370)
20 Abercromby 1889, 218
21 Abercromby 1889, 287
22 Abercromby 1889, 89-91
23 Mamatsashvili 2001
24 Bell 1840, 1, 194; 2, 486
25 Bell 1840, 2, 407, Pl. between 404-405.).
26 I am extremely grateful to Casper Meyer for this identification and the parallel from Princeton University Museum. https://artmuseum.princeton.edu/collections/objects/38924
    Colchis had passed from the control of the Kings of Pontus into Roman hands in the late 1st B.C. to early 1st millennia A.D. until the 3rd century A.D. when it came under the sway of the Byzantines.
27 Telfer 1876, 1, 292-297
28 Bryce 1877 e.g. 48-52
29 Bryce 1877, 75ff.
30 Telfer 1876, 1, 109-110, 115
31 Telfer 1875, 1,182

32 Telfer 1875,2, Appendix VII, 245-247
33 Telfer 1875, 2, 25
34 I am particularly grateful to Irina Demetradze-Renz for her contact Keteran Ramishvili who identified this piece and gave the following reference: M. Lordkianidze, *The Ancient Finger Rings of Colchis*, Tiflis 1981, 25-37, figs. 1,2
35 Abercromby 1889, 287, fig.15
36 Cunynghame 1872, 207
37 For the bronzes see Ward 2015, 9-12. Ibid Pls. 112-138. For clay and ceramics see Pls. 142-155
38 Abercromby 1889, 207-208
39 Abercromby 1889, 209
40 Abercromby 1889, 218
41 A history of the wall found in Persian, Arabic and Turkish versions, including extracts in a Russian one by Alexander Kazem-Beg, St. Petersburg 1851. This includes accounts of the Arabs subduing the Caucasus
42 Abercromby 1889, 224. It is one of the many sources for the wall: see Pourjafar 2003; Kettenhofer 2023
43 Poujafr 2003, E. Isl. Online, 3
44 Gadjiev 2008; 2017, E.Ir. online: the wall had three main periods: mid 6-8th, 9th to the beginning of the 11th and from the 11th to the beginning of the 13th century.
45 Abercromby 1889, 213-217
46 Abercromby 1889, 222
47 Abercromby 1889, 228
48 Abercromby 1889, 235-236
49 Abercromby 1889, 236--237
50 The 8th century Friday Mosque, restored and added to at various times, Shikhsaidov 2009, 17-19
51 Abercromby 1889, 240
52 Abercromby 1889, 230
53 Abercromby 1889, 231
54 Abercromby 1889, 234
55 Abercromby 1889, 238
56 Abercromby 1889, 251
57 'The Wall of Derbend', *The Scottish Geographical Magazine* 6/3, 1890, 135-145.
58 Wixman, R. E.I. 1986 Vol. 2, 285. The entry is disappointingly identical that of the first edition 1927.
59 Vassal and independent rulers of the area of Shirvan, eastern (Caucasus, now Azerbaijan) from the 9th to the 17th centuries
60 Alexander 2015, 99
61 Lebedynski 2008 76,80,82
62 Christian Martin von Frahn 1807-1815 orientalist, Professor at Kazan University, Director of the Asiatic Museum at St Petersburg. I have been unable to verify this claim.
63 Abercromby 1889, 265ff.
64 Abercromby 1889, 265-266
65 Mammaev 2018, 2022 for examples of Kufic writing on Kubachi stones

and stelae. Unfortunately Russian publications on these stones are not available here.
66　Abercromby 1889, 267, fig. 2
67　Abercromby 1889, 266
68　Abercromby 1889, 269-270, 271 rubbing Fig.6
69　Abercromby 1889,271, Fig.4
70　Johannes Albrecht Berhard Dorn (1805-81), orientalist, Academician, Professor at St Petersburg University, Director of the Asiatic Museum, 1842, and of the Ethnographic Museum, 1855; Abercromby 1889, 272
71　Abercromby 1889,271-272
72　Mammaev 2020
73　Trever and Lykonin 1987, Hermitage Museum, fig. nos. 17, 27, 37, 84, 112)
74　Abercromby 1889, 272
75　Abercromby cites Abu Hamid el Andalusi in Dorn. *Melanges Asiatiques tires du Bulletin de l'Academie Imperiale des Sciences de St. Petersbourg*, VI, 1871, p. 699. I have been unable to find this publication, but it was in a series that Dorn printed in the journal (from 1869-1874) on inscriptions from the Caspian and surrounding regions. See Dorn 1873
76　Abercromby 1889, 273
77　Abercromby 1889 ,Figs 7-11
78　Abercromby 1889, 276
79　Abercromby 1889, Fig.10
80　No. 1 A copper box (2.1/2 inches x 2.1/2inches): fig. 7 showing a central band with a wild boar pursued by three lions with a band of ornament above and below. Cf. e.g. Melikian-Chirvani 1982, no. 104 p. 223 from Fars (south-west Iran) for the band of animals and fig. 63 from 15th century Khorasan, for the foliate decoration. No. 2 a nine-sided brass stand, 5 inches high, 9 inches at the base. Fig. 8. 18 pentagonal fields filled with decoration each containing with 'aureolated' horsemen above and seated cross-legged figures holding cups or musical instruments below, with key pattern ornamentation and geometric rosettes. His comparison with the St. Maurice collection is accurate. The museum bought this piece (Melikian-Shirvani 1982, no p.92 fig. 88 in 1884 for £10.00) from the St Maurice collection alongside others donated or bought later in the 19th century (Melikian-Shirvani 1982 Index p. 444). Melikian-Shirvani comments that the stylized costumes were derived from the 13th century. Number 3 (fig. 9): a circular pot c.7 inches high, once part of a lampstand. Its decoration was similar to that of no. 2. The main ornament was a belt of figures, standing in pairs at the top and facing each other, one holding a wine flask the other reaching out, while below were seated cross-legged figures, with a circular medallion between each figure. The provenance and date thus seems to be similar to that of no.2. Number 4 (fig. 10) the base of a candle-stick12. $^{1}/_{2}$ inches, turned into a pot, with eight belts of ornamentation and four short Arabic inscriptions divided the area into four compartments. In one (fig. 10) a crowned aureolated rider hunts down a bear surrounded in a foliate design within a scalloped shaped rosette. A lower band shows foxes and cheeta chasing hares through foliage, and an upper band shows wild geese. It had been inlaid with gold and silver. The form of the rosette occurs in 13th or early 14th century brass work from west Iran fc. Melikian-Shirvani

1982 , Figs. 81, 82 87 but not (in those examples) with royal riders. The foliate motif however seems slightly later e.g. Melikian-Shirvani 1982 Fig. 63 a from Fars 14th-15th centuries. Number 5: The base of a candelabra (fig. 11), 9. ½ inches was similar in style to nos. 2 and 4. Six figures were contained in circular frames, each with a word of Arabic interlaced with floral motifs. Three figures were on horseback, there seated cross-legged holding hoop-like objects over their heads. Cf. Melikian -Shirvani 1982 p. 208 no. 94 a for a similar seated figure, on a 14th century tray from Fars. Number 6. A twelve sided brass vase 8.1/2 inches high, diameter 6 inches, with six bands of ornament in medallions consisting of human headed winged lions, with perpendicular wings, spiral lines and an inscription. Above the band of inscription was a band of running long backed animals and birds. Abercromby thought this piece 'decidedly inferior' to the others both in terms of design and execution. He thought it might have been made locally. It had no remains of silver. It is difficult to assess this piece without any illustration. Number 7 A brass ewer, c. 11 inches high with a handle and spout, with two rows of figures round the body of the ewer and another round the neck. The lower figures consisted of twelve aureolated figures in a seated of crouching position, facing left with arms raised at the elbows, as if beating time or clapping. Cf. a very similar figure in Melikian-Shirvani 1982 on a casket from early 14th century western Iran, showing attendants seated on either side of an enthroned king. The headdresses are Mongol.

81 Abercromby 1889, 284
82 Abercromby 1889 Fig. 14, 285
83 Abercromby 1889, 286
84 Abercromby 1889, 288
85 i.e. pre-Safavid, Turko-Mongol and Safavid periods: Golombek 2014, 214, 180-181 thinks the bulk of the ceramics were made in Isfahan at the Qumisheh workshop, inspired by Isfahan painters. How they ended up in Kubachi can only be speculated on, she writes.
86 Abercromby 1889, 287-288

PART 5

The Great Outdoors

After the decimation of much of the indigenous population and the defeat of Shamil (trumpeted as the 'pacification' or 'conquest' of the Caucasus) the region began to attract enthusiasts of a new kind. Self-serving and determined, they were keen to investigate new territory in which to make their mark as sportsmen, some as professionals.

Geographers and sportsmen were particularly associated with two institutions: the Royal Geographical Society and the Alpine Club. The Royal Geographical Society, founded in 1830 as the Geographical Society of London, was created for the advancement of geography as a science. William IV and Queen Victoria were patrons and many of its presidents were aristocrats, with a male only membership until the early twentieth century. As a supporter of exploration the RGS was associated with many famous colonial explorers of the time, such as Charles Darwin and David Livingstone. Most travellers who had published books on their travels, particularly to exotic or relatively unknown places, belonged to the RGS or aspired to be members and to be published in the *Proceedings* of the RGS or its journal. The Alpine Club was founded in 1837 by British Alpinists and naturalists to promote and widen the scope of alpinism away from the Alps. Both institutions were highly competitive and drove not only exploration but travel publishing.[1]

'Stupendous Peaks': Mountaineering

Douglas Freshfield, who was twenty-three at the time of his visit, had three goals: to climb Mount Kazbek, to follow the mountain chain west and to climb Mount Elbruz. He was not alone: François Devouassoud, Adolphus Warburton Moore and Charles Comyns

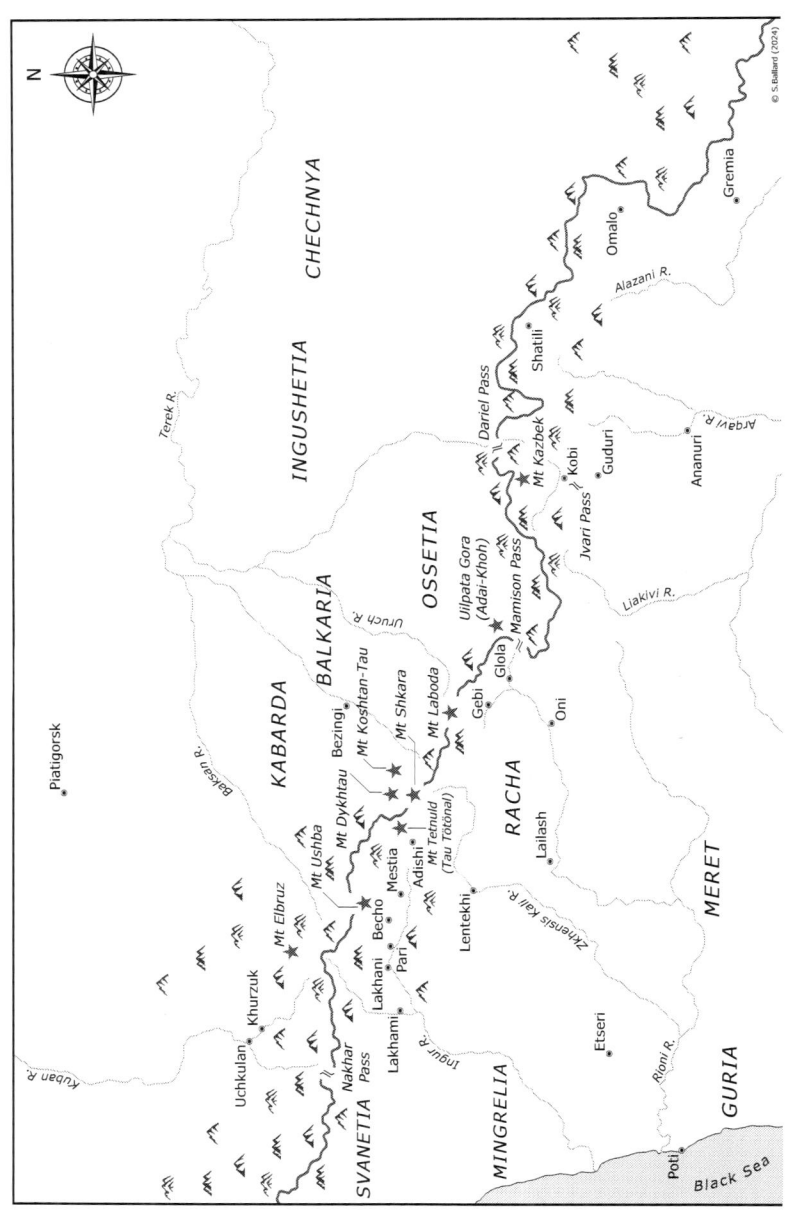

'Kazbek, from the Post Station'

Tucker were part of the group, but the publication of Freshfield's *Travels* and his subsequent efforts in print and lectures ensured that his was the name to be remembered for opening up a 'new Switzerland'. Freshfield acknowledges that others had attempted the ascent of Kazbek before them (Klaproth in the early nineteenth century, Parrot in 1811, Moritz Wagner in 1844, Russian officers) but none had been successful.[2]

Having trained for one day studying the twin peaks of the 'magnificent mass of rock and snow,'[3] the party set off for the ascent proper from Kazbek village at 5 a.m. on 30 June 1868 through gentians, rhododendrons and grasses until they reached the snow, climbing up to 11,000 feet. They opted for the eastern peak because it seemed about level with the western one and was easier for bivouacking. At 2.45 am the next day they set off via the Ortvizi glacier, climbing through rocks and broken *névé* (compacted snow) until crevasses became large and had to be dodged. Devouassoud was in the lead, then Freshfield, followed by Moore and Comyns Tucker. They had some lucky escapes (Comyns Tucker finished head down a chasm) and trudged - sometimes crawling - for four hours before reaching the saddle between the summits. In raging wind they thought that from here it was evident that the eastern peak was the highest (but see Grove below), reaching the summit without too much difficulty at midday.[4] Freshfield, with characteristic restraint, does not wax lyrical about the summit: 'the apparent grandeur of the range to the east was a surprise'.[5] Preoccupied by their potentially dangerous descent down the ice slope they spent very little time on the summit and descended via Dariel and the Terek back to Kazbek. Here they were hailed as heroes (instead of 'humbugs') as they had been thought lost. They wrote an account of the ascent to the Commandant of Duschet and it eventually appeared in *Kafkas* (not soon enough, hinted Freshfield).

The competitiveness of this sport was evident: they wanted to be the first to climb the two mountains but also the first to follow the route along the mountain range between the two peaks.

They left Kazbek station towards Kobi in the Terek valley, through 'gloomy villages', continuing up the Terek valley pass (c.10,000 feet) towards the Res, crossing the Ardon river towards the Mamisson pass.[6] Here they saw 'the stupendous peaks' of the Adai Khokh, whose southern face they wanted to inspect. They scrambled up through 'beautiful forest trees' and rhododendrons in full bloom and stood before the two peaks supposed to be of the Adai-Khokh: they observed 'huge seracs hung in a curtain under its crest' through a telescope. At this point Freshfield points out the total confusion over mountain names (Radde differed his nomenclature from that of the Five Verst map, but had not yet published his findings.[7]) They headed for the Uruch valley, through magnificent forests, sub-alpine flowers and valleys of the Rion down to Glola village. Thence they followed the right bank of the Rion to Chiora.[8] Freshfield goes on to describe slow progress through the glaciers, snowfields and forests of the central Caucasus (Karagan glacier 'wild but not grand' and the 'immense' and 'magnificent' glacier on the north side of the Adai-Khokh - Khatschi-Dau). The glaciers were larger and more complicated than any they had met before: they struggled through trenches, up walls, under towers of blue crystal 'fair to the eye but likely to topple over', great chasms in what seemed to be labyrinths, and were unable to recognize any peaks on sight until they came down the watershed and passed onto the southern side again.[9] They were satisfied with what they had learnt by this passage, enabling them to form an idea of the general character of the chain from west of the Mamisson pass to the sources of the Rion. Tau Burdisula was taken as a point of division, but no attempt had yet been made by the 'authors' of the Five Verst map to name any of the ridges and peaks of the area.[10]

After provisioning at Gebi they reached the ridge of the pass of the Pass-Mta (which contrary to the map was not a peak but a rocky buttress, partly due to a confusion of names).[11] They continued to the banks of the Zenes-Squali (Zhensis-Kali)[12] discovering local names for mountains and correcting the map, and reached the Scena valley above it through a scene unimaginably 'savage and unseen' except in some of the landscapes of Gustav Doré. They finally reached Svaneti, and here Freshfield concedes that the nature of the country and its great barriers had 'a great share in forming the savage and wild character' of its inhabitants.[13]

After a stormy stop at the village of Jibiani they continued up the glaciers of the Ingur (Adish, Göröscho), the pass of Dschkumer to Latal (whence they saw Mount Uschba, the 'Caucasian Matterhorn') and Tau Tötönal (an 'elegant snow pyramid'). The idea of climbing either of the twin peaks of Mount Uschba 'seemed insane', and they continued through meadows, circumventing ravines to Pari.[14] Their goal, via the Baksan valley and Uruspieh, was finally within reach. They acquired 'geographical information' about routes into Svaneti: one through the Nvka valley, the other south of Uruspieh to the Becho district.[15] They continued to where they saw the source of the Baksan and the glacier filling the head of the valley, and from here they had their first sight of Elbruz (known locally as Minghi-Tau).[16] They inspected the mountain and settled for the night pitching their tent on a ridge resembling an 'inverted tea-cup'.[17] Their view from their 'eyrie' that night (at 12,000 feet) from the trough of the Baksan to the central chain and east to Uschba 'was superb'.[18] After a freezing night, the 'sudden kindling' of the eastern ranges and 'rose-suffused' crags warned them of the 'unearthly splendour' of the sunrise. This sudden lyricism suggests that Freshfield was truly moved. By 7.30 am they were at a height of over 16,000 feet still in bitter cold wind, with an imminent risk of frostbite. They faced the final struggle on a broad crest, marching in procession until they reached the summit at 18,500 feet - actual height today 5,642 metres or 18,510 feet according to climbinggeorgia.com - at one end of a horseshoe ridge, crowned by three distinct eminences, which suggested an old crater. They looked at the panorama and concluded that the Caucasian peaks were sharper and finer than the Alpine ones.[19] They remained for about twenty minutes: they had achieved their second goal, but it was not for the character of the mountain, but for its height. Freshfield called Elbruz 'at best' a 'bloated monarch' which had little to recommend it beyond its size, whereas Koshantau Tau

'Our Camp-Fire in the Forest'

and Dychtau were respectively the worthy king and queen.[20] The ascent from 6.500 feet had taken seven and a half hours, but could have been done faster, Freshfield thought.[21] They returned to camp where they had to 'submit' to congratulatory 'hugging and kissing', and went to bed satisfied with their triple achievement.[22]

Next day they continued to Uruspieh and Piatigorsk, filthy and exhausted.[23] Their return journey was on the northern side of the range, via the Terek and its source and the ridge over the Uruch, noting the 'great peaks' of Koshtantau (17,095 feet) and Dychtau, which they left 'unscaled' and 'un-attempted' and free for others.[24] Their last camp was in a peasants' hut close to a crag and a stream (which joined the Uruch) marked 'Kut' on the map. Here they had their last mountaineering meal: fresh milk and liquor (between beer and sour cider) brought by a peasant, essence of beef and a tablet of Chollet's dried vegetables (their standard fare) cooked on a portable apparatus brought from England.[25] Meals had been occasionally supplemented with cheese, bread and the occasional piece of meat obtained locally. Their equipment was not itemized, but the *Alpine Journal* (1884) outlined the essentials (a list which grew in time): field glasses, pocket knives, boot nails, small pistol (as gifts), small cooking apparatus, tin plates, knives and forks and Whymper's tents (one for every three men). By 1887 the list had grown to include a mountain aneroid (to 20,000 feet), a clinometer, a prismatic compass, a telescope, and luxury items such as wine gourds and air cushions. The greatest requisite, wrote W.F. Donkin (see below), was 'infinite patience'.[26] The party returned to Tiflis via the Uruch valley, whose scenery they did appreciate.

The completed ascent was to prove controversial and unpopular with the Russian authorities. In Appendix I[27] Freshfield gives an account of a previous attempt at climbing Elbruz led by General Emmanuel and others, one of whom, Herr Kupffer published an account in 1830 (*Voyage dans les environs du Mont Elbrouz dans le Caucase*). Kupffer and his companions 'loosely' claimed success, while others turned back. But meanwhile General Emmanuel who was observing the proceedings through a telescope observed a lone Circassian named Killiar reach what he thought was the summit.

The general offered a reward of 400 roubles, which Killiar claimed. Freshfield stresses how difficult it would have been to see such a detail from a telescope and suggested that the general's claim was only to prove that the expedition had been a success. We can hardly expect Killiar to be the Jacques Belmont (the first to reach the summit of Mont Blanc in 1876) of Elbruz, concludes Freshfield.[28] If Killiar was indeed a Circassian, how likely was it that the general would have attributed the honour to him if it were not what he believed? This Freshfield did not ask, although he could argue that a native conquest was preferable to the Russians than a British one.[29]

Freshfield insisted on keeping the victory to himself and his party to the end. Demonstrating either competitiveness or ignorance or both, the book engendered correspondence about the correct locality of the two mountains and a German report (discussed in *Pall Mall*) denying that Elbruz was where Freshfield said it was. There was also controversy about whether the mountain was the highest in Europe or belonged to the Asian range. This is still being debated today.[30]

Freshfield's account was essentially for mountaineers and climbing enthusiasts: he constantly references the Alps (as does Grove, see below) or the Dolomites, he gives local altitudes, names (or not) of peaks and mountain ranges, the occasional sketched outline of peaks, details on paths, rivers, outcrops, ridges, natural landmarks, corrections to the highly inadequate Five Verst map (and occasionally Radde), and uses specialist vocabulary. On one occasion he asks the reader to open a map and 'look at the disposition of ridges and valleys' and gives a lesson on the watersheds of the west Caucasus from south of Elbruz to the Adai-Khokh group (west of the Ardon valley), which was an uninterrupted granite ridge, never below 10,000 feet, traversed by glaciers and passes.[31] The contribution of this book to the opening to the west of mountaineering in the region and to geographical knowledge cannot be denied: besides the details in the main text of the book, Appendix II gives the heights of peaks, passes, towns and villages in the Caucasus provinces they travelled through and

Appendix III gives a list of local plants collected by Radde and arranged by Trautvetter. Such detailed information was no doubt hugely informative and novel for geographers and mountaineers, but leaves the ordinary reader trudging across many a figurative glacier. In this account the people of the Caucasus were very much secondary to mountains. The endurance and skill of the group and their achievement in the face of hunger, atrocious weather, lack of information, danger from ice, the perennial problem of finding porters, loss of equipment and not always friendly villagers, however, should not be made light of. The *Saturday Review* of 17 July 1869 time acknowledges how unknown the Caucasian range was at the time and praises the book for opening up new ground for mountaineers and for its simplicity, clarity and freedom from sentimentality.[32]

Freshfield returned to the Caucasus a year later with Maurice de Déchy: they crossed two passes over the main chain and climbed several summits including Tetnuld at c.16,500 feet.[33] While approving of certain specialists such as Radde and Abich, who had been in the field, Freshfield was also keen to stress that only climbers were competent to write about glaciers. 'Ice-craft' and 'glacier knowledge' were essential and he derided the ignorance of some specialists, 'savants of societies' and 'doubters' like Professor Heim of Zurich or Mr Muromtzoff.[34] Freshfield had clearly been piqued by past controversy and criticism.

After the publication of the *Travels* and subsequent trip, Freshfield became the reviewer par excellence (in England) of anything on the Caucasus: while commending others he never misses a chance to correct them and, in lectures to the Alpine Club or RGS, to remind his audience of his initial feat. Freshfield's subsequent two-volume book, *Exploration of the Caucasus* (1896, 1902) became a classic. It was dedicated to William Frederick Donkin, Hon. Secretary of the Alpine Club, who perished in 1888 while ascending or descending Koshtantau.[35] The book was not a narrative of travel: its aim was to make accessible to geographers and mountaineers, in carefully organized topographical and subject based chapters, knowledge of the central Caucasus areas and chain (e.g. Kazbek and the Ossete district). Included was a chapter on mountaineering in Svaneti from 1868 (the time of Freshfield) to 1889. Vol 2 also included sections written by others: H.W. Holder, Hermann Woolley, J.G. Cockin, and Maurice de Déchy. Appendices by Professor T.G. Bonney cover topographical notes, climbers' records, a table of temperatures and rainfalls, the heights of the termination of glaciers, and a Bibliography. The glory of this book for the general reader, however, were the photographs, mostly by Vittorio Sella, but also by Woolley and de Déchy (see Part 6).

Freshfield became President of the Alpine Club, Honorary Secretary of the RGS, and has a lasting reputation as a distinguished geographer, traveller and writer.[36]

'Traversing new ground'

Florence Craufurd Grove and his companions from the Alpine Club (Horace Walker, Frank Gardiner and Adolphus Warburton Moore, the latter having accompanied Freshfield in 1868) had similar ambitions to Freshfield: they wanted to make their mark by climbing peaks and 'traverse new ground, at least to Englishmen'.[37]

Grove sets out his itinerary: to leave from Kutaisi for the Rion and its source, then to explore the mountain group at the head of the Tcherek (Terek) valley and its gorge on the northern side of the range and pass into Svaneti if possible; to continue from Bezingi via Tchegem to Uruspieh and Mount Elbruz, return via the Nakhar pass through the valleys of the Klütch and Kodor to the Russian post of Lata and thence to Sukhum-Kale.[38] They intended to climb Elbruz, but not attract the controversy of Freshfield's claims: they wanted the company of Russian officers to verify the climb. They thus arranged to meet a Lieutenant Bernoff at Uruspieh in order to attempt the climb together.[39] They were to use the same Five Verst map as used by others in the Caucasus, with knowledge supplemented by Moore, who knew the terrain from before.

The expedition was soon successful; reaching the Rion (after porters from Gebi had guided them to the wrong river valley) and its glacier, Grove makes claim to 'being the first travellers from the west to have seen the Rion issue from its parent ice', grandly stating that they had thus completed the work of exploration which Jason and the Argonauts began a long time ago.[40] They explored and passed on to the huge glaciers of the 'Tcherek' (Terek) fighting the 'black tempests of the Caucasus'.[41] The upper parts of the valleys were barren, dull and covered in 'shin breaking' boulders, while lower down they were filled with 'crimson mountain flowers' or poppies.[42] Grove describes peaks as he sees them far and wide (Dych-Tau to the north-west of the Terek) and, like Freshfield, compares them to the Alps to give an idea of features and scale.[43]

They reached the greatest glacier system of the Caucasus, to the east of the peak of the Kotchan Tau (Koshtan-Tau) extending eight to ten miles north-east, headed by a vast cirque, beyond which rose an immense peak. Here Grove allows himself to use the 'often misused word sublime'.[44] This had only been seen by Freshfield. The longest axis of the glacier was to the south-west, while its breadth and widest part was three to four miles. They did not explore further as the weather threatened mists and storms, and crossed 'the vast untrodden solitude', a 'virginal mystery' not even trusted by hunters.[45] They headed for Kunim (again unvisited by Freshfield), explored and headed due north, hoping to climb Tau Tetnuld, but the weather did not allow it.[46] They proceeded to the 'wonderful mountain' of Dych Tau, (together with Dych Tau called Djanga by the 'natives'). In 'the severest form of mountain grandeur' they ascended the glacier uniting the two mountains.[47] From here they saw Kotchan Tau, (the highest peak after Elbruz) and proceeded to Bezingi leaving Bezingi via the Chegem pass to the gorge of the Djilki Su,[48] where they were impeded from exploring because of mist,[49] until they reached Tchegem (Chegem). Here Grove saw the potential of going up Tau Tetnuld and Tungsorum, where paths could be made, but needed time and inspection.[50] He then conveys the mountains' impregnability, 'beyond the reach of the best of his fellows' and 'forever virgin to a man's tread'.[51] They walked in pouring rain (it was the end of July) up the Baksan valley towards Uruspieh and their goal: Mount Elbruz or Minghi-Tau as it was known locally.[52] They were short of time, but allowed themselves four days for the ascent and the return to Uruspieh.[53] They approached the two peaks of the mountain, toiling up 'a valley of rocks' and saw the higher western peak and determined this was to be their objective (Freshfield and party had ascended the eastern peak). Walker, Gardiner, Grove and Peter Knubel (a mountain guide) assaulted the steep but flat-topped mountain at 1 a.m., leaving Moore, who 'gallantly' lost the season, having climbed the mountain before, in order to remain with the Russian officers who did not know what to do.[54] The slopes were tedious and wearing, but the moon, nearly full, entranced them as did the rising sun.[55] They rose to 17,000 feet reaching the col at 17,350 feet, continuing up the final slope amidst snow until reaching the little peak of the highest point via an easy slope and past a crater (¾ mile in diameter). Ice had taken the place of lava. 'Delight in

'Crossing the Chain'

reaching an untrodden summit may seem a childish pleasure to many, but never to those who have once experienced it,' Grove enthused.[56] The day was now perfectly clear and they could see all the great peaks in their 'stern majesty', possibly even as far as Mount Ararat.[57] To the south were huge valleys over the main chain and towards the south-east the Black Sea. To the north was 'the green country', 'like the waves of the sea'. The view surpassed anything in the Alps.[58] This led Grove, perhaps unnecessarily, to reflect on the indigenous 'ancient but declining' race on the one hand and on the other 'a mighty country in...its youth...whose power for good and evil was beginning to be recognised' and how the vast ashes of the volcano around made a mockery of the rise and fall of empires.[59] The group came to the definitive conclusion that the western peak was indeed the higher (the eastern peak is lower by 5,261 feet) but Grove was at pains not to offend Freshfield by stating that the two peaks were 'all but equal in height'.[60]

The adventurers were exhausted from fatigue and the thin air and concluded it was from not having practised enough.[61] They returned to camp after four hours then came down the valley to Uruspieh. After resting at Uruspieh they continued north of Elbruz to the 'Mahommedan' 'green country' and the valley of the Khuds-Su to Uchkulan hoping to find men to bring them over the Nakhar (Nakhra) pass and to Lata.[62] They left Uchkulan via a glen of 'great beauty' and reached the col of the Nakhar pass (free from snow) and the southern side of the chain and a zigzag path to the head of the Klütch valley. Descending steeply to 2000 feet, they were suddenly in 'another land', 'another climate': they had left bare rocks, dull grass land and a bracing climate to find a vegetation of almost tropical richness and a varied profusion of beautiful colour and a hot southern atmosphere accompanied by swarms of mosquitoes and horse flies. A 'mighty' and 'magnificent' forest leading to the Kodor valley covered most of the valley. Walking through birches at first, then giant pines and Levantine oaks, and through a glen of 'great solitude' called by Grove 'the valley of the shadow of death' they came to a waterfall at the end of the valley.[63] On the approach to Lata they abandoned solitude and found the 'wonderful fertility' of wild peaches, plums, walnuts and raspberries. They came to a point where the Tchkhalta flows into the Kodor and finally reached the 'fever-ridden' Russian post of Lata. Here they rested before proceeding to Sukhum-Kale.

Grove concludes by urging hunters and others to visit 'the magnificent, untrodden glens' of the woodland hunting grounds of the north-east.[64] Freshfield had also noted good hunting in the region.[65]

As pointed out earlier, *The Frosty Caucasus* is more discursive than Freshfield's books. Atmospheric descriptions and interest in local life would have been more attractive to a general readership, but perhaps not so much to the professional mountaineer. It lacks some of the data provided so profusely by Freshfield. The use of photography by Horace Walker turned into lithographed prints in the book was, as far as can be ascertained, a first for the British in the high Caucasus (see below).

The book was reviewed as a travel book, not one of exploration, but Grove was not a tourist of the baser kind, wrote the *Edinburgh Review* in 1877 (the time of the Russo-Ottoman war). He was amusing about Caucasian habits and avoided needless details. The most interesting parts were those that gave information on the 'tribes' of Caucasian villages; while not pretending to offer solid information on political or practical topics and although much impeded by weather, he was able to supplement some geographical knowledge.[66] Freshfield, in a wide-ranging review of new writing on the Caucasus, acknowledges the slightly higher western peak of Elbruz, and approves Grove's 'lively and interesting' account.[67]

Hunting: *'A Very Lively Time'*

While Freshfield was at pains to show how serious mountaineering and geography were - both as a science and the former as a sport - the writer and big-game hunter Clive Phillipps-Wolley was determined to make his books on the Caucasus entertaining and to turn his exploits into a series of daring-do adventures with men and beast.

The Great Outdoors

Phillipps-Wolley asserts that the main reason for writing *Savage Svanetia*, his second book, was not to analyse whether the Caucasus was a suitable base for operations in India and Central Asia, but, after encouragement from 'a reviewer', the desire to offer information on the people and game in the 'least known' corner of the Caucasus.[68] Not all thought that this aim was achieved (see below). His first book (1881) deals mostly with Dagestan and the Caspian, the second (1883) with Svaneti.

Phillipps-Wolley was ready to track, stalk and shoot anything of the animal kingdom (from bear to bird), particularly if it was rare or could be brought home as a trophy. He was accompanied in Dagestan by a Tartar guide and also hired a local Lezgin (Allai) who offered to find him chamois, *tûr* (mountain sheep) and other game.[69]

The area near Kuriur near Elizavetpol (on the way to Dagestan and the coast) teemed with wildlife: there were bustards, wild duck, sand-grouse, antelope. Here he stalked a large flock of 'reddish birds' (which he was unable to identity), but they were very shy, and he was unable to procure a specimen.[70] He was keen to observe hunting locals and in the same area he mentions the method of Persian dog-hawking, where greyhounds and hawks were used in the hunting of hares, sand-grouse, partridges and even antelopes, instead of a fowling-piece, as these were too unwieldy.[71] He mentions the dreadful roads and in fear of 'brigands' was in a hurry to get to Dagestan. On the way he observed starlings being chivvied by hawks. Coming across game and skins in local bazaars reinforced his determination to kill *tûr* and chamois in the wilds of Dagestan.[72] Approaching the 'Lesghian mountains' towards Gerdaoul he indulged in shooting squirrels, whose skins were prized by Tiflis furriers, and partridges. From Gerdaoul his party proceeded to the mountains with Allai where they found bear tracks and heard the cry of red deer (known locally as *marral*).[73] He noted that the natives needed nothing where meat was concerned: there were plenty of pheasant and red-legs (hares), mountain sheep, red deer and wild swine (the latter a menace to harvests). They made use of these resources: bear fat was used for lamps, hog skin for moccasins and moss to make dye.[74]

The party (Phillipps-Wolley, Ivan the Tatar guide, Allai and two other Lezgins) started for the higher peaks around Christmas time.[75] In very difficult, slippery terrain (coming across the occasional shelter used by shepherds) they found themselves surrounded by potential game: flocks of wild goats, the tracks of bear and mountain-sheep, deer, black pheasants and broad winged lammergeiers (vultures).[76] They chased red deer until they gave up.[77] On Christmas eve in a mountain hut Phillipps-Wolley was amused by the shrill whistling of the mountain turkeys, who were tame and very easy prey.[78]

They returned from Gerdaoul and set off for Shemakha and Aksu having 'a very lively time' shooting at vultures, red-legs and pheasants.[79] After Tchaillee he witnessed the passage of the lesser bustard (*otis tetrax*) 'in millions all over the steppe', which he was able to shoot and bag as there were so many, also foxes, wild-fowl and, as they approached Lenkoran (Lankoran), which was full of lakelets, ponds and estuaries, water-fowl.[80] Some of this game was for food, but Phillipps-Wolley does not specify what they did with the rest they massacred. Near Salian they saw a vast flight of pelicans 'in wondrous keeping' with the crimson evening sky, and as they approached the Caspian they were deafened by the noise from mandarin ducks, swans, pelicans and flamingos.[81] At Lankoran Phillipps-Wolley searched for a gun-smith and gave him his 'fowling piece' for repair.[82] They spent days at Lankoran shooting wild-fowl (not identified but long-legged and long necked and 'strange to a British eye'). Wild-fowl was very cheap at the bazaar,[83] and he was horrified by a Tatar fowler's practice of not killing birds outright but breaking their legs and wings (kept at the bottom of his boat alive and 'in dreadful pain') until he sold them. He remonstrated with him but to no effect. They spent more shooting days at Eryvool, with the same routine: cock-shooting in the morning and a run at wild boar with the dogs in the evening until they got tired of it. Dogs were essential to ease the hunters' first shot and avoid the 'gnashing ivory bayonets'[84] but the hunt was not so easy, the dogs struggled with a sow and her young got away. Around New Year a there was report of a tiger having killed a cow at Eryvool and the hunters settled down for a long, uncomfortable vigil among eagle owls and the occasional badger to wait for 'Mr. Stripes'. The tiger did not show.[85]

Phillipps-Wolley returned to Tiflis via Lenkoran and dreadful post-roads, stopping at Shemakha to shoot antelopes 'for the sake of the pot as much as the sport'.[86] Nearing Tiflis they witnessed a Tatar antelope hunt on horseback. Having found a herd, the riders surrounded it and tried to separate it, each man choosing his own prey until the beast was exhausted and the hunter closed in. There was no escape route for the antelope as it would 'get headed' by one of the other hunters if the original hunter was not successful. The Tatars had trained dogs with them.[87]

Leaving Tiflis for Poti they spent the day hunting wild boar with sixteen dogs and able bodied 'roughs' of Poti, one of them armed with a blunderbuss. Phillipps-Wolley also noted the number of stag-horns (and roebucks) for sale. These, he writes, had been purposefully slaughtered by Mingrelians in order to deprive the Russians of their favourite sport. Brought from neighbouring villages, the horns, along with boar-tusks, made for 'a roaring trade'.[88]

He indulged in 'sport' until the steamer left Duapse for Kerch.

The 'success' (a rather guarded recommendation in a review by Freshfield in the *Saturday Review*, see below) of his first book spurred Phillipps-Wolley to investigate Svaneti, 'a hungry land inhabited by an angry people,' he wrote in his preface to *Savage Svanetia*.[89] Phillipps-Wolley arrived from the Black Sea via Kerch and Poti and headed for Kutaisi. Here the Prince of Mingrelia had arranged a great mountain drive where as many as sixty head of *tûr* (*Capra Causica*) and chamois could be killed, he was promised, but it fell through. He then hoped for a dawn wolf-hunt, which was impeded by rain.[90] After several days of princely entertaining and 'wine bibbing' Phillipps-Wolley was keen to head for the mountains and revel 'in wild sport'.[91] He wanted bear and chamois.

Phillipps-Wolley and his friend Frank left for Oni in Racha in miserable 'screws' provided by a Jewish horse dealer. En route to Oni he observed the number of butterflies (referring to Radde's collection). The road from Kutaisi onwards was through densely wooded country, with occasional patches of agriculture, climbing to boulder strewn ravines and mountain torrents. At Glola he was told that this was the home of Bruin bears 'par excellence' (attested to by the number of bear skins spread out in all cottages) but despite all the villagers being hunters, none was forthcoming as a guide. Phillipps-Wolley was particularly keen to find a bear with a collar mark on the neck, to check whether it was a species of brown bear as stated by Radde.[92] He pushed on to Gebi, noting the cries and clatter of gongs made by armed locals on watchers' platforms protecting their maize from bears.[93] At Gebi he hired two guides, including one who had been with Freshfield in 1867 and they left for the 'tûr haunted' mineral springs of the neighbouring mountains and Keertescho (Kirtischo, north-west of Gebi) via cornfields up to 2,000 feet in the vicinity of the Tchosura glacier. Here they met 'the genius of the place': a renowned hunter named Simon (see Part 3),[94] who was appointed hunter in chief. They settled near a spring (in what was to be many a watch on this expedition) to wait for *tûr*. The secret was to be out of sight and as quiet as possible. Here they woke and slept and woke for three days, constantly alerted to the animals by small falling stones from above, but were reduced to only seeing chamois from afar.[95] They forded the River Tchosura in pursuit, but after several missed shots they returned to Gebi crestfallen.[96] Here they were alerted to nearby activity and despite it being a Sunday they set off for a bear hunt[97] and finally saw its 'long tawny shape' (so different from 'the poor spiritless beasts that disgrace the name of Bruin in the (London) Zoo').[98] Phillipps-Wolley fired into the indistinct shape but the bear appeared untouched. His companion also wasted the opportunity. Bear slides through tangle and bush, where the bear slithered down from his lair to 'seek the fruit bushes of the valley', were all around. They continued to the spur of the mountains to look for chamois and came across a bear's lair, 'a luxurious shelter from the noonday sun', where they rested, surrounded by bilberry bushes. He noted a tame scarlet bullfinch.[99] Waiting till night for something to materialize Phillipps-Wolley reflected on the eerie nocturnal behaviour of the Bruin, to whom he attributes an almost human character: the bear emerging slow and solemn in absolute silence from the dark recesses of the woods in contrast to the grunts of boars and howls of wolves and jackals. But bears were also 'blind at night' and as one emerged, the hunters shot at him, but wounded, he escaped into the night. Early next morning they found him 'gashed and gory', dead and close to where he had been shot. They skinned him and left him as he lay,[100] shooting a small sheep on the way back to camp. Yet another vigil produced another dead bear.[101]

Still hungry for more sport they left for Svaneti, recommending Gebi and Shukachalo (before harvest or at the end of August) for bagging bear and chamois, as in spring bears were too gaunt and their coats rough and thin.[102] They stayed for three days of 'fasting and bad luck' at Lapar, but were happy to bathe and drink in the cleanest, coldest water coming down through a birch wood. They sought game at night, tried stalking, but to no avail.

This was glacier land, filled with crags, streams and rocky ledges, 'destitute of herbage', with mountains looming overhead.[103] They ravenously ate a small sheep trapped by Simon.[104] Phillipps-Wolley lamented that in three weeks he had killed a couple of bears but no chamois or ibex. As they climbed up the glacier they constantly heard the cries of Caucasian snow-partridges (*Tetrao Caucasicus*). They wandered searching for ibex along 'ruinous paths of former avalanches' coming across hunters' lairs, and, tired and hungry, headed towards Lukhanova peak in the Lukhan district.[105] Looking down at the glacier they saw ibex, and here Phillipps-Wolley comments, a long-range rifle would have done the trick rather than his 'Express' (a comparatively new rifle of higher velocity). They returned to Lapar, counting the steps of the '*via diabolica*' to find that the herd had arrived at last. Fortune ended up being kind to them that day and Phillipps-Wolley shot his first buck. He brought the head back home with him to hang in his dining room.[106] On the slow road to Ushguli[107] they saw more bear thoroughfares and out-of-reach chamois amidst beautiful purple crocuses.[108]

As they approached Svaneti and Ushguli, Simon the hunter, 'the best fellow I ever met in the Caucasus', was coming to the end of his contract[109] and left to go back home. At Ushguli, high on the crest of a table land, they hired horses (against their instinct but at the insistence of the porters) and headed off to between Svaneti and Racha to find *tûr* again. The reason for not bringing horses was made clear when a horse crashed through the scrub of a steep mountain to fall below. The 'poor animal' was left there still alive as the Svans would not hear of it being put out of its misery. They later had to compensate the penniless owner.[110] Phillipps-Wolley noted the abundance of snow partridge due to the scarcity of vultures and other big birds of prey characteristic of Dagestan.[111] Toiling up the glacier they saw *tûr*, were partially successful but were disrupted by the light from a Svan camp's fire and returned to the village 'soaked, crestfallen and hungry'.[112] They hired horses and left for Becho. The scene was 'cheerless', 'of savage desolation' and enlivened only by rosemary and juniper bushes and 'a prickly bush with bright red berries'. They reached 'the miserable collection of hovels' that was Becho and observed Mount Ushba. Both the pejorative language (hovels) about Svaneti and note on Mount Ushba seem to have been nods to Freshfield as future reviewer. At Becho the local prince made them compete in a shooting match - much to Phillipps-Wolley's regret as it wasted his cartridges.[113] The area was rich in trees and potential mines, but the only export from Svaneti, Phillipps-Wolley ascertained, were the grand horns of the *tûr* (made into drinking cups in Kutaisi) and a large number of marten skins.[114]

Impatient as ever for more kill they set off for Latali and Becho and a last attempt at *tûr*, of which (according to Radde) there were two kinds: one with deeply indented horns (seen as trophies at Latali) and another almost smooth.[115] The porters made a pact among themselves about how to divide the pay in case a *tûr* was killed, but later almost came to blows about the route they were to follow into the mountains to catch them.[116] On the third day's ride they came to a small cove at the foot of the snow peaks where the animals were said to be. Their objective was to drive the animals along the top of the mountain ridge.[117] Despite all efforts they missed three herds which passed out of range. After a week they 'crept' back into Becho, frustrated by toil, deprivation and the frustrating evidence of *tûr* and bears all around them.[118] By this time, Frank, his companion, had had more than enough and headed back to Kutaisi while Phillipps-Wolley determined to continue to the forest of Lankoran. On the surprisingly good road from Etseri and approaching Lachamul they spotted a she-bear and her cubs; determined to have 'their jackets', he killed the 'old lady', who tumbled into a stream, and one of the cubs. He skinned them with the help of woodmen.[119] They entered the forest, which was the only way in and out of Svaneti in winter, and followed the Ingur, coming across summer log huts (*tchalashe*) and small patches of cultivated maize. So desperate was Phillipps-Wolley for more killing that he offered an ample reward for anyone who could take him to the *tûr* and double the reward if successful. They set off and ran into a small herd standing 'like statues': 'what a lovely mark they made…feet all together and head turned back.' He wounded three, killed another.[120] They tied the dead animal up (others were to collect the rest) and Phillipps-Wolley carried the beast (complaining of the heavy burden) and returned to the camp in triumph. They proceeded to clean the heads (for Phillipps-Wolley) and the bones for the others. Mercifully for chamois, the weather was now against the party and prevented further butchery. They set off for Ipari and Djuaria. On this road along the riverbed and at night they were accompanied by bears (two old and two cubs) and heard every sound they made. Phillipps-Wolley reflected on respect for the bears' fighting spirit (not having come across it) but he stressed that he loved 'the old forest droll, comic good natured face and cunning ways' and the manner in which the bear gathered as many maize stalks as he could, piled all his harvest in a heap and then set down amongst it 'to eat his supper at leisure'.[121]

The party finally gave up the bear hunt and proceeded to Djuaria and Zudgdidi. The hard times 'were over', there was a good road and a train from Novo Senachi to Kutaisi and the coast. But far from sated once they reached Poti, Phillipps-Wolley indulged in snipe shooting and at Batum joined a military shooting party for boar, jackal and roe deer.[122] The one 'bag' that day was a roe deer (shot by the colonel); Russian soldiers, Phillipps-Wolley thought, had 'as little idea of carrying a drive to a successful issue as has an Easter holiday maker of stag-hunting'. Finally tired of the coast and its dreadful climate they left, 'longing for the civilized world' for Sukhum-Kale and Odessa, to Austria and thence to London's Victoria Station.[123]

Phillipps-Wolley's anecdotal contribution to ethnography was worthwhile, as, he no doubt hoped, was his information on the type and whereabouts of game and local hunting practices to future hunters. Yet the books were hardly manuals of the genre, lacking maps (he used the Five Verst map) except for a very crude outline on the cover of the Svanetian book, and pertinent illustrations. There was little attempt to systematize information, to be precise about hunting techniques or to identify species and be consistent in the use of Latin names. The author seems to have attempted more 'scholarly' information such as references to Radde and a more discursive style in his Svaneti books than in his first (perhaps at the prompting of his publisher), resulting in two volumes and unnecessary detail. Here the general reader might be forgiven for appreciating the details of mountain life and peoples rather than the long descriptions (much abridged above) of endless vigils and missed shots among the bare rocks and ridges of Svanetian glaciers.

The author's cavalier attitude was to be criticized from the first. Freshfield approved of Phillipps-Wolley's amusing anecdotes in *Sport in the Caucasus*, a book that was satisfactory and worth reading but also disappointing as a book of travel. Having been vice-consul at Kerch, Phillipps-Wolley's ignorance of the Caucasus was surprising, nor did he seem to know anything of previous publications (implying his own among others), wrote Freshfield in the *Saturday Review* in November 1881.[124] This omission was probably deliberate on the part of Phillipps-Wolley.

Freshfield was even more guarded when reviewing the Svaneti book. The author made himself out to be a noble barbarian,

Freshfield wrote, but again the book lacked information, re-used illustrations (similar but not identical to ones used before) and was too lengthy in its details of hunting. Although this may well be true, Freshfield ignores the fact that his own *Travels* were also too lengthy in details of his own sporting exploits.[125]

1. https//www.rgs.org; Band 2006
2. The Russian attempt on Mount Elbruz was reported in the *Alpine Journal* of 1865, H.B. George, 168-177
3. Freshfield 1869, 185
4. Official height of summit today: 5,054m 16,581.36 ft, climbinggeorgia.com
5. Freshfield 1869,201
6. Freshfield 1869, 220
7. Freshfield 1869, 234
8. Freshfield 1869, 238-244
9. Freshfield 1869, 258-262
10. Freshfield 1869, 267
11. According to Radde, Freshfield 1869, 279
12. Freshfield 1869,283-286
13. Freshfield 1869, 286-297
14. Freshfield 1869, 332
15. Freshfield 1869, 355
16. Freshfield 1869, 359
17. Freshfield 1869, 361
18. Freshfield 1869, 362
19. Freshfield 1869,367
20. Freshfield 1869, 417
21. Freshfield 1869, 368-369
22. Freshfield 1869, 370-373
23. Freshfield 1869, 379
24. Freshfield 1869, 413
25. Freshfield 1869, 421
26. Freshfield 1884, *Alpine Journal*, 471-474;Donkin 1887, *Alpine Journal*, 258
27. Freshfield 1869, 497
28. Freshfield 1869, 499
29. earthobservatory.nasa.gov
30. Fisher 2001, 91. My thanks to Vanessa Winchester for making me aware of this publication.
31. Freshfield 1869, 209
32. Saturday Review 17 July 1869, 89-91
33. Freshfield *Proceedings of the Royal Geographic Society*, 1890 8/2, 257
34. Freshfield 1884, *Alpine Journal*, 1884, 320-339
35. An account of the search for Donkin was given in in Freshfield 1896, 59-92, esp. 85-87
36. Fisher 2001; see Biographical Notes.
37. Grove 1875, 30
38. Grove 1875, 29-30
39. Grove 1875, 27ff.
40. Grove 1875, 84
41. Grove 1875, 84-85, 89-101
42. Grove 1875, 98-111
43. Grove 1875, 90-91
44. Grove 1875, 99-100
45. Grove 1875, 102-105
46. Grove 1875, 129
47. Grove 1875, 134-135

48   Grove 1875, 136
49   Grove 1875, 152
50   Grove 1875, 170
51   Grove 1875, 171
52   Grove 1875, 211
53   Grove 1875, 210
54   Grove 1875, 225
55   Grove 1875, 232
56   Grove 1875, 235
57   Grove 1875, 238
58   Grove 1875, 240
59   Grove 1875, 240
60   Grove 1875, 237, 243
61   Grove 1875, 238
62   Grove 1875, 293
63   Grove 1875, 325
64   Grove 1875, 341
65   Freshfield 1869, 282
66   *The Edinburgh Review* 1 January 1875, 49-50,56
67   Search and Travel in the Caucasus, Proceedings of the RGS 1890, 257
68   Phillipps-Wolley 1883, 1, ix
69   Phillipps-Wolley 1881, 206-207
70   Phillipps-Wolley 1881, 198
71   Phillipps-Wolley 1881, 196-197
72   Phillipps-Wolley 1881, 205
73   Phillipps-Wolley 1881, 221
74   Phillipps-Wolley 1881, 224
75   Phillipps-Wolley 1881, 228
76   Phillipps-Wolley 1881, 230-234
77   Phillipps-Wolley 1881, 231
78   Phillipps-Wolley 1881, 233
79   Phillipps-Wolley 1881, 237-238
80   Phillipps-Wolley 1881, 245
81   Phillipps-Wolley 1881, 250-251
82   Phillipps-Wolley 1881, 255
83   Phillipps-Wolley 1881, 258
84   Phillipps-Wolley 1881, 260-263
85   Phillipps-Wolley 1881, 269
86   Phillipps-Wolley 1881, 274
87   Phillipps-Wolley 1881, 279
88   Phillipps-Wolley 1881, 281-282
89   Phillipps-Wolley 1883, 1, vii
90   Phillipps-Wolley 1883, 1, 54-65
91   Phillipps-Wolley 1883, 1, 72
92   Phillipps-Wolley 1883, 1, 97
93   Phillipps-Wolley 1883, 1, 105-106
94   Phillipps-Wolley 1883, 1, 128-129
95   Phillipps-Wolley 1883,1, 147
96   Phillipps-Wolley 1883, 1, 154
97   Phillipps-Wolley 1883, 1, 165ff.

98 Phillipps-Wolley 1883, 1, 168
99 Phillipps-Wolley 1883, 1, 173-174
100 Phillipps-Wolley 1883, 1, 185
101 Phillipps-Wolley 1883, 1, 180-190
102 Phillipps-Wolley 1883, 1, 193
103 Phillipps-Wolley 1883, 1, 217
104 Phillipps-Wolley 1883, 1, 211
105 Phillipps-Wolley 1883, 1, 222
106 Phillipps-Wolley 1883, 1, 233-234
107 Phillipps-Wolley 1883, 1, 241
108 Phillipps-Wolley 1883, 1, 253
109 Phillipps-Wolley 1883, 1, 264; 2, 21-22
110 Phillipps-Wolley 1883, 2, 103
111 Phillipps-Wolley 1883, 2, 38
112 Phillipps-Wolley 1883, 2, 43-53, 62, 70
113 Phillipps-Wolley 1883, 2, 135
114 Phillipps-Wolley 1883, 2, 142
115 Phillipps-Wolley 1883, 2, 147-148
116 Phillipps-Wolley 1883, 2, 148, 15-151
117 Phillipps-Wolley 1883, 2, 154-155
118 Phillipps-Wolley 1883, 2, 163
119 Phillipps-Wolley 1883, 2, 177
120 Phillipps-Wolley 1883, 2, 197-199
121 Phillipps-Wolley 1883, 2, 221
122 Phillipps-Wolley 1883, 2, 324-239
123 Phillipps-Wolley 1883, 2, 248-250
124 *The Saturday Review* 1881, 26, 672-673
125 *The Academy* 15 December 1883, 390-391

PART 6

Images

Illustrations were an integral feature of nineteenth-century travel books. They had the power to considerably influence the value of a book and, together with size and binding, could turn it into a luxury item. None of the books discussed here belongs to this category, although the binding of some (Ussher, Freshfield, Telfer), with images of indigenous mountain peoples or equestrian subjects, embossed and picked out in faux gold, are more elaborate than others. What will be assessed below is whether the type (drawn, lithographed, photographed) and manner (vignettes, plates, colour) of given illustrations contributed to and or enhanced the narrative or message of the books and contributed to the overall image of the Caucasus.

British illustration in the early part of the century was dominated by artist-engravers using standard sized box-wood blocks for vignettes and the transfer of pen and ink drawings on blocks. By mid-century electrotyping and lithography became dominant in the printing process.[1] From the later 1860s onwards photography began to make its impact on illustration: these would be engraved, reproduced and lithographed and used together with traditional engraved woodcuts.

What cannot be known and is outside the remit of this book, was to what extent the choice of illustrations was the authors' or the publishers' or both, the copyright and financial arrangements or the relationship between the authors and publishers with lithographers and artists, all of which would have had an influence on the number and eventually type of illustration.

Early photography in England and the Caucasus

Photography in England went through several processes (daguerreotype, calotype, wet-plate process, dry-plate process)[2] before it was viable to be commonly reproduced in books, even though these cumbersome methods did produce good photographs. In the Caucasus, the impetus for the use of photography in the books discussed here came from the Alpine Club and its photographers (see below under travellers).

In the Caucasus itself, photography was linked to Imperial expansion and colonization from the outset through state bodies such as the Military Topographical Department (photographic branch opened 1855), the Imperial Geographical Society (1851) and the Caucasian Army (see below).[3] Photographers were commissioned to research the latest techniques abroad and such links, mainly with France, were to stimulate and initially hugely advance the craft in Russia and the Caucasus. Another spur was the quality of the European Crimean War photography (by the likes of Roger Fenton), which prompted Nicholas I to order the Military Topographical Department to research the latest wet-collodion process used.[4]

One of the earliest to document the Caucasus was Sergey Levitsky (later famous as a portrait and court photographer), who worked in the Ministry of Internal Affairs and was commissioned in 1843 to accompany an Academy of Sciences expedition to make landscape views in the northern Caucasus to be used for the development of the region. His daguerreotypes are among the first of this genre in Russia.[5]

Tiflis, for Imperial logistical reasons and as the capital, was an early draw for photographers. A number of daguerreotype workshops are said to have existed there in the 1840s and 1850s, but few examples of this work survive.[6] Alexander Ivanivsky, who was responsible for setting up in 1863 the Photographic Unit of the Russian Army in the Caucasus (after his return from France with equipment and materials), also produced some of the first extant views of Tiflis (1858).[7] Tiflis drew not only those in the service of the state but also freelancers from abroad, such as an individual called Werner (in the 1840s) or Simon Moritz (in the 1850s) in the early periods[8] and the likes of Edward Westley from St Petersburg, who set up the first permanent workshop in Tiflis in 1863.[9] Nicolai

Heiten opened a studio in Vladikavkaz in 1864.[10] By the 1860s photography in Tiflis had taken off as a craft and from the 1870s as an art form, with local artists (part of the Society of Caucasian Artists set up in 1873) taking it up as a hobby. Photography became lucrative and studios opened in Kutaisi (a major centre, where Dimitri Barkanov had started out before opening a studio in Tiflis in 1873), but also Telavi, Gori and other places.[11] Besides the lucrative fashionable portrait photography, photographers were developing their own interests, such as Nicolai Sagnardze from Kutaisi who had a particular interest in western Georgia.[12]

Photographic units not only recorded topographical and military subjects but also archaeological and ethnographic ones, and despite them being a state enterprise at first, many photographers trained in such units became professionals and famous in their own right. Thus the next generation of photographers, such as Alexandre Roinashvili (1846-98), Dimitri Barkanov (1826-92) and Dimitri Ermakov (1846-1916) as well as being photographers of the Russo-Turkish War 1877-78, together with Dimitri Nikitin, travelled widely in the Caucasus, Iran, Central Asia and Turkey and became internationally known.[13] Both Ermakov and Barkanov produced a huge body of work (albums, negatives, plates) of peoples, monuments, landscapes, roads, infrastructure and antiquities as well as portraits that covered the last quarter of the nineteenth century and early twentieth century. This work is highly skilled, not only technically but also compositionally,[14] and is invaluable for recording the life, peoples and places of the Caucasus and beyond at the time. Roinashvili also had the already mentioned travelling museum and catalogue of stereoscopic views showing Caucasian antiquities and scenic views, which he took to Russia.[15] Amateurs were also on the rise. In 1897 a gold medal was awarded to the head of the Tiflis Society of Amateur Photographers' laboratory, Sergei Margulov.[16]

Photography and ethnography

Photography was not only used for recording topography and infrastructure, but in ethnography, where it was to serve the

Empire in casting its indigenous people into types. The approach was spurred by the naturalist Karl Ernst von Bauer, who relied on Paul Broca's method of physical anthropology in which facial and (naked) body types were recorded for taxonomic purposes. Some of Broca's specifications had been used in the 1867 All Russian Ethnographic Exhibition in Moscow and published in the *Journal of the Royal Geographic Society* of 1872. The Russians adapted this system to clothed subjects in indigenous dress, sometimes with work implements[17] and a background. Such typologies lent themselves to albums and the making of individual cards showing different indigenous types (calling cards or *cartes de visite*), from the early 1860s. The same method, used for society portraiture as well, was also current in Europe at the time. In contrast with society portraiture, however, which promoted the elite, showing men in heroic poses or women in graceful ones, calling cards depicting indigenous peoples played a very different role in the dissemination of what was purported to be ethnographic or scientific knowledge.

The cards had two faces, actually and metaphorically. The obverse showed a figure, sometimes a group, usually facing frontwards in indigenous dress (ranging from festive to rags), numbered and annotated, against a natural or blank background or posing in a studio. The faces are frequently expressionless or sullen, even angry, and whether alone or in groups are like the mannequins in the Tiflis Caucasus Museum, as if fixed in backward time. Other images showing girls dancing or statuesque with water jugs veer towards the erotic, while male Caucasians armed to the teeth (but now disarmed and impotent) indulge other tropes.

The reverse of the cards had elaborate inscriptions promoting the photographer, royal patronage, any medals received, with floral or other designs, such as an artist's easel, paintbrushes and photo apparatus (see Appendix). These cards became commodities, curiosities and collectors' items, reprinted in books and as postcards, passed around and relied upon, thus promoting the prowess of the state and photographer over an indigenous population reduced to mere objects. The 'reality impact' of such photography to use a phrase of Edwards[18] was hence highly ambivalent.

IMAGES

Picturing the Caucasus

All the British travellers' publications discussed above give a list of illustrations. Full plates, half plates as well as vignettes interspersed in the text or at the beginning and end of chapters were used. The illustrations were very much of their time in terms of technologies used: they show a progression from images made into woodcuts and lithographed to actual reproductions of photographs. Not all artists, woodcutters, lithographers and photographers are mentioned on the plates or vignettes nor is the process that that went into making them indicated. The authors (and publishers) were slightly backward, given what was possible at the time (both in Tiflis and in Britain) in the use of photography, which only came into its own in these publications with the work of Vittorio Sella and others in Freshfield's (*et al*'s) 1896-1902 *The Exploration of the Caucasus*. This may have been partly due to the authors' inexperience, the impracticality of carrying heavy and fragile equipment, lack of preparation and potential printing costs back home.

The travellers' illustrations (dealt with chronologically below to give a sense of developing techniques and their usage or not and potential influences from one publication to the next) fall into two groups: those specific to the books' narrative (subject and aims), and those that are more general. The illustration of Robert Lyall's general *Travels in Russia, the Crimea, and Georgia* (1825) comprises carefully chosen, small woodcut vignettes at the head of each chapter in a wide-ranging book. They suggest a mood of travelling by carriage but mostly focus on the main subject of the chapter with views such as the Castle at Tiflis or a fortified village near Kasbek,[19] and later Russian subjects. There is no indication (to the naked eye) of who the artist-engraver was and the use of small woodcut (i.e. a small block) vignettes was very much of its time.

The early publications dealing with Circassia (Spencer, Bell, Longworth in the 1840s) predictably depict overwhelmingly Circassian subjects, but with particular focus and care. Some of Spencer and Bell's plates are coloured, and those of Bell are especially telling and valuable as they give actual portraits of eminent Circassians (Frontispiece Hadji Ghuz Beg, and Tchurukh-oku Tughuz, Hadji-oku Mehmet and Vordezav-oku Zepsh in a later plate).[20] Equally his views of Russian camps, local hamlets and illustration of antiquities are all relevant to the area and narrative (focusing on warriors in the field, even though somewhat idyllic) and are referred to in the text. The only concession to exotic norms and domesticity is the Frontispiece of vol. 2 showing two slender Circassian maidens with long tresses (see below).[21] Longworth's scenes are group based showing tribal gatherings (p.24) and Circassian interiors, and together with views of forts and bays they give a strong sense of the setting and the local topography defended by the Circassians and of who attended such gatherings (gleaned from the costumes: mullahs, nobles, warriors, commoners). The latter convey an idea of the numbers that could be gathered.[22]

'Circassian Maidens'

IMAGES

Spencer's illustrations, the earliest of the group, veer from being overtly political (such as the illustration of the Urquhart-designed Circassian flag[23]) to more general and romantically themed illustrations such as 'A Circassian Chieftain and his Family', 'The Warrior's Return' or 'Guerilla Warfare in the Caucasus') to interiors (Reception Room of a Circassian Prince) and costume illustrations ('Circassian Chief in Gala Costume') - or himself in one edition (see below).[24] These were geared as much towards popular appeal and book promotion as much as the Circassian cause.

Bell's illustrations were based on his own drawings made into woodcuts by various artists (mostly H. Warren and G. Bernard) and lithographed by Day and Hague, lithographers to the Queen. Spencer used the painter and engraver Zeiter for his own sketches drawn from nature.[25] Longworth does not acknowledge who made the sketches for the woodcuts (the assumption is it was himself as they are of the same style), also using Day and Hague as lithographers.

'The Author in Circassian Costume'

Cameron travelling in 1844 had no illustrations.

Ussher's *A Journey from London to Persepolis* (1865) was a very different type of publication from those above; it was a semi-luxurious general travel book (the cover shows riders picked out in faux gold and has coloured plates), possibly in competition with Sir Robert Ker Porter's monumental *Travels in Georgia* of 1821, which had also included Persia. It was meant to impress and divert rather than inform; the Frontispiece is a coloured plate of the Fire Temple at Baku, Georgian damsels in costume,[26] Circassian dance,[27] Circassians now transformed into marauders.[28] Of eighteen images, six are of Georgia and Dagestan. The latter would have been particularly pertinent for those interested in the Caucasus as the book came out very shortly after the so-called end of the war against the mountain peoples and show an image of Shamil (p. 45) and of Gunib from a distance attesting to a touring westerner's actual presence in what had been a war zone (see Part 3).

The majority of the illustrations are from lithographed drawings (artist not named, lithographed by Vincent Brooks) except for the portrait of Shamil which was lithographed from a photo,[29] but the photographer is not specified. The amateur Count Ivan Nostitz is credited with having made one of the earliest portraits of Shamil.[30]

Freshfield's illustrations in *Travels in the Central Caucasus and Bashan* (1869) were above all specific to mountains and landscapes, with plates and half plates and panoramic sketches (eleven out of twenty-two): for example, Mount Elbruz, twice, once as coloured Frontispiece, Ararat, Kasbek, peak in the Terek valley, Adai-Khokh, panoramas of the Koshtantau group,[31] but also included are indigenous peoples.[32] These illustrations, in stark contrast to Bell's, do nothing to celebrate and romanticize the people. They reflect Freshfield's negative attitude; the woman of Uruspieh, for example, is shown huddled against a wall and scowling in a passage ironically describing 'Uruspieh beauty' and prematurely aged and wrinkled women. Images of the Khevsurs, the natives of Jibiani and the Ossetians all convey primitiveness, and how he perceived them.

There are no indications as to who the original artist or artists were (there are different styles) in this book, except for one showing a campfire in the forest,[33] which suggests that some must have been by members of the group. Some sharp images, such as that of Mount Ushba above Latal shown in a circular frame (Frontispiece),[34] may have been taken from an existing photograph, and some vignettes may have been lifted from larger images. Freshfield's 1896-1902 publication was in a completely different league to this one and will be discussed below.

Mrs Harvey's *Turkish Harems and Circassian Homes* (1871) was a diverting travel tour aimed at a female audience. It has only two pretty illustrations in chromolithography (M. and N. Chromolithographers) drawn by Anne Harvey the author, showing A Distant View of El Barouz on the front page (with embellished epigraphy) and with a Frontispiece of a mountain gorge above Sukhum-Kale.

Arthur Cunynghame's *Travels in the Eastern Caucasus* (1872) was also a general travel book but interesting for its group of illustrations of Dagestan (of twenty-five images six are of Dagestan): they show Gunib ('Shamyl's village'), a characteristic Lezgin village hanging from a mountain side (Inkulluk), a Lezgin soldier, mountain passes and a Tatar house at Chok.[35] All convey the isolation and atmosphere of the place. They were drawn by Cunynghame's son Henry Harding (the lithographer's name is not given) and most are in the form of unframed vignettes. Two are reminiscent of photographs: the cloaked Lezgin soldier standing in driving rain and a plate and half-plate view of Tiflis, which are both framed in the manner of photographs. Plates were usually framed[36] but not other vignettes inserted in the text: the framing of the former may have been to convey the influence of photography.

Grove's illustrations in *The Frosty Caucasus* (1874) are balanced and suit the subject both in terms of primary aim (mountaineering and geography: two of Elbruz, the valley of the Baksan, Tungsorun, the gorge of the Djilki-Su) and the representation of people and their homes in this landscape (a house at Bezingi) respectively and as a group (men of Gebi).[37] They are significant because for the first time in the Caucasus they showcase the use of photography throughout by a British mountaineer: Horace Walker, a member of Grove's party (lithographed by Edward Whymper). The lithographs are sharp and reveal the impact of photography on, for example, the rush of water (The Valley of Baksan) or the scale of mountains, and in the case of the group photograph of the men of Gebi, whose expressions can be seen with some smiling, unlike in current ethnographic 'visiting cards'.[38]

The Alpine Club and Photography

From its early days in the 1860s, the *Alpine Journal* had charted the use of photography in Alpine settings in various articles, from the wet-collodion process through to the first daguerreotypes and the snap-shot camera. Ruskin boasted that he had been the first to take a photograph of the Matterhorn in 1849 (not survived), wrote Douglas Milner in 'A Century of Alpine Photography'. Milner also describes the extremely heavy equipment (c.500lb) used by Aimé Civale in the Alps around 1860, using twenty-five mules but limited to where the animals could get to.[39] In 1859/60 good daguerreotypes were available of Mont Blanc. By the later 1860s the field was opening up and photographs were being taken annually. A *Note* in the Journal from 1865 states that the best cameramen at the time were Mr Braun of Dornach and a Mr England but it does not specify which camera or method was used.[40] It must have been the wet collodion process, which had replaced the calotype. By 1870 H.B. George in 'Notes on Photography in the High Alps' showed how things were changing and how things could be adapted. He reported that Mr Edward's apparatus was indeed a marvel of portability, but things could be even better. His own apparatus weighed less than four pounds (without a tripod) and that the 'royal road' to photography involved 'satisfactory dry plates' (which could be used after any interval of time). This would dispense with a dark tent and ill-smelling chemicals and would allow for enlargements. Black velvet to cover the apparatus (3½ inches) was all that was needed. A dozen plates (kept in a zinc box in a leather case 7½ x 4 x 7½ inches) would suffice. This may have been the method used by Horace Walker but there is no record of it in the *Alpine Journal*.[41]. With other fittings and a tripod the whole load would weigh approximately 5½ pounds.[42] The first highly rated (by the Club in England) photographer was W F. Donkin, the Hon. Secretary of the Alpine Club, who died in a climbing accident in 1888 (see Part 5). In 1882 Donkin himself wrote an article stressing that accuracy and sharpness were essential to delineate form, snow and rock (and thus geology) and that scale should be captured correctly. Avoiding blurring atmospheric conditions was essential. When compared to painting, colour was lost, but accuracy made up for the exaggeration of painters. For Donkin, photography was as much a science as an art. He recalled the toil of transporting 7lb of apparatus and plates, but now things had changed with sensitive plates and Mr. Hare's changing box of twelve plates. Good landscape work could now be done with a half-plate field camera (5 x 4 inches, or 7½ x 5 inches) and a changing box. They could be enlarged with the carbon process. But it was acknowledged that better pictures were taken with larger plates and larger lenses. Plates could be transferred to a slide, exposed and returned to the box with no damage from light. It could all be packed on top of a rucksack. But development had to occur in situ and not on return to Britain.[43] As the century wore on the *Alpine Journal* reflected public interest in photography with frequent photographic exhibitions showing the photographers' own techniques.[44] In 1890 there was an exhibition of equipment recommending the latest apparatus.[45] A new hand-held camera (Kodak no. 3 Junior) could give good but not memorable work, wrote Walter Leaf in 1891. Such cameras could catch incidents whereas setting up a tripod etc. 'took the truth out of the picture', but holding a camera also impeded the climber, and the film was so rapid that it was easy to overexpose.[46] In 1893 the telephoto lens produced the star photograph of the photographic exhibition, Mont Blanc taken from fifty-four miles away.[47]

Vittorio Sella, in Freshfield's book of 1896-1902, was to follow his own path where apparatus and equipment was concerned.

Technical challenges

Experience in photography was clearly needed and this is clearly demonstrated by Phillipps-Wolley's mishaps in *Sport in the Crimea and Caucasus*. He sets the scene: after a two-hour climb with Rouch's patent dry plate apparatus[48] to photograph some of the scenery of Dagestan, his party chose excellent views and took them very carefully, going away satisfied that those at home would be able to share in their enthusiasm for the scenery of 'Lezghia'. They also photographed a *babushka*, the elderly female family tyrant known to all locals. Upon their return, however, it was necessary to develop (amidst an admiring and expectant crowd of locals) and here 'it was easy to stand over a tripod with a black rag over your head, but when dealing with chemicals and other diableries' they had to pretend they knew what they were doing, and put on a brave face. They washed the plates and poured on developing fluid backwards and forwards but no sublime peaks nor picturesque village appeared on the glass. Phillipps-Wolley recalled an equally disastrous incident in Kerch, where they had attempted to photograph a group of Tatars (making them sit still for a quarter of an hour) but then found that no plates had been inserted in the slides. This time the plates had been inserted but still the plates remained the same. One dark spot eventually appeared. They mumbled excuses to the expectant throng and resolved to give away their photographic equipment at the earliest opportunity.[49]

As a result, Phillipps-Wolley's 1881 book has no illustrations. *Savage Svanetia* does have illustrations from lithographed photographs (by Pearson) but they are inserted in the text with no references, using subjects that since Freshfield had become fairly standard (the Valley of the Rion as Frontispiece to vol. 1; Svanetian villages of Mulach and Mugal Frontispiece to vol. 2; Mestia p. 114, Moulachi with Uschba mountain p. 226 in the text of vol. 2.[50] Arguably the most interesting ones are a Svanetian dwarf on the front cover of vol. 2, itinerant Persian gypsy musicians from a series of types of musicians of the Caucasus[51] and a group photo of indigenous people with a Russian official on the front page of vol. 1. The identical photo (not cropped) from

'Persian Gypsy Musicians'

the Abercromby collection brought back from Tiflis shows these men to have been Ossets (see Appendix).[52] Incomprehensibly, there are no illustrations at all of the main subject of Phillipps-Wolley's book: hunting and game, and if a reader had to guess the actual subject of the book they would be unable to from the illustrations alone.

Wardrop's goal in *The Kingdom of Georgia* of focusing on Georgia and its history and intellectual heritage was made possible by the wide array of images now available, including photographs, postcards or reproductions of paintings. Thus prominent people (Queen Tamara, Irakli II, the poet Rustaveli, Prince Ivan Machabeli) and landmarks (Tiflis, Vladikavkaz, Dariel, Ananur, Signagki) were reproductions or lithographed from photographs.[53] Various engravers' names appear: A. Brabant, D. Langlot, A. or H. Sirouy, an A.T.

Wardrop's personal collection of Georgian material shows an abundance of such images (many coloured) collected in albums, including many of the ethnographic calling cards mentioned above and like those brought back by Abercromby in 1888.[54]

Abercromby's illustrations were all focused on two of his main interests: ethnography and antiquarianism. Antiquarianism was dealt with by rubbings and drawings and ethnography by photography, reproduced in the book. Abercromby was inexperienced. He bought a 'photo apparatus' in Moscow on the recommendation of a 'commis voyageur' who accompanied him as his translator and would be photographer for a while. The man turned out to be incompetent with a camera and had to be got rid of. On arriving in Tiflis, at a time when photography was widely used and thriving, Abercromby found to his regret that he could have engaged someone competent, but it was too late, he writes.[55] The bonus of this bad luck was that he purchased over thirty calling cards of Caucasian types in Tiflis (see Appendix) and of antiquities, some by the celebrated Barkanov, which he brought back to Edinburgh. He showed the former at a public lecture. These were possibly the first of this kind of the Caucasus to be physically handled in Edinburgh. Six from the collection were printed as plates in the book: 'Group of Lezghians' (Frontispiece), 'a Lezghian', 'a group of Chechents', 'a group of Chechents women', 'a group of Tush men', 'a group of Tush women'. The final photo in the book shows a photograph of the author with his two guides and helpers Majid and Akim done on the spot (p. 247). Unfortunately he does not tell us who the photographer was.[56]

The illustrations of the final book of this group, Freshfield's *The Exploration of the Caucasus*, are overwhelmingly of mountains and landscapes but also include local people in their setting, as well as the travellers themselves. The book is dominated by photographs or vignettes derived from photographs, inserted in the text, the majority of which are by Vittorio Sella (only seventeen out of two hundred and sixty-nine illustrations are by others: M. de Déchy, H. Woolley and A.W. Moore). The scale and detail of the mountain and landscape photography reveal the true nature and challenges of the area, while those of the indigenous people, whether at work, taking part in a ceremony or lying in a field or at home, convey the reality of these peoples' lives in the mountains and their character,

'The Author, Mejid, and Akrim'

without judgement and far closer to ethnographic reality than any calling card.

Sella (1859-1943) understood mountains and was a keen mountaineer as well as a photographer, travelling from Europe to North America and Africa, making three trips to the Caucasus (1889, 1890, 1896). His excellence, both in his documentation (precision) and artistry (composition, tone) was achieved by the deliberate use of large plates (18 x 24, 24 x 30, 30 x 40 cm). These were carried in specially adapted equipment (making for very heavy loads) and needing an assistant. He used both the wet and dry collodion process and gelatine silver or silver bromide prints.[57]

Sella profited from the times in which photography offered a choice of cameras and technologies, but it was his individuality, determination and technical understanding that made him stand out.

Reflections

Which of the above illustrations and techniques contribute most to the narrative and/or aims of the books? Is it even a legitimate question to ask given the restrictions of technologies (and publishing)? A trawl through the above books' illustrations has shown that the answer is far from clear cut.

There are nuances between subject, technology and size. Thus, precision and impact for mountains and landscape was best achieved through photography, for as Donkin said, artists could exaggerate; equally, lithographed photos of places and mountains showed more accuracy but when drawn show a different, longer and considered kind of engagement. The representation of people was complex: lithographed, probably hand coloured drawings, such as those of Bell, show intimacy with the subject and details (costume, physiognomy), but also add an element of story-book romance to the publication. This is particularly evident in Spencer's illustrations, which tend to heighten drama by the figures' exaggerated movement. Intimacy could not be achieved by the photography of calling cards, but could be captured, even though at a further remove, by individual photographers such as Walker (in Grove) or Sella. For details of antiquities and archaeology the established norm of drawing was best.

General images used in the wider touring books were derived from different sources and different historical subjects (as in Wardrop) and serve their purpose but do not make a particular impact, whereas Bryce's single image of Ararat (frontispiece) focuses on his specific cause at the time, the Armenians. Phillipps-Wolley's images seem to have been inserted for the sake of convention, and could have been informative but are not because they are not referenced in the actual text.

If a test were applied as to what any book was about by only looking at the illustrations, those of Bell, Longworth, Spencer, Freshfield (twice), Grove, Bryce and Abercromby and to a lesser extent those of Lyall, Ussher, Cunynghame and Wardrop would not leave the reader at a loss as to their aims. The size of images conveys importance: as such, Frontispieces announce the key to the book, coloured plates stress particular subjects, some with an emphasis on the dramatic (e.g. Ussher) while the various shapes of lithographed photographs (rectangular, half rectangular, oval) introduce variety. Vignettes are sometimes too small to be appreciated, but act as fillers, chapter heads or ends. Others if large or original enough give a quick impression of the subject.

A feature introduced to arouse interest in the authors themselves were images of the travellers in situ. This trend also informed the reader on context. Freshfield's 1869 *Travels in the Central Caucasus and Bashan* contained an illustration of the group's native guides by a campfire in the forest (p. 212), Grove combined the climbers and a guide (or surveyor) with a view of Elbruz (back cover0, Abercromby showed himself accompanied by his two guides and helpers. The height of vanity was Spencer's illustration of himself in Circassian costume as Frontispiece to his 1839 edition of *Travels in Circassia* (p.239). This was captioned as 'Circassian Chief in Gala Costume' in the 1837 edition.

Reviewing the books in question it is possible to see which images became stock (but not identical) features of the genre, whether in terms of subject or placement within the book. A mountain (Elbruz, Kazbek, Ararat) repeatedly placed as Frontispiece (Freshfield, Grove, Harvey, Telfer, Bryce, Phillipps-Wolley) became an obvious symbol of the area. Other stock images were of the Dariel pass or fort (Lyall, Freshfield, Cunnynghame, Wardrop), Svanetian villages with towers (Freshfield, Telfer, Phillipps-Wolley), Tiflis (Lyall, Freshfield, Ussher, Telfer, Cunnynghame), costume and dance (Bell, Ussher, Telfer, Wardrop), Lezgin soldiers (Cunnynghame, Phillipps-Wolley, Abercromby, as Frontispiece), etc.

As the century wore on so images started to repeat themselves, despite greater availability through photography. This gave greater choice to some, which Wardrop took full advantage of, but not others. This may have been because of the influence of tourism and itineraries set by travel guides such as John Murray's *Handbook for Travellers in Russia* (1888, 1899 etc.) which contributed to the fixing of places and images in peoples' minds. While earlier images conveyed novelty and variety, later ones (except for Sella's) began to reiterate an established image of the Caucasus they had seen.

The impact of illustrations on readers of the time is difficult to gauge as illustrations are hardly ever referred to by reviewers (except for Sella's photographs in Freshfield, which gave a particular cachet to that book). Anything new, such as Bell and Longworth's illustrations, which attest to personal engagement over and above that of a traveller, or early images of Svaneti and Dagestan or the early portrait of the celebrated Shamil must have resonated with the public. Sella's images of the landscapes and people of the Caucasus would also have provided a dose of reality. Their contribution to knowledge was undeniable: images of Circassians in situ, of Dagestan, of indigenous peoples in their settings, of history and architecture (both in mountainous regions and Tiflis and other parts of Georgia), of geography, landscape and mountaineering all provided a glimpse into a world that many would not know about, nor have a chance to really understand.

IMAGES

1. Electrotyping: an engraved block impressed onto lead or a metallic face imposed on it to produce a mould and an electrotype. Lithography: moistening a polished stone surface, applying the drawing, pouring acid to elevate the image and applying ink. Various stones could be used to produce different colours. Victorian victorianweb.or/Victorian/art/illustration.
2. Daguerreotype (1835): a copper plate exposed to iodine vapour and placed over heated mercury to create an image fixed with thiosulphate (1835) producing and inverted image, which could not be reproduced. Calotype, patented by Fox-Talbot (1841): a sheet of paper coated with silver chloride exposed to light in a camera obscura, yielding a negative. The image was developed with gallic acid, with much shorter exposures. Wet-plate collodion process (1851): a mixture of collodion and potassium iodide were poured over the plate, then immersed in a sensitizing solution of silver nitrate, developed, fixed and dried. Dried-plate process (1871): a glass plate coated with a gelatin emulsion of silver bromide. Stored until after exposure. Victorianweb.org/photos/chron.; online Encyclopaedia Britannica
3. Gorshennina and Sonntag 2018, 324-5
4. Gorshenina and Sonntag 2018, 327-329
5. Gorshenina and Sonntag 2018, 326-327, with references
6. Mamatsashvili 2014, 19
7. Mamatsashvili 2014, 19-21
8. Mamatsashvili 2014, 19
9. Mamatsashvili 2014, 22
10. Solovyova and Kouteivikova 2016, 135-136
11. Mamatsashvili 2014, 26
12. Mamatsashvili 2014 26
13. Mamatsashvili 2014, 28-4
14. Mamatsashvili 2014, e.g. nos 109, 113,187, 189, 205 205
15. Mamatsashvili 2014, 23, see also Mamatsashvili et al 2015 Roinashvili and his Museum, Tbilisi
16. Mamatsashvili 2014, 24-26
17. Gorshenina and Sonntag 2018, 330
18. Edwards 1988, 26
19. Lyall 1825, Chapters XII, XVI, XVIII
20. Bell 1840, 1, Frontispiece, and 242
21. Bell 1840, list of Plates,1, 154, 2, Circassian Maidens Frontispiece, Russian camp at Sashe 12-13, relic of antiquity with seated warriors, 58-59, view of Toapse 92-93, Greek cross and warriors, 254-255, embarkation 276-277, assembly of tribes, 344-345, silver cup 404-405
22. Longworth 1840, List of illustrations, from vol 1 front, Frontispiece, Interior of a Circassian house, Genoese Castle 9, Circassian hospitality, 45, assembly of Circassian chiefs 90, Vol.2, Frontipsiece Gathering of Circassians, Bay of Semez 1, Peasants of Tougouse, the Wolf 47.
23. Spencer 1837, 2, Frontispiece
24. Spencer 1837, 1, Frontispiece Circassian chief in gala costume; 2, A Circassian chieftain and family, front page; Frontispiece; 1837 2, 232 Reception room of a Circassian prince; 1838 1 Frontispiece The warrior's return, Guerrilla warfare in the Caucasus, 1838, 2, Frontispiece; 1837 2,

232 Reception room of a Circassian prince
25 Spencer 1837,1, xix
26 Ussher 1865, 2, 79
27 Ussher 1865, 5, 150
28 Ussher 1865, 4, 107. For full list see front of book.
29 Ussher 1865, 6, 163
30 Mamatsashvili 2014, 21
31 Freshfield 1869, for mountains: Full page 125,185,197, 2 Panoramas 381, Woodcuts, mountains and nature:328,411, 237, 282,
32 Freshfield 1869, mountaineers in armour 195, an Ossette 227, a native of Jibiani 300, a woman of Uruspieh 357, an Osette village 213, view of Tiflis 104, Fort of Dariel 442. For full list see front of book.
33 Freshfield 1869, 288
34 Freshfield 1869, 329
35 Cunynghame 1872 186, 198, 199, 201, 211, 223; Shamyl's village, 198, Tatar house 199, Pass near Gunib 186, 201, Inkulluk village 211, Lesghian soldier 223. For full list including Pass of Dariel 244 and Tiflis 257 see front of book.
36 as were other Plates in the book e.g. City of Sebastopol, 96
37 Grove 1875, mountaineering and geography, 152, 186, 226, 298, title page, house at Bezingi, men of Gebi 75
38 Grove 1875, Baksan 186, Men of Gebi 75
39 *Alpine Journal* 1957, 157-164
40 *Alpine Journal*, 1865, 48
41 Only the itinerary of this journey is given in the journal of 1874, knowing presumably that a book on the expedition was to be written by Grove
42 *Alpine Journal* 1870, 402-410. Liverpool dry plates were recommended.
43 *Alpine Journal* 1882 63-71
44 *Alpine Journal* (all online) 1892, 1893, 1897, 1899 etc
45 *Alpine Journal* 1890, 136-138
46 *Alpine Journal* 1891, 472-479
47 *Alpine Journal* 1893, 347
48 W.W. Rouch's apparatus, 180 Strand, London a firm founded in 1863, later joined by Henry Burfield.
49 Phillipps-Wolley 1881, 225-228
50 1883, List at front of each book
51 1883, 1, 162; Aleksidze 2018, 16; Mamatsashvili 2014, 240
52 Abercromby no. 24 (Appendix)
53 Wardrop 1888, List of illustrations at front of book. A number of his illustrations can be compared to Roinashvili's photographs, with or without amendments: eg. Queen Tamara, Rustaveli, Irakli cf. Mamatsaschvili 2001 36, 37; the castle and fort at Dariel: bid 13. For portraits of clerics: ibid 123.
54 See Aleksidze 2018 figs 9-11 and e.g. Wardrop 13.67 in the Bodleian collection.
55 Abercromby 1889, 2
56 Abercromby 1889, 52, 124, 134, 174, 178, 206. He acknowledges that all were from photographs
57 Fondazione Sella; Andrew Smith Gallery

Conclusion

What were these British up to in these parts of the Caucasus during the nineteenth century? The region was virtually an unknown to them in the earlier part of the century and was either at war or unsettled for many years. The travellers' and consuls' texts discussed in this book show a mix of motives, on the one hand confusing and on the other clear-cut with a division between Britain's geopolitical involvement or interference, exemplified by partisan travellers such as Spencer and Bell, an interest in discovery (mountaineering, ethnography, antiquarianism) or touring for curiosity. The latter often included Crimea as well as Russia.

In geopolitical terms, an open Black Sea trade and maintaining the status quo of the Ottoman Empire were of strategic importance to the British. The idea of promoting Circassian independence became caught up in these objectives and was championed by enthusiasts. Russia's ongoing brutal colonial mission was also clear: this was witnessed pragmatically, while at the same time the threat to India and Constantinople from Russia was stressed by those who championed the Circassian cause.

The question arises as to why the British government chose to toy with the idea of Circassian independence. It was clear from Dr Riach and others' reports from the early Caucasus wars that the mountain 'tribes' could not be unified to provide a consistent and reliable resistance to the threat that Russia posed. Even if they did unite, it would not last for long. One of the problems was how they would be governed and by whom. London covertly sent agents and arms to Circassia, but never enough, nor was there any indication of any forward planning. This frustrated Bell and Longworth as they waited for instructions from London in the late 1830s. Reports to the Foreign Office (and the travellers' books) again reveal how willing the Circassians were to fight and how they could be helped on the ground, but also that the prospect of maintaining unity and discipline among the tribes was not really viable. As the Russian war against the mountain people was raging, the Circassians bombarded London with a deluge of petitions asking for help. But it became evident that it would be difficult to harness them to any British scheme and that the British would not threaten war nor go to war over the cause.[1] Yet the strategy of sending agents and arms continued during the Shamil wars, when there was the added complication of Shamil's envoys to Circassia only partially rallying the Circassians to his cause. The Crimean War might have been a real opportunity for the Circassians, but again they were let down both by the Ottomans (whom they resented and did not want as masters and who had poor leadership) and the British, who were now wanting to use the Circassians for their horses and fodder, while investigating the viability of co-opting them and Shamil. Shamil and his envoy refused at first to accept British interference.

Longworth's reports describe the volatile reality on the ground, the fear of Shamil's unpalatable 'theocratic principles' spread by his deputy in the western Caucasus, and the ultimately unrealistic prospects for any settlement with the Circassians. By now the Foreign Office needed reminding of its previous relations with Circassia. It thus appears that it was not a question of the British hedging their bets but that there never was a British strategy towards the Circassians. What remained became merely a form of information gathering and agitation against the Russians. The show of petitions and Circassian envoys to the Foreign Office and the Crown would have been an added taunt to the Russians as well as a form of colonial kudos.

Black Sea trade had ostensibly opened up post-Crimea, and relations with Russia, even though fractious, were on a different footing and the Circassian affair no longer relevant. The decimation of the Circassians and other mountain peoples in the 1860s was witnessed and deplored by the British on the ground and overseas, but while it could be argued that the British (and the French, who were also sending agents and arms) were not responsible for the genocide of the Circassians and other mountain peoples, they were guilty of prolonging the duration of the war against them. The insurrection during the 1877-78 Russo-Ottoman War took place among wider geopolitical priorities, and with official British

CONCLUSION

neutrality and the future of the Ottoman Empire at risk, the insurrectionists' cause was now lost.

A new cause emerged for some: the future of Armenia and Armenians, in which the colonial Bryce, with suggestions of building up western institutions supported by Britain in Ottoman lands, was invested. Transcaucasia was left to ferment in a surge of nationalism.

With regards to other aspects of relations with Russia at the time, the establishment of consuls on the old Circassian coast, and later Tiflis, was a new start for the British in post-Crimea Caucasus. The consuls reported from lamentable, badly paid posts and both consuls and travellers portray a Russia that that was despotic, inefficient and backward. But they made do. The travellers depended on Russian administrative help for parts of their journeys, which was not refused, although their ambiguous relationship with Russia was also evident in their summary attitude to Tiflis. Except for Wardrop, they not show much interest in its culture: the Museum at Tiflis, for example, which expressed in multiple ways Russia's Imperial, civilizing mission vis-à-vis primitive mountain tribes, did not impress them. The travellers were mostly keen to get away from Russian officialdom (and probably policing) in Tiflis.

Anti-British feeling came to a head during the Russo-Ottoman War, with trade being particularly threatened, but this was also partly posturing, as a number of British firms were involved in Russia at the same time. The consuls' reports give an insight into Russia's development and domestic problems: the building of ports and railways in which foreign firms were involved, its poor roads hampering trade, its ruinous focus on wars both as a means of conquest and of placating the populace, co-option of elites and adversaries through repeated bribery by the Tsar down to ordinary officials. They also observed grave social discontent and resentment against the ruling class, rising authoritarianism, nationalism, unreliable troops, and chaotic, corrupt and ultimately collapsing administration in the Caucasus. Consul Lyall was able to foresee both the revolution and the future conflict that was to be the First World War.

Learning and general knowledge of the northern Caucasus were enhanced by the travellers in several ways. Geography was advanced by Freshfield and Grove through their observations of the topography, the nature of glaciers and map making. This was acknowledged by the *Encyclopaedia Britannica*, which uses their publications to inform on the mountains and vegetation of the central chain of the Caucasus.[2] Equally, a new field for mountaineering enthusiasts away from the Alps was opened up by Freshfield and Grove and their ascents of Kasbek and Elbruz. Ethnography, or cultural anthropology as it was known at the time, was not a field the travellers were interested in *per se* and nor had Britain any engagement with the discipline as regards the Caucasus. The subject was still generally understood as 'customs' and was late in developing in Britain, although observation on 'customs' was expected in travelogues. Thus the travellers' observations give rare insights into the way of life of the indigenous mountain communities, the structure of Circassian clans and their war tactics, some religious practices (indigenous, Christian, Muslim and mixed), differences between Muslim and Christian groups, their remoteness, the poverty of some and riches of others, their tradition of hospitality, and evolving relations with Russians. In Dagestan they were able to observe the lives of local governors, mixed communities (Jews, Armenians and others) as well as contributing to the myth of Shamil.

Abercromby focused mainly on language and physical anthropology. But he did make it to Chechnya and observed its people as well as the Russian stranglehold on the area. He was also the first (or among the first) to bring back to Edinburgh a collection of ethnographic 'visiting cards' of the peoples of the Caucasus and images of antiquities (see Appendix).

Antiquarianism was also mostly incidental, but Bell, Telfer and Abercromby all contributed to knowledge by highlighting what could be found in the landscape or while farming or building roads, whether kept in private collections or in remote villages. Abercromby was able to recognize valuable Islamic metalwork at Kubachi on the basis of having seen a precedent in the Kensington

Conclusion

Museum and reported on unique local stone reliefs. His deliberate charting of the Derbent wall was also an advance on what had gone before. Telfer even conducted his own excavations at M'zhett (Mtskheta).

It cannot be argued that a complete picture of the Caucasus was given, nor could it be given by these individual travellers[3]. Their time there was too short, they faced the obstacle of not knowing the relevant languages (except for Telfer and Wardrop), the country was unknown to them and they were of their time. The colonial mindset was inevitable although this was more prevalent in the attitude of some (Freshfield, Cameron, Bryce) than others. All were aware of the inevitable Russian domination of the area and it cannot be denied that they saw most indigenous people as backward and doomed. The travellers also perhaps subconsciously adhered to evolutionary ideas of human progress prevalent in the nineteenth century. The relentless march of colonialism was part of their world. This attitude was directly addressed only by Cameron, occasionally accused of pro-Russian bias, who argues in his preface that 'acts of British rule…oppression and injustice… were not surpassed by any Russian authority.'[4] The consuls saw things the travellers did not nor perhaps wish to see: the latter also had to consider the appeal of their books, balancing entertainment with fact.

The British nineteenth-century travellers did not romanticize the Caucasus as the Russians and to a certain extent the French did, but they did contribute to the idealization of Circassians (in text and illustration) and Shamil, to tropes of beautiful and ugly Caucasian women and to the cliché of turning a decimated Abkhazia into a lost paradise. Nevertheless, individuality and engagement with current affairs was demonstrated by some: partisanship with regard to Circassia by Spencer and Bell, by Longworth in his analyses of the situation, by Bryce with regard to Armenia, Wardrop with regard to Georgia. Geopolitical events influenced ideas, but nothing concrete came of them. Other travellers such as Abercromby chose not to engage with such events and took the opportunity of travelling in peacetime.

Towards the end of the century, the popular image of the Caucasus was changing and becoming more standard and narrower due to the opening up of certain touristic routes (to which the travellers' work had certainly contributed). Areas that had been remote were opened up while others were being closed. The travellers' image of the Caucasus was, however, salvaged by Sella's spectacular photographs in Freshfield's *The Exploration of the Caucasus*, which allowed the viewer to feel as well as to properly see the landscape and some of the people of the northern range of mountains.

The events at the beginning of the twentieth century contributed to separating and alienating the Caucasus under a regime considered worse than that of the old Russian Empire. In the wake of this nationalism came not only the chaos of the Russian Revolution and the First World War, but the potential of a unified body of independent states in the Caucasus was briefly seen. This took shape in 1918 in the ephemeral Trancaucasian Democratic Federative Republic, formed of Georgia, Azerbaijan and Armenia. The state failed, perhaps predictably, after a few months because of the power play between the historical associations of the different sides (Georgia against Germany, Azerbaijan allied with Turkey, Armenia threatened by Turkey) and due to internal wranglings between Azerbaijan and Armenia. Wardrop's dream of an independent Georgia was also crushed by the realities on the ground: in February 1920 the Red Army occupied Tiflis. Azerbaijan had facilitated this development by joining the Bolsheviks and letting them pass through contested parts of Armenia into southern Georgia.[5]

Having endured Bolshevik and anti-Bolshevik wars, religious alienation, Stalinist terror, the German advance of the Second World War and tight communist rule under the USSR (as autonomous republics or regions), independence finally came to Azerbaijan, Georgia and Armenia after the break-up of the Soviet Union in 1990-91. The Caucasus remains divided and fraught: Dagestan, Chechnya, Ingushetia and North Ossetia are Russian republics, the first three prone to insurgency if not

CONCLUSION

tightly controlled. Georgia is divided internally between a pro-Russian leadership and a pro-European population. The region is vulnerable to historic ethnic tensions (Georgia and Abkhazia, North and South Ossetia, Armenia and Azerbaijan), so-called frozen conflicts (likely to erupt again) and Russian interference. It is cut off from others, and remote as an entity. In the competition for oil and gas, allegiances are also changing. Azerbaijan's offensive against Nagorno-Karabakh in September 2023 is evidence of its new resolve over an Armenia that has been gradually abandoned by Russia. This has led to massive displacements (reminiscent of the nineteenth century) and Armenia looking to Europe for support. Russia's war in Ukraine and its occupation of Crimea have made the Black Sea a contested area once more. Meanwhile vibrant Circassian, Abkhazian, Chechen and Ingush among other diasporas refuse to let their past histories be forgotten.

There is little to suggest that in the foreseeable future a status quo that satisfies all elements of the region will prevail.

1. It is worth remembering that there was not a year during the nineteenth century when Britain was not at war somewhere in its empire (apart from the Napoleonic Wars and Crimea): eg. Burma, Afghanistan, China (Opium wars), Ashanti, Zulu, Boer, India.
2. *Encyclopaedia Britannica*, 9th ed. 1875-1889, vol. v, 252-254, 256, 258-259. The Encyclopaedia also expected that future explorers would make the public aware of further recesses of the chain.
3. Travellers and others whose focus was India, Persia or Central Asia and who passed through the southern Caucasus (south Dagestan, Azerbaijan and the Caspian) are discussed in a forthcoming, separate piece of work.
4. Cameron 1845, xiv-xv
5. Aleksidze 2018, 125-137. I have relied heavily on this abbreviated account (of an extremely complex situation) as it is the most succinct and based on original documents. See also Forsyth 2015, 374-427.

Appendix

These are part of the collection of 'calling cards' and photo reproductions brought back by Abercromby from Tiflis.[1] The calling cards come from Dimitri Barkanov's Tbilisi studio (see Part 6) and here show mostly ethnographic subjects and a few antiquities.

The calling cards are marked with Barkanov's name front and back, with the elaborate backs acting as an advertising board for his patronage by the Grand Duke Michael, his international renown through various exhibition medals (Paris, Moscow) and diplomas (Vienna, Toulouse) and the location of his studio (Erivan Square).

---

1   Edinburgh University, Abercromby Papers Gen. 1841/21.

One of the photo reproductions (Abercromby 15) is also by Barkanov (written on the cardboard or paper frame), as may have been the unattributed ones, as Abercromby seems to have bought the whole lot together. The cards are of different sizes: the standard size for the ethnographic ones is c.10.5 x 6.5 cm and larger ones for precious materials and manuscripts 10.5 x 16.5. The latter's black back and faux gold writing makes them appear lustrous and almost as luxury objects in themselves. They presumably would have been more expensive.

The cards were part of a series, as indicated by the numbers written on the cards themselves and annotations in Russian, sometimes giving the name of the village or town the subjects came from (not always identifiable now). The numbers on the cards and photo frames are by Abercromby. Most appear to have been taken in a studio with props, although the background of some of the mountain ones seem to have been blacked out at a later stage. Those taken in the field show details such as fences, a dry-stone wall or a large sheet hung as a backdrop, ground coverings and/ or earth.

The ethnographic cards and photos show the social standing of the subjects, distinguished by dress and demeanour (e.g. the Abkhaz princess, the Georgian prince versus the groups of Abkhaz men or Mingrelian women). Dress was an important ethnic, rank and class distinguishing criterion in the Caucasus, but varied regionally even among ethnic groups themselves (mountain or coastal dwellers). The poorest, however, were often shown in rags, with the women wearing indistinct textiles wrapped around their heads. Head coverings of various sorts were worn by most ethnic groups, whether Muslim or Christian.

The cards have been arranged alphabetically. Some photographs are noticeably damaged at the edges with unclear figures.

Ethnography

seated Abkhazian Princess wearing a ess with a densely embroidered bodice. e has a long flimsy veil attached to r head and long plaits, some of which ve tassels on them. Her strongly arched ebrows are noticeably joined. (Barkanov, dio, Abercromby 17). See Parts 1 and 3.

Three seated and one standing, affluent Armenian women wearing embroidered aprons over their dresses and flimsy veils hanging from florally decorated head pieces, one with a tassel. They wear beads and one woman a cross. (Barkanov, painted background to the left, Abercromby 20). See Parts 2 and 3.

A group of armed Abkhaz men, possibly traders, with full cloth sacks hanging from peaked bonnets on their heads secured by frontal straps. (Barkanov, Abercromby 16). See Parts 1 and 3.

Chechents men

Circassian women

Three armed, bearded Chechen men, in sheep-skin hats. The man on the right has a *kinjal* and pistol. All have cartridge holders at breast level across over-tunics. Their shoes appear soft. (Damaged photo reproduction, possibly originally in the field, Abercromby 6). See Part 3.

A group of seven Circassian women weari plain kaftans or overdresses, the two on t left with embroidered fastenings. All we shawls or scarves as head coverings, so: over another scarf or headpiece. (Fai damaged reproduction, Abercromby See Part 3.

Chechents dancers

A Chechen male and female dancers w raised arms. The bearded male danc wears a tunic and is fully armed, the fem: dancer wears a long, belted silk or sa overcoat with cartridge motifs at the lape The male wears a sheepskin hat and t female a long hanging scarf drawn ba The left hand and long sleeve of the fem: dancer is blurred suggesting moveme Two young women with headscarv are seated between them to the rear. carpet is just visible. (Photo reproductic Abercromby 5). See Part 3.

APPENDIX

1

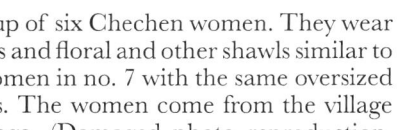

Chechents women

23

A group of six Chechen women. They wear clothes and floral and other shawls similar to the women in no. 7 with the same oversized sleeves. The women come from the village of Ataga. (Damaged photo reproduction, blurred on the left, cropped and used in Abercromby's book, Pl. III. Abercromby 1)

A wealthy Georgian woman in fur trimmed velvet cloak with slit sleeves. She has ringlets and wears an embroidered headpiece with a lace veil hanging over it. A cross hangs from a beaded necklace. (Barkanov, Abercromby 23)

3

Chechents women

Two young Chechen women, dressed differently. The one on the right wears an overtunic with cartridge motifs on the lapel gathered at the waist showing a frock underneath. She wears a large shawl or scarf with a rectangular pattern over a headpiece. The one on the left wears a similar tunic gathered at the waist but with different fastenings. She wears a floral shawl over her head. Both outfits have extra wide, long sleeves (cf. the woman dancer of no. 7). The women, named (?) Genjuevi, come from the village of Voznesiena. (Photo reproduction, indistinct floor covering, Abercromby 3)

265

A bearded Georgian prince wearing a flat embroidered cap and a tunic with cartridges on the lapels. An amulet hangs below his beard. (Barkanov. Abercromby 22)

An Imeretian Georgian dancer holding tambourine. She has a similar headdre and ringlets to the woman in no. 9. T details of the dress are not clear because t photo is overexposed. (Imeretia: coastal a mountain region, capital Kutaisi.) (Pho reproduction, Abercromby 27)

An Imeretian fruit and vegetable b vendor holding two small wicker bask in his hand and a large one on his ba He wears a sheepskin hat and indistin clothes. (Photo reproduction, in the fie Abercromby 11)

Appendix

An Imeretian cart pulled by two bullocks with a massive wine jar and a smaller one hanging from a large stake. The owner/driver stands by the cart. A fence to the side shows a depot of stakes, used for fencing but also to manoeuvre the wine jars. (Barkanov, in the field, Abercromby 19)

[A] moustachioed Gurian officer in a short [tun]ic with cartridges on his lapels, metallic-[loo]king epaulettes and a striped sash belt [hol]ding his sword and other accoutrements. [He] holds something indistinct in right hand. [He] has a cap on his head and wears trousers [and] light boots. Guria: a small coastal and [inl]and area between Poti and Batum.) [(Ba]rkanov, Abercromby 28)

Two men and two Mingrelian boy traders. One holds a wicker basket on a staff, and another a rolled bunch of produce (maize, tobacco?). The boy on the left holds a piglet, and the one on the right a bird or small hawk. They wear ragged tunics and trousers, dark woollen cloaks, soft leather shoes and different head coverings (sheepskin hat, round cap, cap with ear pieces and indistinct rags). Mingrelia: south of Abkhazia, north of Guria (see Part 1). (Barkanov, Abercromby 29)

A group of modestly dress[ed] standing and seated Mingreli[an] women of different ag[es] wearing different types [of] long tunics over dresses. [All] wear head coverings, so[me] wrapped over embroider[ed] head pieces. The women ha[ve] folded arms or crossed han[ds] and the majority are noticeab[ly] looking down rather than at t[he] camera. (Photo reproductio[n] Barkanov written on the fram[e], Abercromby 15)

A bearded Lezgin notable in a white and black sheepskin hat, wearing a belted tunic with cartridges on the lapels, armed with a *kinjal* and a sword. (For Lezgins see Part 3) (Barkanov, Abercromby 18)

A group of five Lezgins, one seated, o[ne] elderly. Four wear black sheepskin h[ats] of different shapes, one white, and [a] variety of tunics, two with empty cartri[dge] pockets on their lapels. Three of the m[en] carry *kinjals* at the waist. The man on t[he] far left has a medal hanging on his che[st]. They stand on a striped textile, against [an] extended sheet as a backdrop, with a wat[tle] fence and roof behind them. (Damag[ed] photo, in the field, Abercromby 7)

Appendix

Three fully armed, bearded Lezgin Cossacks. All wear the same outfit: tall black sheepskin hats, tunics with full cartridge pockets over an under tunic and striped trousers. The central man holds a rifle, two *kinjals* attached to his waist. The other two hold similar *kinjals*. The contrast between these serving men and those of Photo 7 could not be greater. The message of the former is that apart from the *kinjals* these Lezgins are poor and disarmed. (Barkanov. Abercromby 25)

group of Lezgin boys, four standing, four ted. They wear a variety of tunics and ite or black sheepskin hats. One boy ars a white and black hat. They may me from the village featured in Photo 18, the setting and ground covering is the ne. The name of the village appears to Kiosuch Usmuk. (Photo reproduction, in field, Abercromby 8)

Two armed Cossack Lezgin men. One kneels pointing a rifle out of an opening in a dry-walled structure, another, barefoot, preparing a rifle, stands behind him. The village, named as Usmuk, is probably the same one as above. (Photo reproduction, in the field, Abercromby 9)

269

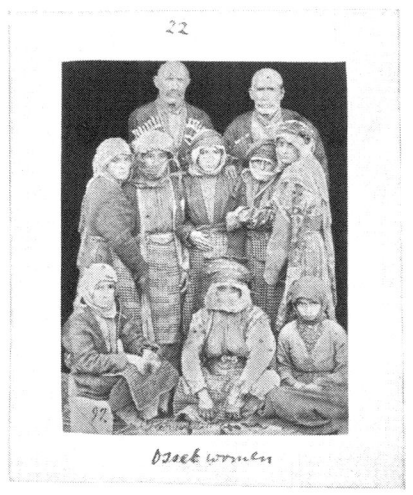

A group of eight Osset girls (five standing, three seated) with two male elders standing behind them. The majority are dressed in similar clothes: long belted over tunics, with chequered aprons. The girl on the far left wears a patterned over dress and shawl. All have head covering, some as plain scarves others as scarves secured by rags. Two of the girls have partially covered faces. (Photo reproduction. Abercromby 22). See Part 3.

A group of Osset women and girls, dress very similarly, with chequered aprons a scarves and rags wrapped in tall, flat-topp bundles on their heads. A young boy pee through on the far left. The girls in the frc are seated. All have folded arms or cross hands and many look directly at the came (Photo reproduction, Abercromby 23)

A group of eight Osset elders stand behind a seated official with a ledger on the left and a priest on the right. The elders wear a variety of tall sheepskin ones and caps. Two men are bareheaded. This image was used by Phillipps-Wolley 1883, vol. 1, on the title page, with no references, presumably with the aim of showing indigenous people and officialdom even though the group represents Ossetians and not Svanetians. (Photo reproduction, in the field with blackened background, Abercromby 24)

Appendix

/o well-dressed Svanetian women, one ted the other standing in front of a oden gate and fence. The one on the ht appears to be wearing a silk dress toned at the front and tightly belted, and olded scarf over a head band or covering. e older seated woman wears a chequered ntle over a dress, and has a bib hanging ound her neck. She holds a finger to her outh as if to keep it closed. She wears listinct scarves on her head. The village ds something like Chanezka. (Photo oroduction, in the field, Abercromby 13). e Part 3.

A group of two standing and two seated Tatar traders or shepherds. Three of them carry cloth bundles. Three wear heavy sheepskin cloaks over tunics and trousers. Two wear black sheepskin hats, one a cap and one possibly a fur hat. The elderly seated man holds a crooked staff. (Barkanov, Abercromby 30). See Parts 3 and 4.

A group of seated Svanetian boys and young men, one with a *kinjal*. Indistinct adults stand behind them. A large white sheet is used as a backdrop with indistinct trees in the background. The boys are either bareheaded or wear a selection of hats: tall bell-shaped bonnets, flat topped hats and sheepskin hats. They wear ragged mantles or vests over trousers, soft boots and leggings, or are barefoot. The village appears to be Chasiuk or Chasimuk. (Photo reproduction, in the field, Abercromby 12)

An affluent seated Tatar woman in stockinged feet from Baku. She has ringlets, and wears a turban-like headdress, a voluminous calf-length petticoats and a patterned (velvet?) mantle, with a shawl or covering over one shoulder. She has earrings and beads on her wrists. Her feet rest on an indistinct carpet or textile. (Barkanov, Abercromby 32)

A Nogai Tatar woman in a floral ou (trousers? and jacket closed at the waist) o undergarments. She wears pointed slipp and has a plain scarf on her head, earrin and a necklace with an oblong attachme (Photo reproduction, Abercromby 31)

Two seated Tatar women. They ha shawls draped over their heads over a or turban, and distinctive pendants in th joined parts made of cloth or metal.
Their very distinctive features suggest No or Mongol origin. The name Hasaika (? written on the frame. (Photo reproductic oval frame, damaged, Abercromby 14)

Appendix

Tush (Chechents) women

A group of three Tush girls or young women seated cross legged on a patterned textile against a dry-stone wall. They wear large plain shawls on their heads covering other headpieces and jackets over dresses. They have ringlets and a variety of beaded necklaces. The central figure wears an elaborate cruciform necklace. (Photo reproduction, Abercromby 4. Used in his book Plate V). Tushetia is in north-east Georgia, hence this grouping with the Chechens. See Part 3.

Tush men

A group of four Tush men, one on a horse. Trees and houses are in the distance. Three are armed with *kinjals*. They wear similar layered clothing: a short mantle with cartridge pockets at the lapels and trousers. Three wear caps and the man on the horse a sheepskin hat. (Photo reproduction, In the field, Abercromby 10. Used in his book Plate IV). See Part 3.

273

Precious materials

An example of a superior Barkanov calling card (black frame and back, back printed in faux gold) showing priestly garments, mitres, church votive offerings, relics (crosses, jewelled arms, bibles or gospels) and altar pieces.

Such pieces showing Georgian churches' treasures and wealth were very much part of Georgian and Christian propaganda at the time. The cards were often annotated with the material provenanced. Other religious antiquities included icons, pages of manuscripts and miniatures, and bindings. Other groups of materials included silver objects, jewellery, various types of metal vessels, oriental vessels, superior items of clothing (e.g. decorative headbands and lace headwear), embroideries, towels, musical instruments, enamels, saddle bags, cushions, carpets). Such cards, for example, were part of Roinashvili's travelling museum (Mamatsashivili 2015, 64-108) and were a phenomenal introduction to and display of the rich heritage of the Caucasus. Similar material was to be found in the Tiflis Caucasus Museum.

Short Biographical Notes

Abercromby, John, Hon. 5th Baron, 1841-1924
Ethnographer, archaeologist, folklorist, author, President of the Society of Antiquaries of Scotland, founder of the Chair of Archaeology, Edinburgh University.
Edinburgh University Information Services online https://www.ed.ac.uk/information-services/library-museum-gallery/crc/collections/special-collections/rare-books-and-manuscripts/rare-books-directory-section/john-abercromby

Bell, James Stanislaus, fl. mid-1800s
Part of a merchant shipping family. Little is known of his life except from the correspondence regarding the *Vixen* affair (see Part One and his book *Journal of a Residence* (1840).

Bryce, James, Viscount, 1838-1922
Jurist, politician, historian, academic reformer (promoting research), traveller, author, mountaineer. Short term Liberal MP, President of the Alpine Club 1899-1901. Partisan to causes (Garibaldi, Armenia, anti-German cruelty during First World War, pro-American, Ambassador to Washington.
Christopher Harvie, online Oxford DNB, 2004
https://doi-org.ezproxy-prd.bodleian.ox.ac.uk/10.1093/ref:odnb/32141

Cameron, George Poulett, 1805-1882
Army officer in East India Company, served in Portugal, on special mission to Persia (Tabriz) 1836-1838, Commandant of the Nilgiri Hills, Retired from E.I.C 1858. Joined the Austrian Italian campaign 1859.
A.J. Arbuthnot, revised by James Lunt, online Oxford DNB, 2004
https://doi-org.ezproxy-prd.bodleian.ox.ac.uk/10.1093/ref:odnb/4441

Cunynghame, Arthur, Augustus, Thurlow, Sir, 1812-1884
Army officer rising to Major General, author. Served in Bengal, Crimea, the Cape, Ireland. KCB in 1869. Besides his *Travels in the Caucasus* he published *My Command in South Africa in 1874-1878*, 1879
H. M. Chichester, revised by James Lunt, online Oxford DNB, 2004
https://doi-org.ezproxy-prd.bodleian.ox.ac.uk/10.1093/ref:odnb/6940

Freshfield, Douglas, 1845-1934
Mountaineer, eminent geographer, educator, advocate of women's membership of the Royal Geographical Society, traveller, author. President of the RGS 1914-1917. Hon DCL from Oxford, 1916, Geneva 1923. Hon. Fellow of New College, Oxford 1925.
H.M. Chichester, revised by James Lunt, online Oxford DNB, 2004
https://doi-org.ezproxy-prd.bodleian.ox.ac.uk/10.1093/ref:odnb/6940

Grove, Florence Craufurd, 1838-1902
Mountaineer, author, President of the Alpine Club 1884-1886
A.L. Mumm, *The Alpine Club Register*, London 1923-1928

Harvey, Annie Jane (née Tennant), 1825-1898
Author of fiction and travel, watercolourist.
Bassett, Troy J. "Author: Annie Jane Harvey." *At the Circulating Library: A Database of Victorian Fiction, 1837—1901*, 19 November 2023, http://www.victorianresearch.org/atcl/show_author.php?aid=2693

Longworth, John Augustus CB, fl. 1830s-1865
Consul at Monastir, employed on several special service mission (Epirus and Thessaly, Albania, Circassia, Crete), author, Consul General in Serbia 1860. CB 1865
Foreign Office List 1869, 126

Lyall, Robert, 1790-1831
Botanist (collector), physician, traveller, author. Worked as physician in St Petersburg, and subsequently published *The Character of the Russians with a Detailed History of Moscow*, Edinburgh and London, 1823, and articles critical of Russian despotism. British Resident agent in Madagascar 1826.
John H. Appleby, online Oxford DNB, 2004
https://doi-org.ezproxy-prd.bodleian.ox.ac.uk/10.1093/ref:odnb/17236

Phillipps-Wolley, Clive, 1853-1918
Vice Consul in Kerch, army captain, sportsman (big game hunter), author. Settled in British Columbia.
Who's Who 1896, 1918

Short Biographical Notes

Spencer, Edmund, fl. 1830s-1867
Prolific travel writer on Europe and the Caucasus, known chiefly from his publications.
Bassett, Troy J. "Author: Capt. Edmund Spencer". *At the Circulating Library: A Database of Victorian Fiction, 1837-1901*, 19 November 2023, http://www.victorianresearch.org/atcl/show_author.php?aid=1794.

Telfer, John Buchan, d.1907
Royal Naval Captain, fought in Crimea, FRS Antiquaries, author.
The Geographical Journal, 30, 1907, 97-98

Ussher, John, fl. 1865
Author. I have been unable to trace any archival information on him.

Wardrop, Oliver, KBE, CMG, 1864-1948
Diplomat, army interpreter in Russian, Private Secretary in St Petersburg 1892-1893. Vice consul in Kerch, Sebastopol, Warsaw. Acting Consul-General at Galatz, Tunis, Port-au-Prince. Consul at St Petersburg 1903. Consul for Bergen 1914. Consul General at Moscow 1917. FO employment on special mission to Transcaucasia 1919. Consul-General at Strasbourg. Member of the International Commission at Paris 1921. KBE 1923.
Foreign Office List 1928, 434-435
Jennifer Donkin, online Oxford DNB, 2004
https://doi-org.ezproxy-prd.bodleian.ox.ac.uk/10.1093/ref:odnb/49215

Bibliography

Primary Sources, Archival

National Archives, Kew

FO (Foreign Office)

FO 65/569 Captain Cameron's Report on the Caucasus, Part 1 and 2. Political, Statistical, Military, 1860
FO 65/570 Captain Cameron's Report on the Caucasus; Parts 3 and 4, Topography, Commerce, 1860
FO 65/590 Consuls at Berdiansk, Soukhoum-Kale, Poti; Cumberbatch, Dickson, Lloyd, 1861
FO 65/613 Consuls at Soukhoum-Kale, Poti, Warsaw: Dickson, Lloyd, Wilkinson, Stanton, White. Jan-June 1862
FO 65/649 Consuls at Soukhoum-Kale; Poti; Dickson, Wilkinson, 1863
FO 65/654 Trade on the east coast of Circassia, Vol 3, 1857-1863
FO 65/ 671 Consuls at Soukhoum-Kale; Poti; Dickson, Wilkinson,1864
FO 65/690 Consuls at Soukhoum-Kale, Poti, Kertch, Theodosia; Dickson, Herman, Wilkinson, Clipperton, Podesta, Barker, 1865
FO 65/712 Consuls at Soukhoum-Kale, Poti; Dickson, Wilkinson, 1866
FO 65/740 Consuls at Soukhoum-Kale, Poti; Dickson, Wilkinson, 1867
FO 65/ 761 Consuls at Soukhoum-Kale, Poti; Dickson, Wilkinson, 1868
FO 65/781 Consuls at Soukhoum-Kale; Poti; Dickson, Wilkinson,1869
FO 65/810 Consuls at Soukhoum-Kale; Poti; Dickson, Wilkinson, 1870
FO 65/826 Consuls at Soukhoum-Kale; Poti; Dickson, Wilkinson, 1871
FO 65/844 Consuls at Soukhoum-Kale; Poti; Dickson, Wilkinson, 1872
FO 65/861 Consuls at Soukhoum-Kale; Poti; Dickson, Wilkinson, 1873
FO 65/894 Consuls at St. Petersburg, Taganrog; F and J Mitchell, Carruthers, Hoyland, Vice-Consuls at Poti; Leslie, Gardner, 1874
FO 65/951 Consuls at St. Petersburg, Taganrog, Viborg; Michell, Carruthers, Lorentz, Vice-Consuls at Moscow, Berdiansk, Poti; Leslie; Wagstaff, Gardner, 1876
FO 65/ 950 Consuls at Kertch, Tiflis, Warsaw; Barrow, Ricketts, Mansfield, Finot, Maude, 1876
FO 65/976 Consuls at Helsingfors, Taganrog, Kertch, Warsaw; Campbell, Carruthers, Barrow, Maude, Vice-Consuls at Poti, Nicolaieff, Sebastopol; Gardner, Wagstaff, Moffat, Political 1877
FO 65/977 Consul at Tiflis; Ricketts, Political. vol. 1., 1877
FO 65/978 Consul at Tiflis; Ricketts, Political. vol. 2., 1877
FO 65/982 Consuls at Tiflis, Warsaw, Poti; Ricketts, Maude, Gardner, 1877
FO 65/997 General Correspondence, 1 Jan 1878-16 January 1878 (Russian Press reports)
FO 65/1015 Consuls at Odessa, Poti; Stanley, Hunt, Gardner, Political, 1878
FO 65/1018 Consuls at Helsingfors, Archangel, Taganrog; Campbell, Shergold, Carruthers, Hoyland, Vice-Consuls at Poti, Berdiansk; Gardner, Lowe, 1878

Bibliography

FO 65/ 1054 Consuls at Helsingfors, Odessa, Tiflis, Warsaw. Campbell, Stanley, Lynall, Maude. Vice Consul at Poti Gardner. Political, 1878

FO 65/1056 Consuls General at Odessa, Warsaw. Stanley, Maude. Consuls at Taganrog, Tiflis. Hoyland-Wooldridge, Lyall. Vice Consuls at Nicolaeff, Poti, Sebastopol. Wagstaffe, Carroll, Gardner, Watson, 1878

FO 65/1093 Consuls at Archangel, Helsingfors, Kertch, Riga, Taganrog. Gellermann, Campbell, Barrow, Colledge, Grignon, Hill, Breslau, Raby, Wooldridge. Vice Consuls at Berdiansk, Poti, Wiborg, Nicolaeff, Lowe, Gardner, Backland, Wagstaff, 1880

FO 65/1095 Miscellaneous FO correspondence 1880 (Europe and Russia)

FO 65/1123 Consuls General at Odessa. Stanley, Hunt. Vice Consuls at Batoum, Poti. Watson, Peacock, Gardner. Political Consular Commercial, 1878

FO 65/1124 Consuls at Taganrog, Tiflis, Warsaw. Wooldridge, Lyall, Lovett, Maude. Vice Consul at Kertch. Colledge. Political Consular. Commercial. 1878

FO 65/1166 Consuls General at Odessa. Stanley, Pakenham, Hunt, Perry, Webster. Vice Consuls at Batoum, Kertch, Nicolaeff, Poti. Peacock, Colledge, Wagstaff, Gardner. Political, Consular and Commercial, 1878

FO 65/1168 Consuls at St Petersburg, Taganrog, Tiflis. Michell, Page, Wooldridge, Lyall. Political, Consular, Commercial, 1878

FO 65/1369 Consul General at Odessa, Sandwith. Commercial. Vice Consuls at Kieff, Poti, Sebastopol. Smith, Gardner, Harford. Consular and Commercial, 1879

FO 65/1427 Consuls at Batoum, Riga. Murray, Mattievitch, Stevens, Wagstaff. Vice Consul at Poti. Sturge. Consular and Commercial, 1892

FO 97/344 Trade on the east coast of Circassia 1834-1843

FO 97/ 350 Trade on the east coast of Circassia, vol. 2 1854-1857, includes letter about Longworth.

FO 195/ 443 From Circassia, Lloyd's mission, 1854-1855

FO 258/4 Tiflis, Letter-book 1862-1863

FO 258/5 Tiflis, book, 1864-1867

FO 418/17 Report by Colonel Herbert, Military Attaché at St. Petersburgh, on a Visit to the Caucasus and the Crimea, 1889

FO 418/136 Russia: reports; Trans-Caucasian provinces; journey down the Volga to the Caucasus; visit to Caucasus and Crimea; 1889

FO 881/510 Report. Frontiers of Russia and Turkey, and Georgia and Caucasus. (Dr. J. P. Riach and Capt. Stoddart). 1836-1837. Bound: Russia 23.

FO 881/545 Affairs of Circassia. (Consul J. A. Longworth). Bound: Russia 23.

FO 881/618 Memo. Circassia. 1739-1857. (Mr. Lewis Hertslet). Bound: Mema, 1857

FO 881/3410 Despatch: Danger to British Interests in the East by Annexation of Armenia to Russia. Views of Russian Press as to Black Sea being made a Russian Lake, etc. (Mr. A. H. Layard), December 1877. Bound: Turkey 67.FO 881/1443 Corres. Affairs of Circassia. Bound: Russia 23, 1855-1857

FO 881/5855 Report. Col. Herbert's Visit to Caucasus and Crimea. Bound: Russia 18, 1889

National Army Museum

NAM 6807/377/3/52 Bundle 1, Rifles for Captain Hughes, return of ordnances, 1854

NAM 6807/303 Raglan Papers, Memoir re Lloyd's visit to Circassian chiefs, 1854

Qatar Digital Library/British Library: India Office records and Private Papers

IOR/L/PS/9/76/214, 2 letters to Hartford Jones Resident at Baghdad re Russian activity in the Caucasus, 1801-1802

IOR/L/PS/9/76/243, 2 letters from an informant of Hartford Jones re Russian activity in the Caucasus and the Caspian, 1802

IOR/L/PS/9/76/260 copy of letter from Harford Jones to Alexander Stratton, Minister to the Ottoman Empire, from Baghdad, 1802 enclosed letter of informant re. Russian military preparations in the Caucasus and planned Russian annexation of Yerevan, 1802

IOR/L/PS/9/70/131 Letter from the East Indian Co. envoy to Persia Lft. Col. John MacDonald Kinneir to Secret Committee of the East India Company, views over the war between Russia and Persia over the Caucasus, 1826

IOR/L/PS/9/70/132 Copies of letters from Lft.Col. John MacDonald Kinneir to various people regarding Kinneir's mission to the Court of the Shah of Persia and the outbreak of war between Russia and Pwersia and the territorial disputes in the Caucasus, 1826

IOR/L/PS/9/69/140 Letter from Henry Willock to George Canning, on Georgia Shirvan, Karabagh, the Caspian, Yermolov and the subjugation of the tribes, Circassia, 1823-1824

Edinburgh University Archives

Abercromby Papers, Gen.1841/7/1-6 Folder with notes on anthropology, history, linguistics, archaeology, including lecture on the Caucasus

Gen. 1841/12/3 Folder, miscellaneous foreign illustrations

Gen. 1841/21 Photographs

Primary Sources, Printed

Abercromby, J. 1889 *A Trip through the Eastern Caucasus, with a chapter on the languages of the country, with maps*. London: Edward Stanford

 1890 'The Wall of Derbend', *The Scottish Geographical Magazine*, 6/3, 135-145

Baddeley, J.F 1908, *The Russian Conquest of the Caucasus*. London: Longmans, Green, and Co.

Bell, J.S. 1840, *Journal of a Residence in Circassia*, 2 vols. London: Edward Moxon

Bryce, J. 1877, *Transcaucasia and Ararat*. London: Macmillan and Co.

Cameron, G. Poulett 1845 *Personal Adventures and Excursions in Georgia, Circassia, and Russia*. 2 Vols. London: Henry Colburn

Chardin, Sir J. 1686, *The Travels of Sir John Chardin into Persia*, London

BIBLIOGRAPHY

Cunynghame, A. Thurlow 1872 *Travels in the Eastern Caucasus, On the Caspian and Black Seas, Especially in Daghestan, And on the Frontiers of Persia and Turkey, During the Summer of 1871*. London: John Murray

Dorn, B. A.1871, in *Mélanges Asiatiques tirés du Bulletin de l'Académie Imperiale des Sciences de St Petersbourg*, VI, 699

Dumas, A. 1858, *Le Caucase*. Paris

1859 *Le Caucase, Voyage d'Alexandre Dumas*. Paris

Dorn, B. 1873 'Auszuege aus vierzehn morgenlaendischen Schriftstellern, betreffend das Kaspische Meer und angraenzende Lander' in *Mélanges Asiatiques, tirés du Bulletin de l'Académie Imperiale des Sciences de St Petersbourg*, VI, 685-716

Erkckert von R. 1887 *Der Kaukasus und Seine Volker*. Leipzig.

Freshfield D. 1869 *Travels in the Central Caucasus and Bashan*. London: Longmans, Green, and Co.

1896 *The Exploration of the Caucasus*, 2 vols. London and New York: Edward Arnold

Grove, F.C. 1875, *The Frosty Caucasus*. London: Longmans, Green, and Co.

Harvey, A.J. 1871 *Turkish Harems and Circassian Homes*. London: Hurst and Blackett

Kazem Beg, A. 1831, 1851 *Derbend-Nâmeh*. St Petersburg

Ker Porter, R. 1821, *Travels in Georgia, Persia, Armenia, Ancient Babylonia during the years 1817-1820*, 2 vols. London: Longman, Hurst, Rees, Orme, and Brown

Klaproth, J. 1827, *Voyage au Mont Caucase*. Paris

1827 *Tableau Historique, géographique, ethnographique et politique du Caucase*, Paris

Lake, A. 1866, *Kars and our Captivity in Russia*. London: Bentley

Longworth, J. 1840. *A Year Among the Circassians*. 2 vols. London: Henry Colburn

Lermontov, M.Y. 1839-40 *Geroi nashevo vremeni* (A Hero of our Time). St Petersburg

Lyall, R. 1825 *Travels in Russia, the Crimea, and Georgia*. 2 vols. London: T. Caddell, Edinburgh: Blackwood

Montperreux, F. DuBois de 1839-1843. *Voyage autour du Caucase*. 6 vols. Paris

Pallas, P.S. 1771 *Reise durch Verschiedene Provinzen des Russishen Reichs*. St Petersburg

Marigny, E. Taitbout de, 1837 *Three Voyages in the Black Sea to the coast of Circassia…with sketches of the manners, customs, religion…*London: John Murray

McNeill, Sr J. 1854 (3rd ed.) *The Progress and Present Position in Russia in the East: an Historical Survey*. London: John Murray

Murray, J. 1888 *Handbook for travellers in Russia, Poland and Finland, including The Crimea, Caucasus, Siberia and Central Asia*. London: John Murray

1812 *Travels through the Southern Provinces of the Russian Empire in the years 1793 and 1794*, London: Longman and Rees, Cadell and Davies, Murray and Highley

Phillipps-Wolley, C. 1881 *Sport in the Crimea and Caucasus*. London: R. Bentley and Son
    1883 *Savage Svanetia*. 2 Vols. London: R. Bentley and Son
Radde, G. 1866, *Berichte über die Biologish-Geographischen Untersuchungen in der Kaukasuslandern*. Tiflis
    1878 *Die Chevsuren und ihr Land untersucht im Sommer 1876*. Cassel
    1878 *Das Kaukasische Museum in Tiflis*. Dresden
    1885 *Kratiky Putevoditel' Kavkazkomy Myzeiyu*. (4th edition). Tiflis
    1885 *Le Musée de Tiflis d'après le catalogue en langue Russe*. Tiflis
    1899-1912 *Die Sammlungen des Kaukasischen Museums*. 5 vols published, 6 intended. Tiflis.
Spencer, E. 1837 *Travels in Circassia, Krim Tartary, including a Steam Voyage down the Danube, from Vienna to Constantinople and round the Black Sea in 1836*. 2 vols. London: Henry Colburn
    1838 *Travels in the Western Caucasus including a Tour through Imeretia, Mingrelia, Turkey, Moldavia, Galicia, Silesia and Moravia in 1836*. London: Henry Colburn
Telfer, J. Buchan 1876 *The Crimea and Transcaucasia. A Journey in the Kouban, in Gouria, Georgia, Armenia, Ossety, Imeretia, Swannety and Mingrelia, and in the Tauric Range*. London: Henry King
Ussher, J. 1865 *A Journey from London to Persepolis, including wanderings in Daghestan, Georgia, Armenia, Kurdistan, Mesopotamia and Persia*. London: Hurst and Blackett
Urquhart, D. 1835 (3rd ed.) *England, France, Russia and Turkey*. London: J. Ridgway and Sons
    Progress of Russia in the West, North and South (5th ed.). London: Trübner and Co.
Wanderer (probably Consul Lyall) 1883, *Notes on the Caucasus*. London: MacMillan and Co
Wardrop, O. 1888 *The Kingdom of Georgia, Travel in a land of Women, Wine and Song*. London: S. Low, Marston, Searle and Rivington
Zisserman, A.L. 1879 *Dvavtsat pyat lyet na Kavkaze 1842-1867*, St. Petersburg
    2018 *Twenty-Five Years in the Caucasus 1842-1867* (covers the years 1842-1851). Translation from the Russian by Irina Kiziriya. New York, London, Tbilisi: Narikala

Basic Secondary Sources

Aleksidze, N. 2018, *Georgia, a Cultural Journey through the Wardrop Collection*. Oxford: Bodleian Library
Alexander, D.G. 2015 *Islamic Arms and Armor*. New York: The Metropolitan Museum of Art with Yale University Press, New Haven and London
Allen, W.E.D and Muratoff, P. 1953 *Caucasian Battlefields*, Cambridge: Cambridge University Press
Arkun, A. 2104 'Into the Modern Age, 1800-1913' in eds. E. Herzig and M. Kurkchiyan 2005 *The Armenians, Past and Present in the Making of National Identity*. Oxfordshire: Routledge
Baumgart, W. 2020 (2nd ed.), *The Crimean War 1853-1856*. London, New York: Bloomsbury

Bibliography

Barthop, M. 2002, *Afghan Wars: and the North-West Frontier, 1839-1947*, London: Cassell

Chanishvili, N. 2008 Nineteenth-Century Architecture of Tbilisi as a Reflection of Cultural and Social History of the City, FaRiG Rothchild Research Grant http://ww.farig.org/images/pdfs/research-architecture-tbilisi.pdf

Chikovani, N. 2018 'Tbilisi as a Centre of Crosscultural Interactions (the 19th-early 20th centuries)' in *Khazar Journal of Humanities and Social Sciences, Special issue* 2018, 233-251

Cvetkovski, R. 2014 'Introduction: On the Making of Ethnographic Knowledge in Russia' in *An Empire of Others, Creating Ethnographic Knowledge in Imperial Russia and the USSR*, eds. R. Cvetkovski and A. Hofmeister, 1-22. Budapest-New York: Central European University Press

Dennis, B. 2011 'Patterns of Conflict and Violence in Eastern Anatolia Leading up to the Russo-Turkish war and the Treaty of Berlin' in *War and Diplomacy, The Russo -Turkish war of 1877-1878 and the Treaty of Berlin*, ed. M. Hakan Yavuz. Salt Lake City: University of Utah Press

Dettmering, C. 2014 'No Love Affair: Ingush and Chechen Imperial Ethnographies' in *An Empire of Others, Creating Ethnographic Knowledge in Imperial Russia and the USSR*, eds. R. Cvetkovski and A. Hofmeister, 341-368. Budapest-New York: Central European University Press

Edwards, E. 1988, ed. *Anthropology and Photography 1860-1920*, Introduction by E. Edwards. New Haven: Yale University Press

Elfimov, A. 2014 'Russian Ethnography as a Science: Truths Claimed, Trails Followed', in *An Empire of Others, Creating Ethnographic Knowledge in Imperial Russia and the USSR*, 51-80. Budapest-New York, CEU Press

Fisher, H. 2001, *From a Tramp's Wallet*, The Erskine Press

Floor, W. 2008 (translator with Hasan Javadi) *The Heavenly Rose Garden: A History of Shirvan and Daghestan*, by Abbas Qoli Aqa Babkikhanov

Forsyth, J. 2015, *The Caucasus, a History*. Cambridge: Cambridge University Press

Gadjiyev, M. 2017 'Dagh Bary' in Encyclopaedia Iranica online, http://iranicaonline.org/articles/dagh-bary

Gammer, M. 1994, 2004 *Muslim Resistance to the Tsar, Shamil and the Conquest of Chechnia and Daghestan*. Oxon: Frank Cass

Golombek, L. 2014, 'The Kubachi Problem' and the Isfahan Workshop,' in *Persian Pottery in the First Global Age, the Sixteenth and the Seventeenth Centuries*, 169-181. Brill

Gorshenina, S. and Sonntag, H.S. 2018 'Early Photography as cultural transfer in imperial Russia: visual technology, mobility and modernity in the Caucasus and Central Asia' in *Khazar Journal of Humanities and Social Sciences*, Khazar University Press, 322-344

Gutmeyr, D. 2017 *Borderlands Orientalism or How the Savage Lost his Nobility, The Russian Perception of the Caucasus between 1817-1878*, Wien: Lit. Verlag GmbH and Co. KG

Jahn, H. 2014 'The Bronze Viceroy, Michael Vorontsov's Statue, Russian Imperial Representation in the South Caucasus in the mid-nineteenth Century', *Russian History* 41, 163-180

2020 'Visits of Tsars to the Caucasus as representations of Empire', in H. Jahn ed., *Identities and Representation in Georgia from the 19th century to the Present*, 169-184. *Schriften des Historischen Kollegs 103*, Oldenburg: de Gruyter

Jaimouka, A. 2009 Circassian Culture and Folklore, Monograph, http://jaimoukha.synthasite.com/circassian-religion.php

Jersild, A. 2002 Orientalism and Empire, North Caucasus Mountain People and the Georgian Frontier 1845-1917. Montreal and Kingston, London, Ithaca: McGill-Queen's University Press

Jones, S. *2005 Socialism in Georgian Colors. The European Road to Social Democracy 1883-1917*. Cambridge Mass., London: Harvard University Press

Kemper, M. 2005 'Adat against Shari'a: Russian Approaches towards Daghestani 'Customary Law' in the 19th century' in eds. Balci, B. and Motika, R. *Religion et Politique dans le Caucase post-Soviétique, Institut Français d'études Anatoliennes*, 97-119

Kettenhofen, E. 2020 'Horn, in: Encyclopaedia Iranica Online, <http://dx.doi.org/10.1163/2330-4804_EIRO_COM_3172>

Khodarkovsky, M. 2011 *Bitter Choices, Loyalty and Betrayal in the Russian Conquest of the North Caucasus*. Ithaca, London: Cornell University Press

King, C. 2007 'Imagining Circassia: David Urquhart and the making of North Caucasus Nationalism', *The Russian Review* 66, 238-255

Knight, N. 2006, *The Empire on Display: ethnographic Exhibition and the Conceptualization of Human Diversity in Post-Emancipation Russia*, NCEER Research program VIII, Washington D.C.

Krivosheina, G. 2014 'Long Way to the Anthropological Exhibition: the Institutionalization of Physical Anthropology in Russia', *Centaurus* 56/4, 275-304

Kurtishvili, I. 2018 'The Hope for Homes. A tour of apartments in 12 places in town'. in eds. P.C. Schmal and I. Kurtishvili *Hybrid Tbilisi, Reflections on Architecture in Georgia*, 160-197. Frankfurt am Main: DOM

Laycock, J. 2009, *Imagining Armenia, Orientalism, Ambiguity and Intervention*. Manchester: Manchester University Press

Lordkiniadze, M. 1981 *The Ancient Finger Rings of Colchis*. Tiflis

Laneri, N. et al 2020 'Reconstructing Funerary Sequences of Kurgans in the Southern Caucasus: the first two seasons of the Azerbaijan-Italian Ganja Region Kurgan Archaeological Region Project', *Anatolica*, December, 103-144

Lebedynsky, I. 2008, *Armes at Guerriers du Caucase, Les Traditions guerrières des peuples caucasiens*. Paris: l'Harmattan

Mamatsashvili, L. 2001 *Alexandre Roinashvili, the first Georgian Photographer 1846-1898*. Tiflis: Litera

2014 'Early Photography in Georgia' in *Dimitri Ermakov, Photographer and Collector*,14-41. Tbilisi: Georgian national Museum

2015 'The travelling Museum of the Caucasus' in *Alexandre Roinashvili and His Museum*. Tbilisi: Georgian National Museum and PILOTS, 27-49

Mania, I. 2014 'Gabriel Tamasmschev's Caravanserai and Islamic Elements in the 19th Century Architecture of Tbilisi', Academia edu. https://www.academia.edu/47712249/plus title

Bibliography

Manning, P. 2009, 'Just like England: on the Liberal Institutions of the Circassians', *Comparative Studies in Society and History*, 51/3, 590-618. Online: https://www.cambridge.org/core/journals/comparative-studies-in-society-and-history/listing?q=Manning%202009%20&fts=yes&filters%5BauthorTerms%5D=Manning&filters%5BdateYearRange%5D%5Bfrom%5D=2009&filters%5BdateYearRange%5D%5Bto%5D=2009&searchWithinIds=3D5C40349E588565CAD30F5A7E08F68F

Mammaev, M.M. 2018 'Monuments of Stone-cutting art and Arabic Epigraphy of the 14th-15th centuries from the settlement of Datsamazhe', History, Archaeology and Ethnography of the Caucasus, 14/2. 50-71. https://caucasushistory.ru/2618-6772/article/view/1434

2020 'New Stone Reliefs from Kubachi-architectural details of the 14th-15th centuries with graphic subjects' in History and Ethnography of the Caucasus V, 16/3, 661-681https://caucasushistory.ru/2618-6772/article/view/1580

2022 'Two Artistically Decorated Muslim Steles of the 14th century from Kubachi: on dating and Its Author' in History, Archaeology and Ethnography of the Caucasus, 18/3, 793-804. https://caucasushistory.ru/2618-6772/article/view/1819

McCarthy, J. 2011 'Ignoring the People: the Effects of the Congress of Berlin', in ed. M. Hakan-Yavuz, *War and Diplomacy, the Russo-Turkish war of 1877-1878 and the Treaty of Berlin*. 429-448. Salt-Lake City: University of Utah Press

Marvin, C. 1891 *The Region of Eternal Fire: an account of a journey to the petroleum region of the Caspian in 1883*. London: W.H. Allen and Co.

Melikian-Shirvani A.S. 1982 *Islamic Metalwork from the Iranian World:8th-18th centuries*. Victoria and Albert Museum. London: Her Majesty's Stationery Office

Mouradian, C. 1995, 2009 *L'Arménie*. Paris: Presses Universitaires

Morrison, A. 2021 *The Russian Conquest of Central Asia, a Study in Imperial Expansion 1814-1914*. Cambridge: Cambridge University Press

Musaev, M. and Alkhasova, D. 2009 'Daghestani 'Ulama' in the Muslim World' in ed. M. Gammer *Islam and Sufism in Daghestan*, 43-69. Sastamala: Finnish Academy of Science and letters and Finnish Society of Science and Letters

Museum Studies abroad 2003, A Brief History of the Opera and Ballet Theatre of Tbilisi.https://museumstudiesabroad.org.opera-ballet-theatre-tbilisi

Museyibli, N. *Excavations of Soyugbulaq Kurgans, KP-432-BTCROW*. Baku: National Azerbaijan National Academy of Sciences, Institute of Archaeology and Ethnography.

Olbrycht, M.J. 2015 'Arsacid Iran and the Nomads of Central Asia-Ways of Cultural Transfer' in eds. J. Bemmann, M. Schauder *Complexity of Interaction along the Eurasian Steppe Zone in the First Millenium CE*. Bonn Contributions to Asian Archaeology, 7. Rheinische Friedrich-Wilhems-Universität Bonn

Ponting, C. 2005 *The Crimean War, the Truth behind the Myth*. London: Pimlico

Poujafar, A. (translated by Alexander Khaleeli) 'Darband', 2017 (online) in Encyclopaedia Islamica, <http://dx.doi.org.ezproxy-prd.bodleian.ox.ac.uk/10.1163/1875-9831_isla_COM_036095>

Rayfield, D. 2012 *Edge of Empires, a History of Georgia*. London: Reaktion

Rosser-Owen, S.I. 2007 The first 'Circassian Exodus' to the Ottoman Empire (1858-1867) and the Ottoman response, based on the accounts of contemporary British observers', MA thesis, Near and Middle Eastern Studies, School of Oriental and African Studies. https://www.circassianworld.com>Isla-Thesis

Sagona, A 2018 *The Archaeology of the Caucasus: From earliest settlements to the Iron Age*. New York: Cambridge University Press

Schimmelpenninck van der Oye, D. 2014 'Paul's Great Game: Russia's Plan to Invade British India', *Central Asian Survey* 33/2, 143-152

Shikhsaidov, A. 2009 'Ancient Mosques of Daghestan' in ed. M. Gammer *Islam and Sufism in Daghestan*, 15-28. Sastamala: Finnish Academy of Science and letters and Finnish Society of Science and Letters

Shkolna, O. 'The Mirrored Decor in Interiors of the Tbilisi Buildings in the middle-second half of the 19th century' *The world of the Orient*, 2, 138-162. Institute of Oriental Studies, Kiev.

Solovyova, K. and Kouteinikova I 2016 'A Different Caucasus. Early Triumphs of Photography in the Caucasus' in *Venezia Arti*, 25 (December), 133-149

Tanriverdi, M. 2011 'The Treaty of Berlin and the Tragedy of the Settlers from the Three Cities', in ed. M. Hakan Yavuz and P. Sluglett *War and Diplomacy, the Russo-Turkish War of 1877-1878 and the Treaty of Berlin*, 449-478. Salt Lake City: University of Utah Press

Tatarashvili N. 2008 *Art Nouveau in Tbilisi* – Guide Book, Map and Routes. Tbilisi: Premier Videopress TV

Teissier, B. 2011 *Russian Frontiers: Eighteenth Century British Travellers in the Caspian, Caucasus and Central Asia*. Oxford: Signal

2017 'Crimean Tatars in explorative and travel writing:1872-1802', *Anatolian Studies* 67, 231-253

Thompson, J. 2004 'Palgrave, William Gifford (1826–1888)' online Dictionary of National Biography https://doi-org.ezproxy-prd.bodleian.ox.ac.uk/10.1093/ref:odnb/21159

Tolmacheva, E.B. 2017 'Early Field Photography and Visual Documents of Northern Indigenous Cultures, Ivan Poliakov's Collection, 1876' *Sibirica*, 16/1, 6-30

Trever, K.J., Lukonin V.G. 1987 *Sasanidskoe serebo: sobranie Gosudarstvennogo Ermitzha: khudozzzhestvennaia kul'tura Irana III-VIII vekov*. Moscow: Iskusstvo

Tsutsiev, A. 2014 *Atlas of the Ethno-political History of the Caucasus*. New Haven: Yale University Press

Vuchinich, A. 1988 *Darwin in Russian Thought*. Berkeley: University of California Press

Ward, R. 'Alexandre Roinashvili's Collection of Islamic Metalwork' in Alexandre Roinashvili and his Museum, multiple authors Tbilisi: Georgian National Museum and PILOTS, 9-12

Wixman, R. 1986 'Kubači', *Encyclopaedia Islamica*, 285

Yavuz, M.H. and Sluglett, P. 2011 'Introduction: Laying the Foundations for Future Instability' in ed. M. Hakan Yavuz and P. Sluglett *War and*

Bibliography

Diplomacy, the Russo-Turkish War of 1877-1878 and the Treaty of Berlin, 1-13. Salt Lake City: University of Utah Press

Zhordania, G. 1951 Istorya voznykovennya Kavkazckogo Museya Кавказского музея: k izuchenyu istorii Gos. Muzeya Gruzii. Tiflis: Akad. Nauk GSSR

List of Illustrations

Front Cover: National Library of Scotland, Bell Vol.1, NLS Special Collections LS K. 160.b

Back Cover: Grove 1875, Frontispiece. NLS SC K 130.f

Frontispiece: Freshfield 1896, 91. NLS SC E 117.c

- p.1   Freshfield 1896, Vol. 2, opposite 6, NLS SC, GB 1288
- p.24   Longworth 1840, Vol. 2 Frontispiece. NLS SC RR K 158e
- p. 45   Ussher 1865, facing 163. NLS SC K 168.a
- p.105   Wardrop 1888, Frontispiece NLS SC K 166.b
- p.142   Wardrop 1888, to face p. 62, NLS SC K. 166.b
- p. 150 Freshfield 1869, facing 300. NLS SC K 168.f/GB 580
- p. 154 Grove 1875, facing 75. NLS SC K 130.f/Lloyd. 456A
- p. 159 Phillipps-Wolley 1883, Vol. 2, Frontispiece. NLS SC K 130.e
- p. 161 Telfer 1876, Vol. 2, to face 121, NLS SC, K.160, f
- p. 167 Cunynghame 1872, 211, NLS SC K. 130.d
- p. 169 Cunynghame, 1872,199, NLS SC K. 130.d
- p. 190 Bell 1840, Vol. 1, facing 154. NLS SC K 160.b
- p. 201 Figs 9 and 10 Abercromby 1889, 277, 280. Edinburgh University Library Special Collections 91. (479) Abe.
- p. 209 Freshfield 1869, facing 185. NLS SC K 168.f/GB 580
- p. 212 Freshfield 1869, 288. NLS SC K 168.f/GB 580
- p. 218 Freshfield 1896, facing 57. NLS SC E 117.c/GB 1287
- p. 238 Bell 1940, Vol. 2 Frontispiece. NLS SC K 160.b
- p.239   Spencer 1839, Vol. 1 (3rd ed.) Frontispiece. Oxford Bodleian (Weston) Library, SC 394.S.7
- p. 245 Phillipps-Wolley 1883 Vol. 1, to face 162, NLS SC K 130.e
- p. 247 Abercromby 1889, Pl.VI, Edinburgh University Library Special Collections 91. (479) Abe.

Index

Abadzekhs 13, 39-42, 51, 53-5, 57, 125
Abercromby, John 3, 257, 275
 and illustrations 245-6, 249-50, 261-73
 and mountain people 123
 and religion 194-202, 256
 as ethnologist 130-1, 175, 179, 186, 191-4
 as linguist 165, 176, 256
 in Caspian 172, 174
 in Chechnya 146-8, 256
 in Dagestan 164-5
 in Svaneti 148-9
 with Avars 165-6, 169
 with Lezgins 171
Abich, Hermann 101, 110, 113, 215
Akhaltsik 11, 43, 56, 76, 85, 89, 126-7
Alexander II 6, 51, 55, 86, 116, 126
Alexander III 6, 86, 112, 116
Alpine Club 153, 207, 215-16, 234, 242-3, 275-6
Alpine Journal 213, 230, 242-3, 252
Anapa 10, 14-15, 18, 23, 26, 35-6, 47, 54, 89, 187, 191, 193
anthropology 111, 113-14, 236, 256
antiquarianism 130, 138, 176, 186-206, 246, 253, 256
Ardahan 32, 76-7, 80, 85
Armenia 2-3, 6, 49, 70, 99, 118-19, 145-6, 195, 255-9
Armenians 5, 18, 31, 66-7, 71-4, 78, 81-2, 85-6, 103-4, 106, 113, 116, 126, 128-9, 144, 171-4, 177, 187-8, 249, 263
Austria 32, 43, 64, 69, 81, 228, 276
Avars 27, 61, 70, 79, 124, 146, 148, 164-9, 176, 178, 191
Azerbaijan 2-3, 27, 99, 107, 116, 119-20, 126, 165, 175, 177, 204, 258-9
Azov 10, 28, 36, 54, 64

Baghdad 5, 11, 26, 73, 91, 280
Baku 29-30, 65, 79, 81, 83-4, 91, 114, 126, 164, 166, 172-4, 185, 240, 272, 285
Batum 32, 39, 43-4, 64, 69, 76-7, 80-5, 117, 228
Bayazit 32, 77-8
Becho 151, 162-3, 211, 226-7
Bell, James 3, 275
 and Circassia 131-3, 135, 237, 257
 and excavations 186, 190, 192, 256
 and illustrations 20, 237, 239-40, 248-50
 and language 136
 and political involvement 20-5, 253
 as merchant 14, 18-19, 64, 131
Beyer, Frederick 109-10
Black Sea
 in geography 1, 6, 99, 162, 187, 219
 in politics 9, 13-14, 16, 22, 25-6, 28, 32, 36, 42-3, 48, 62, 73-4, 259
 in trade 3, 44, 47, 82, 119, 253-4
Bosnia 69, 81
Bosphorus 49, 73, 80, 192
botany 110-11, 113, 138
Brosset, Professor 138, 141, 187
Bryant, Admiral 33, 40
Bryce, James 3, 65, 275
 and excavations 186, 191
 and illustrations 249-50
 and railway 67, 145
 as Christian 69-70
 in Poti 66, 68
 in Tiflis 102-3, 106-7
 political views 71-3, 118, 255, 257
Bulgaria 69-71, 80-1

Bulmer, Sir Henry 62
Bzhedug 37, 41

calling cards 138, 178, 181, 236, 245-6, 248-9, 261-74
Cameron, Captain Charles Duncan (Consul) 30, 48-9, 66, 69, 91, 93, 278
Cameron, George Poulett 3, 25-7, 142-3, 182, 240, 257, 260, 275, 280
Canning, Lord George 34, 91-3, 280
Caspian Sea 1, 6, 11, 27-9, 31, 75, 79, 99, 107, 119, 126, 164, 166, 172-3, 185, 195, 205, 221-2, 280, 285
Cathcart, Major 43, 92
Catholics 32, 59, 81, 85, 104
Caucasus Museum 109-14, 125-30, 187-9, 236, 274
Chavchavadze dynasty 38, 92, 115-16, 166
Chechens 25, 28-31, 35, 61, 70, 79, 91, 126, 137, 140, 146, 148, 176-7, 246, 264-5, 273
Chechnya 10, 27-9, 60, 77-9, 124, 136-7, 146, 165, 256, 258
Chilaeff, Colonel 191-2
Christianity 2, 28, 30, 66, 77, 113, 124-5, 130, 132, 138-41, 152-3, 158, 178, 186, 188-9, 274
Christians 15, 44, 69-70, 72-3, 81, 84-5, 127-8, 172-3, 256, 262
Circassia, *passim*
Clarendon, Lord 33-4, 36, 38, 40, 44, 46-7, 93
coins 30, 109, 192-3
Colchis 112, 157, 203-4
Constantinople 5, 14-16, 18-21, 26, 33-5, 39, 41-2, 46-7, 50-1, 55-6, 62, 64, 72-3, 75, 83, 168, 253
Cossacks 10, 13, 27, 44, 52, 54, 59-60, 78, 102, 126, 143, 151, 157, 164-5, 269
Crimea 1, 5-6, 9-10, 17, 32, 43, 108, 130, 186, 188-93, 253, 259
Crimean War 5, 32, 39, 48-9, 63, 79, 234, 254

Cunynghame, Arthur 3, 275
and illustrations 241, 249
and railway 67
in Caspian 172-3
in Dariel, 142, 144
military reporting 68, 168, 194
on forts 166
on Kurds 171
on Russia 149
Curzon, Lord 120

Dagestan 2, 6, 21, 27-35, 44, 57, 60-1, 70, 76, 78-9, 109, 119, 124, 126, 128, 134, 146-7, 164-73, 177, 186, 189, 191-2, 194-202, 221, 226, 240-1, 244, 250, 256, 258
Dardanelles 16, 49, 80, 89
Dariel pass 10, 142-3, 145, 159, 193, 210, 245, 250, 252
de Déchy, Maurice 215-16, 246
de Montperreux, F. DuBois 5, 138, 141, 281
de Redcliffe, Lord Stratford 35, 38, 46-7, 63
Derbend/Derbent 27, 29, 79, 171-5, 186, 192, 194-5, 197-8, 204, 257
Derby, Lord 70, 73, 95-7
Dickson, Charles Hanmer 48-51, 53-4, 56, 59, 64-5, 69, 93-5, 278
Donkin, W.F. 213, 215, 230, 243, 248

Erivan 11, 29, 44, 76-7, 79, 127
Erzerum 49, 67, 73, 75-8, 80-1, 85
ethnography 6, 50, 107, 110-11, 113, 123-85, 228, 235-6, 246, 253, 256, 263-74
Euxine, *see* Black Sea
Evdikimov, General 52, 54

Fedorovna, Grand Duchess Olga 102, 112
Five Verst map 101, 136, 196, 210-11, 214, 216, 228
Foreign Office 5, 14, 21, 35, 42, 50, 70, 73-5, 78, 87, 134, 253-4
Fort St Nicolas 23, 43

France 16, 18, 32-4, 37, 42-3, 45, 53, 64, 67, 81, 234, 254, 257
Freshfield, Douglas 3, 257, 275
 ethnography 131, 137-8
 illustrations 233, 237, 240-1, 243-4, 246, 249-50, 258
 mountaineering 136-7, 207, 209-20, 224, 226, 256
 on Abkhazia 58, 65, 68
 on Poti 66
 on Svaneti 126, 141, 148-53, 155-6, 163
 on Tiflis 100-1
 reviewing Phillipps-Wolley 223, 228-9

Gardner, Vice-Consul Thomas 74, 81-3, 97-8, 278-9
Gebi 149, 153-4, 160, 211, 216, 224-5, 241-2, 252
geology 110-11, 113, 243
Georgia, *passim*
Germany 81, 84-6, 119, 125, 188, 258
 German nationals 100, 103, 107, 127, 131, 171, 174, 214
 German products 102, 166, 192, 202
Ghelenjik 15, 20, 23, 35, 53
Grand Duke Michael 55, 112, 155, 188, 261
Greeks 66, 83, 191, 198
Grove, Florence Craufurd 3, 65, 276
 ethnography 153, 155-8
 illustrations 241-2, 249-50
 mountaineering 136, 149, 210, 214, 216-20, 256
 on railway 67
 on Tiflis 101
Grozny 29, 77, 144, 166
Gunib 45, 78, 146, 164-9, 172-3, 191, 194, 240-1, 252
Guria 11, 58, 66, 118, 125, 267

Harvey, Annie Jane 3, 65-6, 68, 95, 241, 276, 281
Herzegovina 69, 81
Hughes, Francis, Captain 33, 36, 40-1

hunting 102, 174, 199-200, 203, 220-9, 245

India 1, 18, 25, 30-1, 49, 70, 73-4, 84, 88, 120, 174, 185, 221, 253, 260, 276, 280
Ingushetia 28, 60-1, 129, 136-7, 140-1, 258
Irakli 119, 245, 252
Iran 1, 27, 175, 191-2, 194, 198, 200, 202, 205-6, 235, 285
Islam 2, 21, 27-9, 35, 38-40, 48, 104-5, 110, 124-5, 130, 133-5, 152, 189, 194-5, 256
Italy 64, 81, 108, 276, 284

Jews 72, 106-7, 126-9, 153, 164, 171, 174-5, 188, 223, 256
jewellery 76, 188, 192, 198, 274
Jibiani 150, 211, 240
Jighett 51-2, 54, 57
Jones, Hartford 11, 91, 121-2, 280

Kabarda 10, 28, 37, 144, 191
Kakheti 11, 31, 38, 102
Karabakh 3, 11, 29, 259
Karachay 10, 177
Karganoff, General 52, 56
Kars 32, 43, 63, 69, 76, 78-82, 84-5, 92, 97, 151, 173
Ker Porter, Robert 100, 142-3, 240, 281
Kerch 56, 67, 83, 191, 223, 228, 244, 276-7
Khevsureti 125-6, 137, 140-1, 181, 240
Khunsakh 164, 166, 168, 191, 194
King David 2, 99, 113
King Khosrow 195
King Vakhtang Gorsalgali 99
Klaproth, J.H. 5, 131-2, 141, 180, 209, 281
Koshtantau 1, 212-13, 215, 217, 240
Kubachi 175-6, 185-6, 194-5, 198, 200-2, 204, 206, 256, 283
Kuban river and province 9-10, 13,

291

17, 19, 22-3, 26, 28, 37, 40, 42, 53-4, 57, 60, 155, 187, 189-90
Kumyks 27, 61, 91, 177
Kurds 44, 70, 72, 77-9, 81, 84-5, 126-8, 171
kurgans 114, 186, 188-92, 284-5

Laba 37, 40, 46, 53
Laks 27
languages 2-3, 9, 27, 35, 66, 68, 70, 73, 101, 106, 116, 118, 123-4, 127, 130-1, 135-6, 141, 155, 164, 169, 171, 173-4, 176-8, 180, 256-7
Layard, Austen Henry 73, 96, 279
Laz 44, 83, 85, 113, 177
Lermontov 123, 139, 145, 181, 281
Lezgins 31, 35, 44, 57, 61, 77-8, 107, 113, 119, 126, 132, 148, 164-5, 169-71, 175, 177, 221-2, 241, 250, 268-9
lithography 220, 233, 237, 239-42, 244-5, 248-9, 251
Lloyd, J.A. 33-4
Lloyd, St Vincent 50
Longworth, John 3, 14, 276
and ethnography 131-5
and excavations 189-90
and illustrations 239, 249-50
and Naib 40-2
in Circassia 18-21, 23, 25, 33-7, 131-4, 136, 237-8, 253-4, 257
Lyall, Robert 3, 9, 142-3, 182, 237, 249-51
Lyall, Walter Tschudi (Consul) 74, 78, 82-3, 85-9, 96-8, 100, 102, 115, 117, 121-2, 255, 279, 282

Machabeli, Ivan 116, 245
Mansur, Sheikh 2, 10, 28
Marvin, Charles 84, 98, 174, 185, 285
Marx, Karl 16, 89, 118
McNeill, John 17, 281
Melikoff, General 144, 172-3
Messageries Impériales 57, 64

Mingrelia 11, 42, 48, 55-6, 63, 65-6, 71, 77, 116, 119, 125, 127, 157, 177, 223, 262, 267-8
Mitchell, John 69, 95, 278
Moldavia 17, 32
Monastir 33, 35, 74, 276
Mongols 2, 99, 113, 177, 191, 195, 206, 272
Moore, Adolphus Warburton 150, 153, 207, 209, 216, 218, 246
Moscow 5, 26, 108, 114, 128, 145, 192, 236, 246, 261, 277-8
Mount Ararat 70, 113, 127, 171, 219, 240, 249-50, 280
Mount Elbruz 101, 127, 137, 148-9, 151-3, 155, 207, 211-14, 216-20, 230, 240-1, 249-50, 256
Mount Kazbek 101, 127, 137, 143, 145, 148, 207, 209-10, 216, 250
Mount Ushba 157, 226, 241
mountaineering 10, 31, 58, 65, 101, 136, 138, 149, 153-7, 163-4, 207-20, 241-2, 248, 250, 252-3, 256
Mozdok 10, 28, 143
Mtatsminda 100, 106-7
Murat, Hadji 168
Murray, John 5, 107, 111, 250
Muslims
  beliefs 37, 107, 133, 140, 152-3, 178, 194, 197, 256, 262
  law 30, 72
  people 31, 39-40, 56, 60, 69, 71-2, 81-2, 84-5, 136
Mustafa Pasha 35-6, 41-2

Nagorno-Karabakh 3, 259
Naib 33-4, 36-42, 46
Napoleonic Wars 10-11, 260
Naqshbandiyya 28-9, 40, 91
Natukhai 20-1, 37
Nicholas I 5-6, 17, 234

Odessa 67, 83, 138, 193, 228
ornithology 111, 113
Ossetia 29, 77, 136-7, 188, 194, 216
  North Ossetia 28, 142, 258

292

South Ossetia 1, 137, 259
Ossetians 61, 70, 91, 107, 116, 124-7, 138-41, 149, 153, 178, 193, 240, 245, 270
Ottoman Empire
historical 2, 5, 9-10, 16-17
nineteenth century 3, 32, 34, 37-40, 43-4, 48-9, 58, 62, 69-77, 80-1, 84-5, 253-5
see also Russo-Ottoman War

Palgrave, William Gifford 49-51, 57-9, 62, 69, 93-4
Pallas, Peter Simon 5, 11, 131-2, 281
Palmerston, Lord 15-16, 26, 32, 34, 89-90
Peacock, Demetrius Rudolph 83, 98, 279
Persia and Persians 2, 10, 29, 31, 67, 91, 99-100, 107, 116, 126, 128, 146, 173-5, 177-8, 187, 189, 195, 198, 204, 221, 244-5
Persianate style 104-5, 110, 163, 166, 171, 192, 201
Petrovskaya, Sophia 87
Phillipps-Wolley, Clive 3, 276
and hunting 149, 160, 169-71, 220-8
and illustrations 244-5, 249-50, 270
in Caspian 172, 174, 221
in Svaneti 160-3, 221, 223
in Tiflis 102-3, 117
reviews of his books 228
photography 233-52
Piatigorsk 145-6, 152, 155, 213
Poland and Poles 18, 30, 32, 37, 46-7, 51, 53, 56, 79, 103, 107, 168
Ponsonby, Lord 15-16, 21-2, 89-90
Poti 11, 23, 48-50, 59-62, 64-6, 68, 74-5, 82-3, 223, 227
Prussia 32, 64, 76
Pshavs 140-1
Pshku 51-4, 57
Pshukei Bey 135
Pushkin 5, 123, 139, 145

Quba 29, 31, 91, 172, 174
Queen Tamara 2, 99, 113, 145, 245, 252
Queen Victoria 47, 207

Racha 160, 162, 223, 226
Radde, Gustav 101, 104, 109-11, 113, 122, 125, 128, 130, 141, 149, 151, 180, 188, 203, 210, 214-15, 223-4, 226, 228, 230, 282
Raglan, Lord 33-4, 91-2, 280
railways 65, 67, 75, 83, 100, 114, 117, 145, 255
Redut-Kale 14, 23, 43, 47, 49
Riach, Dr 17, 23-5, 31, 90-1, 253, 279
Ricketts, George Thorne 74-7, 79-80, 87, 95-7
Rion River 66-7, 127, 149, 187, 210-11, 216-17, 244
Roinashvili, Alexandre 181, 192, 194, 235, 251-2, 274, 284, 286
Royal Geographical Society 49, 207, 230, 236, 275
Russell, Lord John 51, 93-5
Russian Orthodoxy 2, 32, 48, 54, 56, 69, 85-6, 108, 114, 124-5, 188
Russian Steam Navigation Company 57, 64-5
Russo-Ottoman War (1877-78) 59, 63, 69-74, 118, 220, 235, 254-5
Russo-Turkish War (1806-12) 48
Russo-Turkish War (1828-29) 10
Rustaveli 100, 245, 252

Samegrelo 118
Samsun 18, 58, 62, 64, 83
Sashe 23,192, 251
Sass, General 22
Sassun 81
Scythians 188-91
Sefer Bey 20-1, 36-7, 42, 90
Sefer Pasha 40-1, 46
Seljuks 2, 99
Sella, Vittorio 216, 237, 243, 246, 248-50, 252, 258
Shamil 2, 21, 28, 30, 33-5, 37-45, 51,

54, 72, 91, 124-6, 128, 145, 154, 164, 166-70, 188, 192, 194, 207, 240, 250, 254, 256-7
Shapsug 17, 19-22, 25, 37, 41, 51, 54
Sheikh Ghazi Muhammed 28
Sheikh Ismail al Kurdumiri 28
Sheikh Mansur 2, 10, 28
Sheikh Muhammad al-Shirvani 28
Shervashidze dynsasty 48-9, 55
Shirvan 28-31, 91, 185, 198, 204
Shura 60, 164, 166, 172-3
Simmons, Colonel John 44
Sinope 18, 26, 50, 58, 64
slavery 36, 46-8, 57, 71, 108, 135
Sochi 46, 53-4
Spencer, Edmund 3, 14, 17-20, 24-5, 89-91, 131-3, 135, 180-1, 237, 239, 248-9, 251-3, 257, 277
St Petersburg 9, 26, 55, 69, 74, 79, 108, 111, 138, 140, 166, 173, 176, 187, 193, 204-5, 234, 276-9
Stanley, Earl Edward 75, 94, 278-9
Sujuk-Kale 14, 23, 35
Sukhum-Kale 9, 22-3, 32, 38, 46-50, 54-7, 59-62, 64-5, 68, 77, 83, 216, 220, 228, 241
Sunnis 28, 39, 84, 104, 174
Sunzha River 27, 29, 61
Svaneti 70, 77, 125-7, 136, 145, 148-64, 169, 187, 211, 216, 221, 223, 225-8, 244, 250, 271

Tabarasans 27, 124, 171, 175
Tarki 27, 29, 60, 171-2
Tatars 79, 107, 126-8, 135, 146, 148, 164, 169, 171-2, 174-7, 222-3, 241, 244, 271-2
Tats 165, 174-5
Telfer, John Buchan 3, 65, 277
   and excavations 186, 190, 193, 256-7
   and illustrations 233, 250
   in Dariel 142, 144-5
   in Sukhum-Kale 65, 67
   in Svaneti 157, 159
   in Tiflis 101, 106

   pro-Russian 138, 149
   on Khevsurs 141
   on religion 139-40
Temir-Khan-Shura 60, 164, 172
Temirgoy 13, 19-20
Terek 27-8, 61, 115, 137, 142, 152, 154, 188, 191, 210, 213, 216-17, 240
Tiflis 6, 26, 32, 38, 44, 56, 65-7, 72, 74-5, 79, 81, 83, 87, 99-122, 127-8, 162, 223, 234-5, 245-6, 255, 258, 261
Tiflis Museum 101-4, 109-15, 125-30, 138, 159, 186-9, 191-2, 236, 255, 274
Times, The 16, 20, 25, 58, 62, 89, 102
Toapse 25, 251
Transcaucasia 43, 70-4, 85, 120, 127, 186, 189, 255, 277
Treaty of Adrianople 10, 14-16
Treaty of Berlin 81
Treaty of Gulistan 29, 31
Treaty of Paris 44
Treaty of San Stefano 74, 80
Treaty of Turkmenchay 29
Trebizond 5, 17, 32, 42, 46, 49-50, 54, 57-9, 62, 64, 67, 83
Tsinandali 38
Tucker, Comyns 207, 209-10
Turkey 1, 11, 15-16, 19, 23, 25-6, 32, 36, 43-4, 46, 53, 58, 61, 63, 70, 72, 84, 86, 109, 135, 144, 152, 191, 235, 258
Turkmen 88, 99, 128
Turkmenistan 87-8
Turks 21, 32-3, 36, 41, 43, 47, 66, 70, 76-8, 80, 83, 85, 151, 174
Tush 125-6, 128, 140-1, 176-7, 246, 273

Ubykh 13, 19-20, 51-4, 60
Ukraine 1, 108, 191, 259
Urquhart, David 15-21, 89, 131, 239, 284
Uruch 152, 210, 213
Uruspieh 151-3, 155, 211, 213, 216,

218-19, 240
Ushguli 150, 157, 160, 163, 225-6
Ussher, John 3, 65-8, 142, 144, 165-6, 168, 172-5, 191, 233, 240, 249-50, 277, 282
Ust Labinskaya 13

Varna 33-4, 36, 58, 62
Veliaminov 22-3
Vixen 14, 46, 275
Vladikavkaz 112, 139, 142-6, 154-5, 235, 245
Vladivostok 153, 191
Volga 108, 173, 192, 203, 279
Vorontsov, Prince Michael 99-101, 103, 108-9, 112, 115, 126, 28

Walker, Horace 153, 216, 218, 220, 242-3, 249
Wardrop, Oliver 3, 6, 73, 100-7, 117-22, 142, 145, 186, 245, 249-50, 252, 255, 257-8, 277
Wilkinson, Robert 50-1, 65, 69, 94-5, 278
Williams, Colonel 39, 43-4, 151, 173
women 39, 68, 77, 79, 83-4, 87, 107, 135, 139, 148, 150-1, 159, 161, 165, 170, 175-6, 178, 196, 199, 236, 240, 246, 257, 262-5, 268, 270-3

Yekaterinodar 10, 13
Yermolov, Aleksei Petrovitch 10-11, 13, 29, 31, 99-100, 280

Zakatali 38, 44, 78, 171
Zaluch 138-40, 143
zoology 110-11, 113